Historical Problems:
Studies and Documents

Edited by
PROFESSOR G. R. ELTON
University of Cambridge

27

TRADE AND INDUSTRY IN TUDOR AND STUART ENGLAND

Historical Problems: Studies and Documents

TRADE AND INDUSTRY IN TUDOR AND STUART ENGLAND

Sybil M. Jack
Senior Lecturer in History, University of Sydney

LONDON: GEORGE ALLEN & UNWIN LTD
RUSKIN HOUSE   MUSEUM STREET

First published in 1977

© George Allen & Unwin (Publishers) Ltd, 1977

ISBN 0 04 942155 7 Papercased
      0 04 942156 5 Paperback

Printed in Great Britain
in 10 on 11 point Plantin
by The Devonshire Press, Torquay

*For my mother, Vera Edith Thorpe
and in memory of my father,
Laurence Henry Thorpe*

ACKNOWLEDGEMENTS

I should like to thank most warmly Professor Geoffrey Elton for all his encouragement and advice and also Dr Chris Challis and Dr Roger Hainsworth who read the script at different stages and offered me excellent advice. I would also like to thank Mrs Wilma Sharp for her endless patience in typing the various drafts and struggling endlessly with my illegible handwriting, Miss Mary Jane Kirkman who helped tidy up the last intractable problems and Mr F. B. Stitt, archivist of Staffordshire county record office, who was most patient in dealing with last minute problems at a long distance. I should like to thank the staff of the Public Record Office, the British Museum and the Institute of Historical Research for their assistance. Without the resources of these institutions, this book could never have been completed.

Manuscript material from the Public Record Office is Crown-copyright and is published here by permission of the Controller of HM Stationery Office: this applies to Documents 21, 22, 24, 29, 30 and 32. I should like to thank the National Library of Wales for permission to print Document 11; the Council of the University of Nottingham and Lord Middleton for permission to print Documents 2, 10, 12, 17 and 25a; Lord Anglesey for permission to consult and publish Documents 3, 4, 8, 25b, 27, 28 and 33; the Countess of Sutherland for permission to use Documents 6, 7 and 20; The Folger Shakespeare Library, Washington for permission to use Document 26; Kent County Council for permission to reprint Documents 13 and 23 (this Crown-copyright document in the Kent County Archives Office appears by permission of the Controller of HM Stationery Office); Yale University Press for permission to use Document 5 and Pergamon Press Ltd for permission to reprint Document 9.

CONTENTS

INTRODUCTION

The Problem of Growth in Sixteenth and Seventeenth Century English Society: the Overall Economic Matrix

Economic historians have always been principally concerned with growth and development or their absence. For the last two hundred years in England growth has been associated with industrialisation and with the transfer of factors of production, particularly labour and capital, away from agriculture. At the same time, there was a transfer of people from the country to the town, so that the growth of urbanisation, the process whereby the typical or average Englishman came to live in a community more than 5,000 strong, has been associated with the process of growth.[1]

What constitutes growth, however, and how is it related to development? Obviously, man cannot consume more goods and services than he produces. Only if man can produce more can he improve his standard of living. A pre-industrial economy, however, is generally characterised by a low level of *per capita* production, and this low labour productivity caught mankind up in a vicious circle of hunger, malnutrition, lassitude, inefficiency and low productivity. There were other reasons for a small output, of course, particularly primitive tools and limited known sources of power. To increase man's output, to raise the productivity of labour, is to generate growth. In part, such an increase is the result of better tools and labour-saving equipment, and such machinery represents one facet of the investment of capital in an industry. Instead of applying labour directly to the end in view it is diverted to making equipment which will ultimately increase the yield of a smaller amount of labour applied directly. This withholding of labour from immediately productive ends is not as easy as it sounds, for such labour has to be fed and housed during the period in which the new work is being made, so an accumulation of resources is a necessary preliminary.

On the whole, new machinery or new processes have had their most dramatic effects in manufacturing industry. The rate of growth in such industry can be geometric, while the rate of growth in agriculture is rarely more than arithmetic. For this reason, the importance of agricultural growth has often been underrated. Some economists have even suggested that the sole significant role of agriculture was to make resources available for use in another, more profitable, area. Few people, however, would now adopt so extreme a view, but the division of the economy into areas is a very convenient analytical tool and one that will be used extensively in this section. Economists generally divide the economy into five sectors:

(1) agriculture, forestry, fishing;
(2) manufacturing, mining and industry;
(3) trade and transport;
(4) domestic and personal;
(5) public, professional and all other.

A pre-industrial economy will typically have a lot of its population employed in sectors (1) and (4). The growth associated with industrialisation is generally marked by a shift of population, measured as a percentage, from those sectors to (2) and (3).

The process of transition to a highly capitalistic industrial society is, however, complex and there has been much learned disagreement over the nature and significance of the various factors involved. Clearly much depends on the nature of the labour force. A sober, educated, hard-working labour force with a propensity to work steadily and reliably at its task and a strong sense of personal responsibility is obviously more desirable than a community of lethargic gamblers of erratic habits accustomed to getting by on hand-outs. More conveniently measurable, however, is its size and composition and what economists term its 'elasticity': the ease with which it can be expanded and mobilised.

Much, too, depends on the capital available, its distribution amongst the various social, economic and political groups and the ease with which it can be accumulated, borrowed or transferred. Much, again, may depend on the technological level of the community and the rapidity with which new ideas can be developed and accepted by the community. Other matters to be taken into account include market conditions, the mechanisms whereby goods can be distributed and the institutions of trade, commerce and finance.

Moreover, to list these elements as if they were autonomous is to beg a number of crucial questions about their interrelations. To give a single but critical example: is invention an autonomous gift from outside the system or is it an induced response to a particular set of circumstances ?

Many historians, moreover, no longer think that economic factors alone are a sufficient explanation for a sudden spurt of growth being transformed into a continuing and constant feature of the economy. State policy, man's acceptance of a particular structure of society and man's perception of his own goals must play a significant, if not a dominating role. Recently North and Thomas have laid stress on what they call 'socio-economic' institutions as a necessary framework without which the individual initiative which we call capitalism is unlikely to flourish. By this they mean, for example, that the law must be structured in such a way that the greater part of the benefit of what an individual does is realised by that individual and not by another. They think that structures which encourage the proliferation of 'free riders', that is, those who benefit from the actions of others without contributing in any way to the risks or costs, are adverse to economic growth in a capitalist system.[2]

Even within a narrower economic explanation, differences of opinion on the nature of the forces for growth have always existed, particularly since the impact of many factors varies from situation to situation. Price rises, for example, may stimulate production or make it unprofitable; population growth can provide necessary additional labour or create a 'Malthusian trap' in which pressure on existing resources becomes unbearable and ultimately results in starvation, famines or war.

Arguments about the relative importance of different factors have, moreover, been accompanied by some argument about when the process could properly be said to have begun. Historians divided into two main schools: those who were gradualists, who saw history as a seamless fabric in which the appearance of new colours and designs, at first scarcely perceptible, grew steadily until they dominated the whole material; on the other hand were those who sought for what are called the 'significant discontinuities', who looked for a moment at which a marked and measurable difference was perceptible.

Until the early 1930s most historians considered that such a difference was first noticeable in the late eighteenth century, the period which Toynbee had labelled the Industrial Revolution. Then in 1930 an American scholar, John Nef, made a new suggestion which threatened to disrupt all accepted ideas, and which caused a lot of people to re-examine more carefully than before the earlier history of the English economy. To understand the enduring debate over the industrial developments of the period 1540–1640, Nef's theory and the objections to it must be examined briefly.

HISTORIOGRAPHY OF THE DEBATE

'There have been two industrial revolutions in England, not one.'[3] 'There have been at least two "industrial revolutions" in Great Britain.'[4] 'The opinion is gaining strength that there was at least one period during which the rate of change was scarcely less striking.'[5] So wrote Professor Nef. This idea first came to him when he was working on his first and least-disputed work, *The Rise of the British Coal Industry*. He was deeply impressed by the increase in coal output between the dissolution of the monasteries and the outbreak of the Civil War; and he found when he examined the impact that coal had had on other industries that a good case could be made for giving it a very important place in various developments, so that he could claim, with some reason, that 'by the beginning of the seventeenth century, men had already begun to count coal a national asset'[6] and that 'the general economic and social development of the period from 1550 to 1700 cannot be understood unless account is taken of the part played in it by the coal industry . . . the process by which the ultimate triumph of industrial capitalism was assured would have been fundamentally different without [it]'.[7]

Much of Nef's case rests on the conviction that there was a major crisis in the timber industry which was both too great and too rapid in its development to be accounted for by the rise in population in England. The crisis was caused, he suggested, by increased demand for timber both as a fuel and as building material in industry and manufacture. To prove it, he sought to show 'that a sharp expansion of native industrial enterprise did in fact occur under Elizabeth and James I', and then to give grounds for believing that this expansion made extensive inroads upon the forests.[8]

In demonstrating the second part of the statement he had ample help in the complaints which streamed from the pens of contemporaries both in lawsuits and in pamphlets, complaints which taken at their face value would suggest that the face of England was rapidly becoming totally denuded of trees. In demonstrating the first part, that there was a rapid development of industry and manufacture 'more than proportionate to the increase of population', he was in greater difficulties, partly because there was, and still is, no satisfactory evidence about how fast that rate of increase was.

Nef, however, confident that he could demonstrate a general industrial development accompanied by technical improvements and changes in organisation, was thus led to his first formulation of the idea 'that the late sixteenth and seventeenth centuries may have been marked by an industrial revolution only less important than that which began towards the end of the eighteenth century'.

His first need was to discount evidence of decline in the period, in such industries as tin mining in which G. R. Lewis had shown declining output. This must be not only untypical but unimportant: the industry must stagnate rather than decline ('a slight decrease'), a movement offset by the rise in the developing brass industry which replaced it, and by the supposedly flourishing state of the lead industry. After this he went on to a demonstration that the iron industry under Elizabeth and James expanded considerably and that even when domestic output of crude iron became stationary, the domestic manufacture of iron goods continued to expand on the basis of imported Swedish iron. The demonstration was partly indirect – an attempt to show that additional demands arose in other 'rapidly expanding' industries such as ship building, house building, saltpetre and gunpowder manufacturing, salt making, alum and copperas manufacturing, soap boiling, sugar refining and the dyeing of cloth.

Ultimately, however, he chose to rest his case on three growth industries: the production of ships, of salt and of glass; and of these he produced most evidence for salt and glass making. In the case of salt, he argued that output from the brine pits must have increased since in Henry VIII's time total domestic consumption was 40,000 wey a year, three quarters of which was imported, while by 1681 production might be reckoned as 20,000–25,000 wey a year from the Cheshire brine pits alone. On top of this came the manufacture of salt from sea water (with the aid of coal) which he felt grew from nothing to 15,000 tons or weys a year, or more by the late 1630s. This progress was maintained under the Restoration.

Both here and in his later works Nef conveys an impression that nearly all the salt England consumed was by the seventeenth century domestically produced. Since salt was a crucial preservative, the industry was certainly an important if minor one. In the case of glass he had greater difficulty since most people were agreed that the monopoly Sir Robert Mansell obtained was a hindrance rather than a help to development, but he tried to show that output grew between 1580 and 1615, and that it recovered after the Civil War, while the Mansell patent for making glass with coal gave the English glass makers a great technical lead over their continental competitors. Finally, Nef went on to the minor industries, where he attempted to pile up instances of improvements.

At this point, however, he was more concerned to show how crucial coal was to the development as a substitute for the increasingly costly wood fuel, and to demonstrate its substitution in various processes such as glass making, soap boiling, beer brewing and the like. Coal, he wrote, made lime cheap, so that the husbandman could improve agricultural production; coal stimulated the shipping industry; coal stimulated improvements in wagon ways; coal was significant in nearly all the patents applied for at the period; coal was breaking down regional isolation in economic matters.[9]

In accordance with current economic orthodoxy, he considered that the investment of large units of capital and the development of large-scale organisations, as well as technical innovations, were signs of an industrial revolution, so he stressed such factors wherever they appeared: the increasing costs of starting a colliery, the introduction of new apparatus (especially the invention of boring rods which helped in prospecting) and the development of sophisticated organisations, especially the need for partnerships and the appearance of joint stock companies. 'There were probably not more than 50 men in Elizabethan England with sufficient wealth to finance single handed the largest colliery of the day, even had they been able to realize all their assets.'[10] The coal industry, Nef claimed, proved 'a fertile field for the growth of capitalistic forms of industrial organisation'[11] and it also, by tending to bring about the concentration of industries in certain districts, and thus by widening the market for the product, made conditions favourable for an increase in the size of establishments.

At the same time, Nef looked at the picture from the consumption side and put forward a view of an increasing standard of living. 'Throughout the country, houses of brick and stone, soldered with lime for mortar, each with its chimney, replaced the older, cruder dwellings of light timber, thatch and straw; the inhabitants, in most cases for the first time, looked out of glass windows, sat in comparative comfort round coal fires in iron grates, set their tables with earthen and china ware, knives, forks, and spoons of metal, and drinking vessels of glass.'[12]

This thesis was received cautiously; most reviewers praised the work on the coal industry, but were only moderately enthusiastic about the wider implications. Professor Lipson, reviewing the book for the *Economic History Review*, spoke of it as a substantial work of great value, and praised Nef for his gift of imagination. Nevertheless, he issued a caution:

'With a pardonable emphasis on coal, he leaves somewhat in the shade the economic progress achieved prior to, and independent of, the rise of the coal industry. While we dethrone the year 1760 from its pedestal, we must resist the temptation to put the year 1558 in its place. It will register a definite advance in the study of economic history when we recognise, in the fullness of its implications, the fact that England had already made great industrial, as well as commercial, strides before the advent of power-driven machinery. But the concept of the continuity of economic development forbids us to elevate even the sixteenth or the seventeenth century to the dignity of a watershed.'[13]

G. N. Clark was soon after to write of 'the half-abortive industrial revolution of Elizabeth's time',[14] while from the opposite camp, H. van Houtte condemned all attempts to hypothesis in the existing state of ignorance.

'Has the time already come to attempt a new interpretation of economic history by following a central principle, such as, for instance, the law of progressive concentration of enterprises, or the subordination of all economic facts to monetary phenomenon, or to the evolution of industrial technique, the development of communications or the density of population? Are we to postulate an unbroken line of development or one where the threads have been frequently broken, the alternation like a pendulum of periods of liberty and periods of regulation? . . . In the actual state of our knowledge, these principles, or these hypotheses rather, lie still exclusively within the domain of scientific polemics.'[15]

Nef was sufficiently encouraged by his reception, however, to continue his investigation. His next project, logically enough, was to consider the comparative progress of France and England, with the idea of pinpointing where England had the superiority at this time. Nef observed that the laws passed by the monarchs tended to be much the same, and that they were not of a kind 'to encourage the multiplication of enterprises employing more than a handful of people under one roof'. England's advantage, Nef concluded in good *laisser-faire* tradition, lay in the Crown's relative inability to enforce such laws in England. The breakdown of the guilds in England and their inability to help the Crown in its policies was an additional advantage. He was not, however, inclined to take very seriously the idea of profit inflation. This argument suggested that as prices rose and the cost of labour inputs did not keep pace, the additional sum which accrued to the manufacturer was a bonus which stimulated him to additional efforts. Instead of adopting this idea, which might have given the French manufacturer a greater advantage than the English, Nef was at pains to find reasons why the real wage of the unskilled labourer might have been maintained at a higher level than appeared likely from the material which Beveridge and his team at the London School of Economics were producing.[16]

The outbreak of war turned Nef's ideas into another channel which since the war has come to dominate his approach. This was first apparent in 1942 when he published in the *Economic History Review* an article in which he for the first time explicitly connected England's comparative success in the period 1540–1640 to the fact that while almost every other nation saw war on some scale within its frontiers, so that its government was concerned with the production of war materials, England was free from such disruptions, and her expenditure on war materials was relatively low. Nef was already sceptical of the thesis that demands for war production were a gain to the economy. He wrote:

'With the one hand, the continental warlords and their marching armies created large new establishments to furnish war materials. With the other, they interfered with the progress of large new establishments designed to cater to peacetime markets. In some cases they drove the rising capitalistic manufacturers out of the war zone and even across the channel. In a variety of ways, the industrial losses of the warring countries were peaceful England's gain.'[17]

Nef was to become more and more convinced that war was of no benefit to mankind and man's industrial progress. The only battle which was important, to Nef now, was the battle for men's minds, and that was more crucial than any development in the material sphere. The period from 1540 to 1640 did not cease to be one of economic growth but, it was in the boost that it gave to man's thought, and in the liberation of that thought from bondage, that its ultimate significance lay. In 1950 appeared a book entitled *War and Human Progress*; in 1953 'The Genesis of Industrialism and Modern Science' in *Essays in Honor of Conyers Read*; and in 1954 *La Naissance de la civilisation industrielle et le monde contemporain*. Many of these ideas were incorporated in other books such as *Western Civilisation since the Renaissance*.

Nef's theme was to explore the question, 'How was the growing command which the Europeans exercised over their industrial resources connected with their growing power of destruction? What relations had the new warfare to the employment of human talents and energies in ways leading towards . . . industrialism?'[18] He concluded that war was only one of many stimuli to scientific and technical progress, and that its disadvantages outweighed the advantages – that peaceful conditions were needed for original thought. He was even prepared to set aside one of his own early criteria, the importance of large-scale enterprise, and stressed that 'to discuss the economic consequences of the production of the instruments of war as if this could be kept separate from the economic consequences of their use is of little service to truth'.[19]

Finally, a number of his earlier essays were reproduced in a volume entitled *The Conquest of the Material World*. In the preface to this, Nef disarmingly confesses them to be 'fragmentary in content, imperfect in detail, and tentative . . . in conclusions. I believe, nevertheless, that the subjects discussed are vital to an understanding of the modern world because the essays touch on some of the conditions without which the industrial revolutions could hardly have come as soon as they did and might not have come at all.' Nef fundamentally believes that the study of history is a moral function, that the historian's role is to guide men 'into the ways of truth, justice, reason, and virtue'.[20] Such ways can only be found, however, by the applications of rigid scholarly methods, and it is as well at this point to consider why his early, specific thesis has fallen into disfavour. Nef's thesis was never, however, universally and whole-heartedly accepted. In the same year that *The Rise of the Coal Industry* appeared, F. J. Fisher was already writing, 'except in mining, draining, and the supplying of water, large-scale production did not, in the pre-machine age, carry with it any very great reduction of costs'.[21] He thought that industry would only provide profits comparable to those to be obtained in trade, finance or land speculation if the industrialist was guaranteed his market. He believed that nonetheless the climate of opinion was coming to see industry as a dynamic element which needed to be encouraged as well as controlled, and that attempts were being made to direct the stream of capital into industrial development.

The main reaction against Nef, however, did not appear until after the Second World War, when attitudes to economic growth were changing. The first blow was struck by those who sought to rescue the concept of industrial revolution for use as a specific description of a particular, and supposedly irreversible, change in the structure of the economy. D. C. Coleman led off by protesting against the ever-widening application of the term to any significant change in an individual industry – a use which was rapidly threatening to extinguish any useful meaning in the idea. It should be reserved, he suggested, for a more carefully defined purpose.[22] This idea was taken up by other modern historians like Miss Deane, who attempted to lay down a series of conditions which needed to be fulfilled before a development could properly be termed a revolution.[23]

Closer examination of the sixteenth and seventeenth centuries was also leading historians to wonder how widespread and perceptible the impact of Nef's changes was on the economy. Studies of the cloth industry and trade suggested that it had undergone periods of quite severe difficulty, often at moments when Nef's study of the coal industry had led him to expect expansion and a buoyant economy. The urbanisation he postulated appeared to be confined to London itself, other towns generally growing in only modest proportions, while evidence for the growth in real value of trade was not forthcoming.

Professor Fisher summed up the growing attitude of doubt in his introductory essay to the volume presented to R. H. Tawney. 'The later 16th and early 17th century constitute perhaps the last period in English history in which economic appetites were remarkably vigorous but in which economic expansion was still slow.'[24] He modified this by adding that it was not an age of stagnation, and that there was 'a widening range as well as an increase in the volume of goods and services available for consumption'. He felt, however, that agricultural production was slow to expand and that the lag of wages behind prices, fears of pauperisation and mounting fears of overpopulation all suggested an economy barely coping with an expanding population. The historians' task, in his view, was 'less that of demonstrating the expansive force of economic ambition, than that of examining the impediments which contained it, less that of proclaiming its successes, than that of recording the strains and stresses to which it gave rise'.

Since then, most economic historians have been engaged in following his precepts to the point of total pessimism. Conrad Russell in a recent general text gave the impression that the growth of the coal industry was the one ray of light in an otherwise depressing picture, which is undoubtedly much farther than Fisher himself intended to go, since he saw many developments which were potentially important and encouraging.[25] Professor Wilson, however, described the early seventeenth century as a society still heavily trammelled by custom, in which progress was bound to be jerky, particularly as the European scene was darkening. He summarised the impediments to which Professor Fisher referred as 'lack of skill, lack of money, lack of transport . . . ambitious projects . . . disastrous failures . . .'.[26] There were, however, redeeming features – the cloth industry was adjusting itself, coastal shipping was increasing, and colonial trade was coming to ease the problems of European trade. In his view, less than half a million earned their living directly from trade or manufactures – 10,000 merchants, 100,000 shopkeepers, tradesmen and artisans – so that the weight of the economy rested very directly on agriculture since half a million, if in 1600 the population was around the 4 million mark, was under 20 per cent of the total. Moreover, industry had not yet anything like its present form:

'we must rid our imagination of the accretions of two centuries that have associated it with urban life, with a clear division of capital and labour, with heavy accumulations of fixed capital in the shape of factories, plant, machinery and so forth. Here and there the beginnings of the later economy may be discerned. Some towns were already centres of certain specialised industries. . . . A few industries like brewing, saltmaking, ironworking and paper mills began in the 17th century to use metal vats, pans, forges and pumps and presses . . . these were not characteristic of the economy as a whole.'[27]

Other writers, piecemeal, in dealing with particular aspects of the period, have echoed these sentiments. That industrial change can only be assessed, is only meaningful, in the light of the overall structure of the economy, is a standard theme.

SECTORAL SHIFTS

What then, can at present be said of industrial change in the context of the economists' division of the economy into different sectors? One of the figures a modern economist expects to have available to him is a calculation of National Income and of Gross Domestic Product, two differently arrived-at estimates of what is ultimately the same thing seen from different aspects: the total amount of goods and services available for consumption or saving in any one year. Some goods produced in the country, of course, will have been exchanged for other goods produced outside the country. The number of these may vary from year to year, and the percentage of the total consumed which comes from the outside may also vary. The percentage of the total which goes into saving, and more particularly into investment, is of considerable importance, because such goods are probably laying the foundation of increased growth in the future. Some of them, however, are only replacing the worn-out investment of the past, so that economists are more interested in net figures if they can be obtained.

If the size of the population is known, it is also possible to work out *per capita* income, a figure which may be more revealing of progress than the gross total. This total income may be produced by varying percentages of the five major sectors of the economy, and the extent to which one or other sector may be more important largely determines the overall nature of the economy. An increase in the output of one sector either at the expense of another or in advance of another may therefore be extremely significant. Nef assumed that the industrial sector was growing faster than the rest of the economy. When people like Dr Ramsey[28] speak of industry 'failing' to absorb the increase in population they are implying that the sector is unlikely to have grown faster, although changes in the distribution of the work force do not necessarily go hand in hand with changes in the productivity of that work force and so in the output of the sector. Moreover, changes in one sector may induce changes in another.

The growth of the industrial sector and the growth of the trade and transport sector often show considerable interdependence because industrial growth, if linked (as it often is) with specialisation, means that as a rule goods have to be carried farther to their market, and so increases demand for transport. Increasing specialisation in agriculture may also increase demand. Increased demand for transport also reflects back on the agricultural sector in a demand for the materials for building ships or carts and for additional pack or cart animals, and therefore for feed for them. These linkage effects can be very important in explaining both the form growth takes and the nature of obstacles.

PROBLEMS OF APPLYING SUCH AN ANALYSIS IN THE SIXTEENTH CENTURY

Unfortunately for the economic historian of any period before the nineteenth century, records were not kept in a form which enables gross or aggregate figures to be calculated in any meaningful way.[29] The major difficulty is that so much that went to sustain the life of the people was imperfectly separated from the home, and much, perhaps most, production was still part of a non-market organisation. Economists, of course, are familiar with the position: at the beginning of most nations' movement towards a 'modern' economic structure comes a time when there is a semi-illusory leap ahead as a higher proportion of the country's production starts for the first time to flow in channels in which it can be counted.

It has, for example, been suggested that only 2–3 per cent of all grain stocks were sold on the market in the Elizabethan period. This figure, which is probably far too low, was not intended to cover grain which changed hands outside the market place for monetary or other considerations, but it does demonstrate one possible end of the scale on which the economy lies.

Division of the economy into major sectors is equally of dubious appropriateness when so much of the economy is still closely tied to the home.

POSSIBLE DISTRIBUTION OF WORK FORCE BETWEEN SECTORS IN THE PERIOD

Nevertheless, it is desirable to keep the concepts in mind as the significance of GDP and of sectoral shifts is not destroyed by our inability to measure them with any confidence. It is also desirable to have at least a rough idea of the percentage of people in the different sectors at the beginning of the period since Nef has offered some estimates of the people employed in different industries. It is commonly said that nine out of ten people worked in agriculture. Now it might be possible to demonstrate that nine out of ten people lived in the country, but that is by no means the same thing. Since residence is not the main issue it may be easier to work from the other end. In any society a percentage of people comes into the professional category – the king's servants, the lawyers, ministers of religion, doctors – and all of these added together must come to 2 or 3 per cent. Again, the categories do not fit the realities of society, but were one to include here – as one might justify doing – most of the gentry, whose unpaid local government service was so important, the percentage would rise to 4 or 5.

In trade and transport, categorisation once again fails: can one distinguish the mariner from the fisherman, the man who made his living carrying goods from the farmer using a wagon in the slack season? Even so, the merchants great and small, the shipowners and masters must have amounted to 3–4 per cent. The industrial sector is harder to estimate. The cloth industry alone – universally recognised as the largest industry in the kingdom – presents insuperable problems. How many of its spinsters were truly 'full-time', and what of the jobs that could enable the 5 or 6 year old to buy his own bread? Contemporary calculations suggest that it took the labours of forty people working a week to produce a broadcloth, but the newer 'draperies' were less labour intensive. Fifty thousand broadcloths exported[30] thus represented the annual labour of 38,500 people, however, and cloth was used within the kingdom too; thus the industry must have employed at least 2–3 per cent of a population of $2\frac{1}{2}$ million. Other industries present even more insuperable problems, yet the numbers of miners in the stannaries and the lead mining districts, even in the 1540s ran into several thousands. Where censuses survive which list male occupations – such as the Gloucestershire census of 1608 – only about 60 per cent have occupations which are directly concerned with agriculture, though many of the other employments are agriculture-related crafts.[31] In these circumstances it might be reasonable to consider that the industrial sector already provided employment for at least 10 per cent of the work force.[32]

These figures are not intended to convey any precise degree of accuracy, but are introduced to suggest that even in a relatively undifferentiated economy like that of the early Tudor period rather more people were engaged in pursuits that were not directly agricultural than is sometimes supposed; any available later figures must not be allowed to exaggerate growth rates by comparisons with an unrealistically low base figure.

Estimates of the gross value of the output of any of these sectors, however, would at present be little more than inspired fantasy. When in 1549 an act was passed which, if it had been enforced, would have produced contemporary figures of the number of sheep in the country, the estimates made before the Act (attempting to assess its potential profit-yield to the government) vary from 800,000 to 2 million.[33] With a range of this sort it is hardly likely that any precision in estimating output will ever be possible. Even at the end of the seventeenth century Gregory King altered two estimates of the area under crop so considerably between one draft and another that he was clearly producing only the roughest of approximations. Yet if one considers that perhaps 20 million acres were in some form of useful employment and that with rents at an average of 6d to 1s an acre a gross output per acre of 4s to 5s in value must have been the minimum normally expected to make it worth the farmer's while, one may have some idea of the order of magnitude of the output of the agricultural sector against which Nef's estimates of output in the industrial sector can be measured.

It is also desirable to have some sort of idea of what order of magnitude might justifiably be described as a 'revolution'. Most attempts of this sort when directed to more recent periods of industrial revolution have been made in terms of the rate of growth of GNP – an impossible task for the sixteenth and seventeenth centuries.[34] It is important, however, to remember that the sectoral shifts accompanying this rate of growth are not necessarily particularly impressive. The industrial sector has never in the course of English history represented the majority of the work force; it has barely and only briefly moved towards that figure. An increase, therefore, from a notional 10 per cent in the industrial sector to 15 per cent would represent a major change in the economic structure. It is hardly surprising, therefore, that in a period when the population may have risen 50 per cent that industry failed to absorb the rise, even if its function is to be viewed as that of a reservoir for surplus labour not required in agriculture and not as an area with its own powers of attraction.

THE IMPACT OF DEMOGRAPHIC CHANGE ON THE DISTRIBUTION OF THE WORK FORCE

A change in the size of the population may lead to a change in its distribution between the different sectors, however, and to some necessary reorganisation to accommodate the gain or loss. The total population may be of less significance[35] but the nature of the change and also the rate of change is important since its impact may vary if it comes from a change in the number of births or from a lengthening of the life of the average individual or from some combination of changes, since nearly every change induces subsequent changes elsewhere. Moreover, since men and women are born, marry and die in a social context the absolute importance of many variables will depend on customary attitudes – to remarriage, to extra-marital childbirth, to the position of women and expectations of marital circumstances. A considerable amount of research time has of late been invested in population studies the detail of which need not concern us except in as much as it demonstrates a significant rate of change in the sixteenth century but one unevenly distributed across the country and across the century, reversing a downward trend which had maintained itself for more than a century since 1348. The explanation for this reversal remains unclear. Despite some contemporary and present-day claims[36] there seems no reason to believe that the country was so blessed over the century as to be notably free from plague and epidemics, while the spread of syphilis is more likely to have reduced fertility than anything else.[37] Current medical research in primitive parts of the world suggests that a protein-deficient diet reduces fertility because women conceive less readily and for a shorter period – but diet should have improved after the Black Death, and it is not clear whether the effects of protein-deficiency linger on to generations which do not themselves experience it. The idea that the birth rate may have dropped in the pre-plague years from natural causes such as diet would also need investigation.

So far as recent studies have gone, they do not show a steady upward drift of births, but rather a sharp upward surge, followed by a lull or a set-back in the 1550s and then by another sharp upswing, which brings to mind the 'wave' pattern of births noticeable in nineteenth-century Norway, or in recent times as the post-war baby boom itself reached child-bearing age. In other words the number of women at risk per thousand of population is higher than normal, perhaps as a result of a number of years in which infantile diseases were less virulent than usual. This pattern, however, may be only localised in appearance. There are regions where the local historians seriously doubt whether the population was growing at all noticeably – parts of Bedfordshire, for example;[38] and other regions like Kent and Middlesex where it may have been growing much faster; and others still where the pattern of growth is a-typical. Both the overall growth and the distinctive regional patterns may cast significant light on the timing and location of industrial growth.

It is worth considering carefully the moment at which the Tudors first started to talk in terms of overpopulation, rather than of simple annoyance at a growth in the number of beggars. In the 1540s and 1550s they are aware only of a curtailment of demand for labour which is generally attributed to the evil consequences of enclosure. Even in the 1560s, though there is increasing concern over poor people needing to be 'set on work', the idea of population pressure is not explicit. It is in the plans devised in the 1570s and 1580s that the writers specifically bring to the fore the idea that the country has too many people for the commonweal. After that these notions become a commonplace until at least the 1620s when feelings that England could use more people become more common again.[39]

This, of course, is only a guide to the moment when population was observed to be a problem; there could have been considerable slack to take up before that point was reached, but it is interesting that it coincides with the first marked upward surge of births.

Religion may have deterred many men at that time from taking a census. Some felt that without the overt command of God as given in the Book of Numbers, pestilence might strike them as it struck the children of Israel after David had numbered the people (II Samuel 24). Nevertheless, they began to feel that the economy was not making full use of the unskilled labour force that was available and that active intervention by the government would be necessary to deal with the growing multitude of the poor.

This is the most important demographic fact for an economic historian to grasp because all the rest must be to a degree uncertain. The jury of the rape of Hastings, returning an answer to the Crown on the question of the number of people who would be deprived of their livings if the iron mills continued, said 'all the inhabitants of the towns and villages aforesaid, whose numbers we be not able to express'.[40] It may well be that what they could not number then we shall never accurately count now, even by the rule of four. The inability to work with precise figures does not exempt the historian from considering the impact of growth on the economy and endeavouring to establish where the additional hands found work and what additional demands for food, clothing and shelter they may have made. An increase in the number of people is virtually bound to result in some growth in the total output of the economy, but growth of this sort without technological and other advances to increase absolute growth *per capita* may lead simply to a crisis point when expanding demand hits a 'ceiling' of supply.[41] Viewed from this angle, industrial growth might be seen as a 'last resort' or least profitable use of surplus labour capacity, and the weakening impetus of its development in the seventeenth century might seem to be the natural result of a return to slight or negative population growth. Nef, however, while very deeply concerned over the wage rates for labour at the time and the possible impact of the loss of purchasing power of the individual labourer on the overall demand for goods, was relatively unimpressed by problems of adapting the economy to providing for additional numbers of people.

THE SIGNIFICANCE OF THE AGRICULTURAL SECTOR FOR AN ASSESSMENT OF THE ECONOMY AT THIS TIME

It may be for this reason that Nef hardly concerned himself with agriculture either, although since agriculture was undoubtedly the largest single employer of labour in the period and arguably absorbed the highest percentage of capital, what happened in that sector is evidently critical to any assessment of the wider economic development of the period. In this neglect, however, Nef may have merely been reflecting the preconceptions of his own time. Even twenty-five years ago it was orthodox economics to suggest that agriculture had a strictly limited role in the growth process. At most it could produce the same amount of output with fewer workers or less capital, and it was thought that this represented a smooth 'shedding' of factors which could be more productively used elsewhere. Today many think that agriculture is a much more critical sector both in the production of raw materials and as a consumer of goods and services produced by other sectors.[42] An increase in farmers' and landowners' incomes might thus stimulate demand for industrial goods.

Moreover, some historians would argue that both labour and capital invested in agriculture in fact brought a higher return than labour or capital invested in manufacturing or trade. If this was the case then although the growth of industrial capital and labour force does not lose its importance it loses some of its primacy, and the nature of its role in the overall growth of the economy will need to be more rigorously assessed. Kerridge claims, for example, that increased output in the agricultural sector was accompanied by a reduction in the labour force in agriculture. Indeed, he implies that it was done also with a reduction in the acreage under the plough at any given moment.

'In the early modern period most of the enclosed land in the plain countries was converted to an up and down system. Employment was increased where permanent tillage was enclosed. Generally speaking, the enclosure of common field townships for up and down husbandry led to a degree of agricultural depopulation. The proportion of tillage was necessarily reduced from about one half to a third or even a quarter. The labour force was therefore reduced.'[43]

He concluded that unit costs were four times as high in common fields as in comparable up-and-down ones.[44]

If this case could be proved not simply for a small minority of farms but for a sizeable number, Nef's industrial revolution would indeed have to be fitted into a matrix of widespread development. Unfortunately Kerridge's 'agricultural revolution' has aroused as much opposition as Nef's 'industrial revolution'. Joan Thirsk is prepared to see farm production making 'rapid strides' and in the seventeenth century to identify 'intensified cultivation on existing lands' by a cycle of fodder crops, stock, manure, more corn and so on, improved seed and sown leys.[45] Professors Jones and Mingay, however, maintain that the period of advance does not gather momentum until the eighteenth century. The problem is a significant one for Nef's thesis because land is a limited commodity which, while it may be turned to a number of purposes, can rarely be used for more than one purpose at a time. An increased pressure for grain production, unless accompanied by Kerridge's postulated improvements, may reduce the area devoted to sheep – and so the available wool – or reduce the area used for industrial crops, or timber.[46] Hoskins pessimistically argues that grain production 'barely' kept pace with demand and much recent discussion about price rises postulates that lag in supply drove up prices, possibly culminating in a crisis which slowed population growth.[47] If this is so, and if labour and capital invested in the agricultural sector are indeed more profitable than similar amounts invested in trade or industry, one need seek no farther for an explanation of the apparent weakening of industrial growth in the third and fourth decades of the seventeenth century.

Even historians who would not wish to adopt so extreme a view, however, feel that Nef's neglect of the greater part of the sector was unwise.

The output of the agricultural sector in this period controlled in many ways the potential output of the industrial sector. Though the merchants could and did import wool, they did so in quantities which were generally too small to make a significant difference, so that the amount of wool available set an upper limit to the amount of cloth that could be produced. The amount of leather and parchment produced was similarly limited by the numbers of sheep and cattle killed. The amount of specialised crops grown also affected the supplies of dye stuffs, teazels, oil, and so on.[48] A poor agricultural season was therefore in all probability followed by a poor industrial season, even if the two did not coincide. Industry was still much affected directly by the season. The flood that drowned the farmer's field flooded the watermills, weirs and dykes, and probably stopped the windmill. The drought that burned the crops also brought the watermill to a halt, though it may have made transport easier. The ice that froze the fields when the ploughs should have been out again stopped the mill, halted building, and held up the ships.

Moreover, so long as man was dependent on the direct effects of wind and water for most of his power, so long was the total volume of that power limited by the availability of suitable sites for mills, and so long were the interests of inland transport on waterways and power likely to be in conflict.

THE PROBLEM OF CAPITAL INVESTMENT IN DIFFERENT SECTORS OF THE ECONOMY

Nef claimed that a significant amount of capital was being invested in industry. He was impressed by the size of some of the individual capital requirements which were being met. Even if the amount invested in industrial development was increasing, however, it may not have kept pace with the increasing amount invested in agriculture or the social infrastructure. Of all the problems associated with a meaningful assessment of capital, that of quantifying agricultural capital remains the most intransigent. So much investment in agriculture, the improvement of natural resources, is represented by effort laid out over a period of centuries, effort which is strictly indistinguishable from the input which produced the yearly crops and selected the seed for the new crop. Moreover, such effort has constantly to be renewed if the land is not to 'fall back' or 'tumble down'. The ways in which additional capital may have been put into farms on a day-to-day basis by the employment of a little extra labour are not necessarily distinguishable in the type of records which remain for us.

Even in the sixteenth century the fixed labour costs were in favour of intensive rather than extensive methods, and the extra hand to spread dung, clear drains, and so on may have made an enormous difference to the final output. The improvement of the capital invested in flocks and herds simply by the slow betterment of the strain is another element which will never be properly measured.

Land itself, unimproved and perhaps unused, had a value, but the rentable value of the land depended partly on the amount of effort that had been put into it. While the farmer might speak of the land being 'in good heart', an owner may think more in terms of the actual improvements that have been made; and in this sense, hedges and ditches, drains and watercourses are significant applications of capital. When writers spoke of enclosure, they spoke in terms of the increased rent that could be obtained after the enclosure, and this increase represents the return on the capital invested. Unfortunately, it is generally impossible to work out the rate of return. Sale of land does therefore represent capital changing hands, though not to the whole value of the sale.

Another form of farm capital generally provided by the landlord are the farm buildings: and it should be realised that the construction of a fine new barn which will protect the grain from the ravages of the weather, rats, mice and other vermin may be as important in increasing the effective supply of the grain as an increase in grain harvested. The improvement of stables, cowhouses, piggeries, may be important in increasing animal reproduction rates, protecting the poultry from predators and so on. Additions to fixed farm capital of this sort are hard to trace, and inventories, which these days are so much in vogue as sources of information, shed no light on the quality of the construction of the buildings, and make no mention of hedges, ditches and manure heaps.

The farmer himself had a considerable amount of capital to provide: the movable farm equipment of ploughs, harrows, wains, carts, spades, hoes, harness and the like generally either belonged to the farmer or was hired by him from the landlord. Once again, inventories are hardly helpful in indicating changes in quality: an early sixteenth-century farmer's equipment, with one or two exceptions, can be described in much the same terms as the early nineteenth-century farmer's, and yet the latter's plough, in terms of efficiency, might be something different again from his sixteenth-century forbear's.

The total amount of capital investment in agriculture on hundreds of thousands of farms of all sizes must heavily outweigh the investment of capital in any other sphere. In addition, the farmer needed working capital. The ratio of the return on capital invested or capital/output ratio has only just begun to be explored. One must be clear that this ratio is not necessarily in any way related to the 'capitalising' of the annual rentable value on the basis of which the ownership of land passed from hand to hand – generally at 'twenty years purchase' – or a 5 per cent rate of return on the money expended. Recently, however, Dr Grassby, working on the returns received by seventeenth-century merchants, concluded that the merchant's return on his capital was lower than that of the man with his capital in agriculture.[49]

The capital invested in the social infrastructure must have been next in size to that invested in agriculture. Despite the notorious deficiencies of the road and bridge systems, their upkeep alone, and that of river and harbour facilities, was considerable, particularly if one costs the 'free' statute labour. This sort of investment yields no measurable capital/output ratio since the direct charge rarely falls on the user, but the capital cost must not be ignored. Seen in this context, the capital invested in industry cannot be as overwhelmingly impressive as Nef suggested, but it was not unimportant. Of fixed capital, more may have been invested in ships and shipyards than in any other industry – Dr Scammell estimates that in the 1540s the east coast fleet alone represented a capital investment of £13,750,[50] so that a total of around £50,000 would not be unreasonable. The shipping industry probably continued to absorb the most capital, although it is possible that outlay on mills, both water and, increasingly, wind driven, may have run it close. Kent alone had thirty-nine windmills in 1600[51] in addition to over two hundred watermills, each of which represents an investment of not less than £100, and while Kent was possibly particularly well endowed the total investment in mills throughout the country must have been considerable. Investment in looms, individually perhaps not very valuable, must also *in toto* have been important, and there was increasing investment in furnaces for various purposes, forges, equipment for boiling or brewing and the like.

Fixed capital, however, was only part of the capital needed. Most capital invested in industry was almost certainly movable. The cloth in its unfinished state progressing through the pipeline, the hides spending their statutory twelve months in the tanner's various vats, the iron awaiting processing: all the inventories suggest that it is this stock which represented the manufacturer's or merchant's greatest capital investment. In some ways this is hardly surprising. There is a close connection between investment in fixed capital and technological changes. A technological innovation generally has to be embodied in the form of capital laid out and results in an increase in the percentage of fixed capital in the total cost structure. This period, however, saw only occasional innovations which required fixed capital outlay. The spread of windmills may have been one. The soughs which were made to drain the more valuable mines is another, but they were insignificant in the total distribution of capital.

If movable capital was more important, it was also possibly in short supply. Economic historians, however, tend to prove this indirectly, by demonstrating the relatively high rates of return which men could make by lending capital. The structure of some industries, such as the tin mining industry, permitted the merchant with money to lend to exact penal rates from his clients. The tinners received money in advance for which they bound themselves to deliver so much tin at the coinage – an arrangement by which the merchant was thought to gain 60 per cent.[52] Similarly, when the tinner delivered tin to the smelter in return for which he was given a bill for so much 'white' tin at the coinage, he might, if he needed money, discount that bill – but the rates were heavy.

However socially undesirable this practice and others like it may have been, it is not good evidence for the general scarcity of capital. The interest rate on good security in the open London market is a better guide. The argument runs that the rate of interest is a guide to the relative scarcity of capital because, as in any other form of market, men will bid against one another for the good, and those ventures which promise a very high return without excessive risk will be able to get satisfaction before those whose expected return is only moderate. Therefore, the rate of return indicates how much of the legitimate market for capital can be satisfied. At the beginning of the period, when the usury laws prohibited such things, the rate of interest was 10 per cent or higher. By the early Jacobean period, however, there are signs that the rate was falling, though the relationship between this fact and the acts supposedly governing such transactions is obscure.[53] It looks, therefore, as if capital may have been increasing.

Nef was quick to mark industrial areas in which capital was invested in large blocks, but he rarely distinguished between estimates which gave a total costing of all the expenditure likely to be necessary before the plant would make its first returns, and estimates limited to the actual construction costs of the physical plant. This failure to distinguish between types of estimates makes the calculation of capital/output ratios difficult. Nevertheless, there are some points which suggest that Dr Grassby may be right in claiming that merchants' profits were not the cream which is often suggested.

Capital invested by a sleeping partner in the business of draping seems to have earned 14–19 per cent, which is hardly startling and does not suggest that capital was wholly confined to high earning projects.[54] The capital/output ratio is impossible to determine but it seems unlikely that it was widely different from the 2:1 which was possible in the early industrial revolution period, in the eighteenth to nineteenth centuries. Ships were usually hired at 2s a ton-month in the late sixteenth century, which at a cost of £3 to £4 a ton and a working year of nine months gives a return of under 30 per cent before repairs and renovations are considered.

If capital was not as scarce as is sometimes suggested, however, it was by no means abundant, and prudent individuals were rarely anxious to invest all they possessed in one venture. The significance of the appearance of joint-stock companies as an indicator of a more advanced organisation of the capital market has been much debated. Certainly, it necessitated more elaborate and sophisticated forms of control. Certainly it introduced a more modern approach to the calculation of profit and loss and one which some men took over in their private and personal financial accounts. Historians have therefore found the calculation of precise profits easier as the joint-stock accountancy approach spread. On the other hand the joint-stock company was long reserved for a very small number of areas which one way or another had peculiar problems. The immediate impact of the method was therefore fairly limited, and its significance related more to the long-term developments of the economy and the growth rate for capital.[55]

THE PROBABLE INTERACTION OF CHANGES IN ONE SECTOR ON ANOTHER

It is not possible to ignore, as Nef tended to do, the way in which industry and industrial development was embedded in the matrix of the wider economy. A sudden expansion (if sudden expansion it was) would be certain to have an impact on other sectors. Nef, however, tended to behave as if those elements in the economy were fixed and unchanging or purely dependent variables operating without friction. From the very nature of the development, however, it must be apparent that such changes cannot take place in such a frictionless manner. At the grass-roots level, diversion of a stream to operate the bellows of a forge may leave too little water for the local corn mill. Heavy use of the highway by carts carrying materials to and from an iron works may destroy amenities normally enjoyed by the local inhabitants (Doc. 3); if a mine is opened up access to it may disrupt local farming arrangements

(Doc. 4). There may be social conflict between the incoming miners and the farming community. In innumerable ways, changing the local use of resources causes friction. Some of the problems may be soluble: a horse mill or a windmill provides an alternative source of power to a watermill; a mining community may become acceptable as it increases the local farmer's profits by providing a new source of demand for his products; heavier use of the roads may make it worth someone's while to improve the whole system, to the farmers' ultimate benefit as well. Such solutions, however, are neither automatic nor guaranteed.[56] In some cases only improved technology can solve the problem about conflict over scarce resources; in others, social tensions can create a permanent barrier to change.

The one aspect of this which Nef did absorb because it fitted his industrial arguments related to the alleged shortage of wood and its soaring cost. Nef harped on the conflicting demands for wood – and wood was certainly essential for many purposes. Heart of oak for ships, and for the best furniture, yew for bows, beech for glass making, apple for the cogs in mills, birch for the wood turner's spring, ash for the handles of tools – the types and requirements were endless, apart from the use for wood ash, for bark, for brushwood in fences and drains. Efficient coppicing and management could solve some problems of supply but not all. Wood could be imported, but then it would have to be paid for by additional exports; the Baltic (whence timber could be got) was apparently taking all the English cloth it wanted, and the balance of payments to the area was still unfavourable.

Until a major substitution of inorganic for organic raw materials took place, however, a shift in the economic structure was bound to changes in all areas of the productivity of agriculture, or to the introduction of cheap raw materials from overseas to be worked up by a larger, cheaper or more highly skilled English labour force. The agricultural sector might increase its productivity so that labour became available for industrial employment, but throughout the period it also had to produce most of the additional raw material for the industrial sector.

Any shift between products, moreover (the most obvious example of which was the shift of land from the production of corn to the production of sheep), if not accompanied by increased productivity, was likely to aggravate the short-term problem, since different types of agricultural produce themselves required different labour inputs, and the need to feed the population was the final imperative. The industrial sector was not, therefore, autonomous, and Nef may be criticised for presenting it for the most part as a sector striving for autonomy.

IMPLICATIONS OF PRICE RISES IN THE PERIOD

One of the indicators which economic historians need to take into account in estimating the pressures on different sectors is the varying rise in prices. Nef took an interest in the rise of prices, but chiefly from the point of view of supplies of the precious metals, seeking to demonstrate the early recovery of silver mining in central Europe in the fifteenth century.[57] He deals less fully with the effect of rising prices on the industrial sector. Whatever one's reservations about price indexes for the sixteenth century may be, and whatever technical problems may arise from the fact that good price series are more frequent for agricultural than for industrial goods, the difference between the sharp rise in price of agricultural goods, and the much more modest rise, or in some cases absence of rise, for industrial goods, is so marked that no one can doubt its significance. Now it is true, that it is easier to hold down industrial prices than the prices of agricultural products where the supply is comparatively inelastic. It is also true that a comparatively lower price brings the product within the range of a wider market and so may lead to an increase in demand, but it is true in addition that if goods are to be valued in terms of their market price, then the total share of the market which the industrial sector holds will constantly threaten to diminish and a certain amount of additional output will be needed purely to keep steady the sector's share of the market, viewed in terms of prices.

Nef, well aware that if a greater percentage of any income is absorbed by basic necessities there will be less left for luxuries, made a determined attempt to show that various factors may have offset the apparent decline in the labourer's wage, since he wished to argue for increased consumption and realised that the existence of a massive drop in the purchasing power of the largest group in society hardly enhanced his case. He paid less attention to the effects of the redistribution of income which this implies and comparatively little to the problems of social structure which may also have affected both demand and supply.

THE ROLE OF CHANGES IN SOCIAL STRUCTURE, SOCIAL INSTITUTIONS AND SOCIAL ATTITUDES

Most historians today will give at least some place to the role of factors which are not quantifiable, as for instance the social structure, even if they argue that these are principally brought about by the insidious effects of income redistribution. Major changes in social structure, of course, do not necessarily accompany shifts in the economic structure, but the social structure does govern the nature and type of goods in demand; and it seems probable that certain types of structure are more likely to throw up a demand for mass-produced goods of the sort usually associated with industrial revolution.

More important even than the social structure, however, are likely to be the dominant notions in society about such things as the nature of ownership of property and relations between master and servant, individuality, the individual and his rights and duties, and the role assigned to government. Recently historians have laid great stress on the need for advance on a wide front and for concurrent changes in other areas. North's and Thomas's emphasis on 'appropriate socio-economic institutions' is only one of these. Most people agree that industrial development is not solely dependent on purely economic forces. Much also depends on the community's attitude to work and to material possessions.[58] The relationship between that attitude and the different social groups' view of themselves and their view of others is also a critical factor. The source of income of the dominant group, the rigidity of the social structure, the extent to which industrialists, entrepreneurs or merchants are acceptable in society, are even more directly relevant to the degree of attention paid to economic developments, and to the encouragement of 'useful' skills and professional attitudes. A government which supports industry and trade can be vital; a labouring class whose expectations of rising a little by thrift and diligence are low may cause frustration because its attitude to work may be one in which the objective is solely the acquisition of enough to buy one's immediate daily bread (or beer), and once this paltry sum is acquired, leisure is overwhelmingly preferred. Economists treat this unaccommodating attitude as a 'backward sloping' supply curve – the higher the wages the fewer days worked, the opposite to the response hoped for. Contemporaries certainly referred to the unwillingness of the poor to work in years of plenty, while in years of dearth they pressed for work, which suggests that there may have been some such tendency throughout the period, but as the same complaints were still heard in the eighteenth century, it is hard to say whether attitudes altered at all in the period.[59]

Study of the social structure provides another approach to our understanding of the economy, and so of the place of the industrial sector within it: if the relative size of the different social groups can be established together with some idea of the average or median income of each group, one is moving towards an approximation of the 'national income' – which is ultimately the equivalent of gross domestic product. Moreover, a shift in the major source of wealth of the dominant groups in society is another important indicator of an economic shift. Work on this aspect of the social structure is still fragmentary. A beginning has been made on the percentage of the population belonging to the aristocracy or gentry, and information is accumulating on the size of the professional classes, but all the work done – as it must be done initially – at the local level on the breakdown of the poorer classes into different wealth and status groupings only serves to underline the very considerable differences that may exist between village and village, parish and parish, town and town – and so emphasises the dangers of extrapolation from the few existing detailed studies.

ALTERNATIVE MEASURES OF GROWTH: THE INCREASING STANDARD OF COMFORT

Perhaps paradoxically, however, one aspect of Nef's original thesis which has received some recent support is his suggestion that the well-being of the individual can be shown to have increased over the period. From the gentleman living in his comfortable well-glazed house[60] to the poor artisan, all could find a greater volume and variety of goods to make life comfortable. Certainly contemporary eulogies of such a life did not stress manufactured goods in quite the way that Nef did. Nicholas Breton, in what must be the archetype of such descriptions, spoke of

'hay in the barn, horses in the stable, oxen in the stall, sheep in the pen, hogs in the sty, corn in the garner, cheese in the loft, milk in the dairy, cream in the pot, butter in the dish, ale in the tub, and *aqua vitae* in the bottle, beef in the brine, brawn in the sauce and bacon in the roof, herbs in the garden and water at our doors, whole cloths to our backs and some money in our coffers, and having all this, if we serve God withal, what in God's name can we desire to have more ?'[61]

As David Crossley has recently claimed, 'Despite this suggestion that the improvement of the product and the reduction of costs led to a growth in the sales of glass, the primary explanation for expansion in demand and the attraction of new workers lies in the purchasing power of important sections of the landowning and farming communities and their changing standards of comfort in buildings and furnishings'.[62] It is true that he has elsewhere qualified this by saying 'there was no real mass market, nor was there any export-led boom in a manufacturing industry as seen in the eighteenth century',[63] but the former statement has considerable weight.

Is it in fact possible to establish that the average individual gentleman, merchant yeoman or labourer had better and greater facilities by 1640 than his ancestor had had in 1540? It is hard to show conclusively that any one class had on average a markedly higher income than in 1540, once allowance has been made for inflation.

(i) *The Aristocracy*
Professor Stone has shown that the mean net income of peers in 1559 was £2,200, and that the mean net income of a peer in 1641 adjusted to 1559 prices as £2,290, which is hardly an impressive rise, though the adjustment may be rather too heavily based on indexes which over-emphasise the element of increased food prices to be wholly appropriate for peers.[64]

(ii) *The Gentry*
Details of the average income of the gentry families are harder to come by, but despite the fragmentary nature of the evidence, it would seem that they were able to keep their rents rising in line with rising prices, while those who went in for direct sheep farming may have done even better. Professor Simpson comments that 'it is difficult to see how landlords who were sheep farmers had anything to fear from inflation. There was nothing to stop them from taking advantage of rising prices and the improvement in their incomes would enable them to absorb a higher cost of living.'[65] Though the individual examples of annual income which he is able to ascertain are rather ambiguous, and though it is hard to establish whether a man increases his income from a particular set of lands or increases his income by adding to his lands, Dr Cliffe, from his systematic study of all the Yorkshire gentry, concludes on the basis of inventories that

'. . . during the period under consideration the values of personal estates tended to follow an upward trend, certainly among the richer gentry. In the reign of Elizabeth a leading squire might have £2000 or £3000 in personal property, in the reign of Charles I between £5000 and £10,000. Although this trend is partly explained by the falling value of money it also reflected a general improvement in material conditions.'[66]

(iii) *The Merchant*
The wealthy London merchant at least equalled the gentleman in the size of his possessions, and it would appear that he was becoming wealthier as the period progressed. On the other hand, Dr Grassby concludes that 'it is doubtful whether the charitable middling tradesmen

improved their real position'.[67] The figures quoted show a rise from
c. £250 to c. £1,000, which Dr Grassby rather roughly deflates by the
price index figures to reach his conclusions. The country merchants
were on the whole much poorer than the London merchants. There
were a few wealthy merchants dealing in overseas trade, and a few
clothiers whose fortunes overtopped the thousand pounds, but the
average merchant's inventory rarely reached £100 in the sixteenth
century, and the rises in money values which did occur Dr Grassby
thinks no more than kept pace with the rise in prices.

(iv) The Farmer

More confidence has been shown in dealing with farmers' inventories:
that is with the inventories of people directly exploiting the land. Any
increased return from higher prices or additional output would after all
flow initially into their hands, even if the landlord was on the *qui vive*
to obtain his share. Miss Finch, for example, praises Brudenell for being
'not content merely to prevent farmers from retaining more than their
fair share of farming profits. He sought to increase the profits themselves
– he saw that the greatest prosperity of the farmers could only be
achieved by a change from open field farming to farming in severalty.'[68]

There seems, in fact, some agreement that the peasant farmer on the
land was doing quite well. Mr Skipp speaks of 'indisputable evidence of
greater peasant wealth'.[69] The table he produces in support of this is
interesting, because he gives mean, median and mid-point figures for
his inventories, which are grouped by decade, thus illustrating clearly
the differences obtained from a different choice of criteria; and he
adjusts the mid-point in accordance with the Phelps-Brown and
Hopkins index, which makes surprisingly little difference, indeed
makes an improvement in the 1610–29 period.

Table	No.	Mean	Median	Mid-point	Mid-point adjusted
1530–49	23	17–05–01	13–04–10	15–05–00	15–05–00
1550–69	54	33–11–00	22–16–00	28–03–06	22–08–00
1570–89	27	34–10–20	31–09–04	32–10–09	22–08–00
1590–09	20	49–11–06	35–04–06	42–08–01	38–07–00
1610–29	51	58–14–00	29–11–08	44–02–10	46–05–00
1630–49	42	69–07–00	52–08–01	60–17–07	54–07–00

Mr Havinden, from his analysis of household and farm inventories
in Oxfordshire, comes to much the same conclusions. He points out
that the analysis applies only to those who had enough wealth to
require an inventory to be taken, a limit legally set at £5 – an amount

which, because of the rise in prices, went lower down the scale as the period progressed. This accounts for the rising number of inventories, as the sixteenth century progressed, of value at under £10. At the other end of the scale, however, there is a steady increase in absolute numbers of people whose estates were worth over £50. To demonstrate a rise in the standard of material possessions between the 1550s and 1580s amongst the farmers, Havinden takes two inventories where the farming equipment and area under the plough were virtually identical to show that while the valuation put on those items had risen even further, the later one was three times more valuable than the earlier.[70]

Interpretation of all these figures, however, depends upon the price indexes. Mr Shipp's comfortable rise in peasant wealth, a fourfold increase in money terms, whichever central point one takes, would become a decline if one assumed that the peasant's expenditure on the sort of items included in the inventories had risen more than fourfold.

(v) The Poor

The problem of the well-being of the poor, however, is a much more vexed question. In theory, it would be quite possible for a rise in *per capita* income and economic progress to go hand in hand with stagnation, or even increasing misery on the part of a section of the community. The artisan, cottage farmer and day-labourer or worker in industry appears at this period to have comprised about 30 per cent of the total population, though the percentage varied considerably from area to area.[71] It has generally been assumed on the basis of established wage rates and the price indexes that the real wage enjoyed by the labourer was halved in the period, despite Nef's arguments. One way of calculating this is to work out how many hours of labour a poor workman would need to put in to earn enough to purchase a fixed proportion of grain for breadstuff – a reasonable assumption for the poor, the bulk of whose food was cereal or cereal products and the bulk of whose income went on food. Most of this work has been done on the Continent with the assumption that a family of four required twelve quintals of corn a year; it concludes that prior to 1543 it took a labourer under 100 hours to 'earn' a quintal but that thereafter the number of hours required rose sharply to well over the hundred, where it remained until the late nineteenth century.[72] This perhaps is the critical point for us, since by 1883 the industrialising of Europe was well under way. It suggests that the purchasing power of the very poor, exiguous as it was and almost wholly directed to the problem of keeping body and soul together, was of minimal importance in providing the effective consumer demand for any other goods.

If this is so, then arguably Nef would have been better advised to concentrate on showing that the size of this group was significantly smaller in England than elsewhere – or that the real purchasing power of the 'have' classes was greater in England than in other areas.

In fact Nef's case for doubting the severity of the impact of rising prices on a worker's real wages may well be vindicated to some degree by a careful study of the justices' policy in the sixteenth century of regulating the wages of workmen against the price of corn in the local market. Professor Phelps-Brown and Miss Hopkins' figures, in an article which was a pioneering effort based on printed material rather than original research, have been accepted perhaps too uncritically by those who have used them. In 1610 the price of grain on the market at Norwich was set at 4s below the price given in the modern price indexes for that year. At the same time, the Norwich justices set the wage rates at what historians commonly take to be the standard rate for the period. The Norwich labourer was thus better off than the historian would suppose. It is possible, therefore, that the absence of a detailed study of the relative balance between wages and prices in specific areas is leading to distortion. This whole subject, however, while of critical importance for social history, may have little relevance to the question of an industrial revolution if the arguments above are acceptable.[73]

One possible reason for considering that the percentage of those wholly dependent on wage labour may have been smaller in England than is sometimes assumed is the apparent prevalence in some areas of bye-employment – the part-time occupation which in some cases became a full-time occupation, but which was not regulated by the justices until in James's reign there began to be attempts to lay down the minimum piece rates to be paid for some jobs in the clothing industry. There were innumerable industries of this sort – lace making, glove making, basket making, broom making – as well as all the rural labour that came to be employed in carding and spinning for the clothing industry, knitting and the like. Nor was all this labour 'exploited' by capitalists for a pittance. The defence which the wool brokers entered to the clothiers' complaints in 1615 makes it clear that large numbers were self-employed, having enough money to get started; they 'weekely buy their woolle in the market . . . and weekely returne it in yarne and make good proffit thereof'.[74] Often a man would have more than one such bye-employment. Men in the midlands who took up nail making or other small-scale metal trades may have been labourers so far as social status was concerned, but may rarely or never have laboured by the day for wages, except perhaps at harvest time, when wages were much higher than normal.

Other men described as labourers owned a horse, and perhaps a cart, and earned money by letting the horse to hire, like Richard Vinedy of Sedgely, or by carting by the day, activities which were better paid than day labour. Charcoal burning was another occupation which appears to have been well paid, and a man apparently occupied full time at wood cutting earned very respectable amounts. Indeed, the people who were very poor seem to have been those who already worked in a community which had only one resource. The poor in Norwich who made their living by spinning needed assistance. The arable farming districts where bye-employments did not develop, the tin miners of Cornwall and Devon who were poor and peripatetic, the lead miners of Derbyshire, all these might have far more poor amongst them needing relief than other areas. Professor Everitt, however, thinks that as the century progressed there was a growing number of labourers who belonged to the lowest category of the property-less and often vagrant poor. Pressure on land, he felt, was also squeezing the poorer of the propertied. A growing percentage of labourers in the population as the population is growing in size is not an encouraging prospect for those who would like to see a really significant rise in absolute consumer demand. If the numbers of the poor who could not support themselves increased too much then the precariously based improvements which the wealthier groups at least were apparently enjoying might have been endangered.

There seems, nonetheless, a consensus of opinion that in some sense the standard of living did improve. If so, it can hardly have done so unless production *per capita* of some goods increased. This, however, gives no direct clue as to what sector increased and by how much. After all, over a period, some goods which have a longer life span than humans, as houses and the like may well have, tend to accumulate. The father may build the house, the son, keeping it repaired, may have energy left to build a barn. In such ways, in times of peace, the kind of goods which are most noticeable in inventories may build up when the increase *per capita* in output may be imperceptible. It is unlikely, however, that this is the only reason for the rise in personal wealth.

THE ROLE OF GOVERNMENT

One of the factors affecting the development of the economy which has been most variously estimated at different times is the role of government. This is very largely due to major shifts in pure economic theory. A generation reared in the belief that, just as Canute could not turn back the waves so a modern government could not divert the course of economic progress, was likely to adopt the fundamental attitude which Nef takes up, that since the outlook on their role and the methods adopted by the English and French rulers were fundamentally similar, one of the reasons for England's supposedly more impressive performance in the industrial sphere lay in the greater impotence of the English rulers to enforce their will. Nef also thought that the English were more lightly taxed than the French, and, rather surprisingly, that such taxation as there was was regressive, leaving the wealthy in a better position to employ capital.

Both historical and economic attitudes have changed in the interval, partly in response to the modern, more highly governed state, and partly in recognition of the fact that a body which handles as high a percentage of the total national income as the government does would make an impact on the economy whether or not it ever issued a legislative act. North and Thomas, however, have recently returned to something akin to Nef's attitude to government because they view the creation of suitable property rights (a government prerogative) as a critical factor in preparing the way for sustained growth.[75]

(i) The impact of government income and expenditure

How valid is Nef's assessment of the role of government? It can be divided into consideration of the role of government spending, and legislation. At one point Nef committed himself to the view that the government of the kingdom handled only 2–3 per cent of total national income. Since at no previous stage had he attempted to calculate national income, this is perhaps surprising. It is not difficult, however, to show that the income of the central government was relatively small. While it is extraordinarily difficult to produce a balance sheet of Crown income for any single year, it is possible to discover what contemporaries thought was an average or normal income. This has to be divided into two parts. The Crown had certain revenues which came in every year. These were the 'ordinary' revenues – the income from Crown lands, from the customs and from the law, including the king's feudal rights. Such revenue was either 'certain' (that is, it came in in an amount which could be precisely known in advance) or 'casual' in the sense that the profits from the administration of justice depended on the relative degree of law-abidingness in the population and the efficiency of the law enforcement, but which 'taking one year with another', in the contemporary phrase, could be assumed to approximate to a known figure. The royal income from such sources in 1540, however, was under £200,000.[76] A very thorough assessment of royal resources in 1551 put the ordinary Crown revenues at just over £168,000.[77] Careful administration, and especially the raising of the rates on customs, increased this figure during Elizabeth's reign some two and a half times. In 1621 James I's ordinary revenue was given as £485,804, which may have been raised in a couple of years to £570,000,[78] and it may not have been much further increased until the very end of Charles I's reign, though the customs farms did rise in the late 1630s.

In addition to the ordinary Crown revenue, the ruler could ask Parliament to grant further help. This might take the form of the traditional late medieval grant of a fifteenth and tenth, or it might take the newer form of a subsidy.

Parliamentary grants, however, were granted rather reluctantly, and the government found itself obliged to make out a special case for each. War was the most common form of 'extraordinary' expenditure in the period, and the grants came irregularly with the advent or threat of wars. It is therefore hard to calculate how much additional spending power thus passed through the Crown hands, but its impact in years of strain such as the end of Elizabeth's reign may in an imperfect market situation have been considerable. Even this frequently left the ruler obliged to cover a deficit by borrowing inside or outside the kingdom, or by realising royal assets by sale of lands – solving present problems by increasing future ones. At least, however, the sale of offices never became institutionalised as it did in some places on the continent.

The ruler also had one or two indirect means of obtaining a benefit from his subjects, such as purveyance. Purveyance was a royal prerogative which allowed the Crown victuallers to take foodstuffs and certain other things for the Crown's use, whether or not the owner wished to part with them. These items were paid for, though not necessarily on the spot, but the rates were fixed by the Crown, and though not outrageously out of line with current market prices were probably low. Tradition and agreement governed the amount which the purveyors could raise in any one county, but it was a source of perpetual grievance even so. When, during the proposals for the Great Contract in 1610, by which a number of the less popular sources of royal revenue would have been exchanged for a more equitable one, the question of purveyance was brought up, James estimated it was worth £50,000 a year to the Crown.

Nef, therefore, is right in his general assumption that total royal revenue is unlikely to have been more than a small percentage of the total national income: it was less, for example, than the most conservative estimate possible of the value of cloth exported in a single year, though a precise percentage is impossible.

The burden of government on the people, however, is not limited to the exactions of central government. Local government also imposed its own burdens. Various rates were regularly levied by justices of the peace or specially appointed *ad hoc* commissioners.[79]

Nef's claim that such forms of money raising were regressive, however, taxing the poor comparatively more heavily than the rich, seems extremely doubtful. The impact of indirect taxation such as customs duties is too complex to investigate fully here, but so long as the main purchasing power of the poor was directed towards basic foodstuffs the onus of proof seems to rest on those who would agree with Nef. The impact of purveyance may well have been regressive but the value of purveyance, though hard to assess as a percentage, was undoubtedly of minor significance. The impact of most direct taxation, on the other hand, seems to have fallen fair and square on the wealthier members of the community. The fifteenth and tenth had by the sixteenth century reached a stage of complexity and local peculiarity which makes them hard to evaluate,[80] but to all intents and purposes it was a fixed sum raised in the localities primarily on a basis of land. While the subsidy was initially a genuine attempt to assess each individual's wealth and to tax him according to his means it did so in a progressive manner, the rate being heavier on the wealthy. It is for this reason that the first subsidies have attracted so much attention from historians. Moreover, as time went on, fewer and fewer people were included in the net of the subsidy, so that by the end of Elizabeth's reign to be a subsidy man meant to be a person of some substance in the community, and the term was so used in an Act of Parliament (39 Eliz., c. 3): 'The church-wardens of every parish and four substantial householders there being subsidy men, or for want of subsidy men four other substantial house-holders . . .' – presumably because with a progressive tax one wealthy man produced so much larger a sum than many poor.[81] Local taxes were also principally imposed on the rich. Where repairs and rebuilding of public utilities such as bridges were concerned either successful attempts were made to impose the burden of upkeep on to the shoulders of the landowners holding the adjoining property or on to the neigh-bouring county or hundred, or the required sum was raised by a general rate on the better-off in the county. The statute of sewers (23 Henry VIII, c. 5) laid the burden of maintaining dykes and drains on the local landowners. In the same session an act was passed for levying a county rate for building county gaols (23 Henry VIII, c. 2) which gives more precise details about how such rates were to be assessed.[82] The justices were to call together the high constables, tithingmen or borough holders of every hundred, lathe or wapentake of the shire and by their 'assents, agreements and discretion' tax every resident in the shires whose lands rents or annuities came to 40s. The problem of assessing the total weight of these taxes is created by the fact that each rate for a different purpose – highways, coat and conduct money, maimed soldiers and so on – was separately levied and assessed. The idea of a single rate levied annually on a regular basis from which various different expenses could be defrayed had not yet been established. It is clear, however, that it was already land, and so either landowners or occupiers of land, who were assessed, especially for parish rates – for the poor and for other good causes such as the provision (24 Henry VIII, c. 10) of a net 'for the destruction of choughs, crows and rooks', and by 8 Elizabeth, c. 15 also to pay rewards for the eggs and heads of vermin, including foxes.

These were not the only powers which the churchwarden had to levy money. Since the church was an established part of the government, and the building itself was used for a number of purposes which today would be carried out in the village or county offices, it is perhaps appropriate to include the levies the churchwardens could make for the upkeep of the nave of the church as part of government income and expenditure. Just how heavy these levies could be is an incidental light provided by Jeffreys' case which was settled in King's Bench in 1589.[83] The £70 needed to put the church of Hailsham in repair was to be raised by a charge of 4d on every acre of marshland and 2d on every acre of arable to be paid by the occupier – a sum which, be it noted, only raised £50 of the total £70. Jeffreys' due for the 30 acres of marsh and the 100 acres of arable which he occupied came to 26s 8d, and he was seeking to evade payment on the grounds that he was not a parishioner of Hailsham (which was not disputed) first in the spiritual courts and then, when he was unsuccessful, equally unsuccessfully in the civil courts.

Such rates, it was established, were due from occupiers of land, not from residents: this meant *inter alia* that the local taxes for government were paid by the relatively wealthy and not by the poor. It is true that they were, for sheer convenience and expedition, due from the occupier and not from the owner, which made the landlord exempt except in his own district, but there seems no reason to consider the tax regressive, any more than the central taxes were regressive.

A serious and detailed study of particular local government areas would be necessary to establish what local rates were levied year by year, and so a rough calculation of the amount which must have been raised per acre. There is no reason, however, for a casual assumption that the burden was light. In practice, most local taxes for such things as gaol money or the relief of disabled soldiers were allocated among the parishes in a manner roughly proportionate to their ability to pay and in amounts which would produce the total sums required. Thus in Kent the rates for gaol money in 1583 were at either 2d, 4d or 6d or in the case of Maidstone 8d a week, 2s 2d, 4s 4d, 6s 6d or 8s 8d a quarter, while the relief for soldiers was usually only half as much.[84] These rates were levied annually at least to the end of Elizabeth's reign, and they were not the only rates levied. They produced annually between £12 and £20 from each hundred. The same source gives the value of a subsidy from Kent at £1,000. The burden of local government, therefore, when all the different levies were added together, may well have been a substantial addition to the total burden of government.

Even if some approximation of the precise burden of local rates could be achieved this does not exhaust the burden of government on the individual – and, generally speaking, the wealthier individual. Certain necessary undertakings were financed by the ruler issuing a proclamation permitting an individual or a corporation to raise money in this way for necessary works, such as the rebuilding of a harbour's protection from the sea (see Doc. 5). The 'voluntary' nature of these contributions was notional, and failure to contribute could lead to official action being taken against the defaulter.

Other necessary provisions were similarly shifted from the government to the individual or locality, the most able being expected to provide for the particular need. Thus when additional ships were needed at the time of the Armada and similar threats, the duty, not only of finding the ship but also of provisioning it and paying the crew for a period of two months, fell upon the ports. They were increasingly succeeding in shifting part of the burden to neighbouring towns, whose merchants benefited from the port's facilities, or to the county. Thus in 1588 Hull forced York to pay £600 towards the total cost of £1,015, and in 1598 it brought within the paying circle the West Riding clothing towns for which it was the principal outlet.[85]

Another way in which the actual costs of supporting a governmental structure were not included in physical payments was the royal habit of employing men who received no salary, or a salary which was supplemented by extensive taking of fees, whether legitimate or illegitimate. Services which in the modern state would therefore be included in the expenditure of the government were pushed back on to the individual in one way or another, so that the real costs of government were higher than they appear to be.

Expenditure on behalf of the government therefore took place in ways not affected by the money that flowed into the central treasury, but also imperfectly controlled by the central government whose reliance on unpaid officials – or officials paid on a percentage basis from what they collected – left it very much at the mercy of local attitudes towards local community interests.[86]

Nevertheless it must be recognised that the money in the central treasury represented twenty times the income of even the richest peer of the realm, so that its expenditure was an important factor in the areas in which it was spent. The Crown's demand for goods could be important to an industry, and could also influence the structure of the firms supplying it. Though the amounts yearly expended by the Crown on ship building and repairs seem almost ludicrously small (when Burghley was at his most parsimonious, he had cut them back to about £6,000 a year) the mere maintenance of royal shipyards on a permanent basis was enough to attract ship building of other sorts to the same areas.[87] Royal requirements of beer on a large scale undoubtedly gave a fillip to the size of London breweries.[88] Provisioning the household with any goods in fact demanded a firm of a fair size and with good capital backing to enable it to await payment. Purveyance and the provisioning of armies also influenced the market structure, though possibly not as much as did the mere existence of London.[89]

(ii) *The impact of government legislation*
Nef, however, was really more interested in the role of legislation in attempting to impose paternalistic restraints or controls on the economy. The laws on the statute book covered virtually every type of economic activity from the type of clothing men and women of different rank and occupation might wear, to the number of threads to the inch in different types of cloth. Nef made two general assumptions about this – the first that the legislation on the statute book had been promoted and sponsored for the most part by a central government with a fairly clear concept of its role in such matters; the second that it was on the whole poorly enforced. Both assumptions have been challenged subsequently, though there is by no means a consensus amongst historians that they are in fact wrong. It has been shown, for example, by Professor Bindoff[90] that the famous statute of artificers (1563), once thought to be the product of Cecil's genius, was in all probability the work of the Commons who altered and amended a modest government Bill virtually out of recognition. It has been suggested that a great deal of legislation – particularly economic legislation – was similarly the work of the Commons. Major towns such as London have been shown to have sent their representatives with instructions for legislation which they would like to see passed. London does not seem to have been conspicuously successful in achieving its objectives,[91] presumably because

these objectives were not sufficiently popular. The idea that much of the legislation was the result of a countrywide feeling that the law needed to be altered to amend some social or economic problem must, however, cast some doubt on the alleged unwillingness of the actual enforcers of the laws – generally the unpaid local justices – to put the statutes into effect. Dr Kerridge, following through cases brought after the inquisitions on enclosures (1517–18), has shown that where the accusations were proved not only true but also within the slightly restricted terms of the Act, there is every reason to think that action was taken, and that the enclosures so pulled down may not have been quickly re-erected.[92]

Establishing the extent to which laws were observed, however, is a tricky business. The number of cases brought under an Act is no true measure of its efficiency or of the degree to which the law was observed. The extent to which a common informer brought cases he had initiated in the courts to a final conviction is also an awkward indicator.[93]

Certainly a general resistance of a county community to government orders prejudicial to the well-being of an important section of the community can be demonstrated.[94] Where it is demonstrated, however, it was generally opposition to some type of patent of monopoly where benefit to anyone except the patentee or the Crown's finances is hard to show. Certainly, too, powerful local individuals or officials might effectively obstruct the Crown's legitimate rights for their own private benefit – but as in the case of the Bishopstone wreck*, the economic significance of the resistance may be marginal.

It seems unlikely that any useful generalisations will be made about the impact of government economic regulations until each regulation has been looked at carefully and individually over a period of time.[95] The vigour and efficiency with which regulations about the distribution of scarce grain stocks in time of genuine dearth were enforced (Doc. 7) is one example of the ability of the government to enforce laws where there was widespread recognition of the necessity to do so. Enforcement of orders prohibiting the export of corn, however, might be remarkably different where no such widespread recognition existed.

On the other hand not all patentees of monopoly met with effective opposition from those whose economic interests were damaged by the patent. The Mansell patent for glass was a grievous blow to the Bagots[96] but there is no evidence that Bagot was able to defend himself.

There is a *prima facie* case that, without naively assuming that the laws and proclamations were uniformly and rigorously enforced, they should be taken seriously and that changes in their general tenor should

* Public Record Office E178/2289; HMC Hatfield II p. 223.

be investigated as likely to be a significant indicator of a change of economic direction on the part of the country at large, not merely the central government.

Attempts to enforce the acts against enclosure, to maintain the control exercised by the guilds, to limit the size of establishments or to inhibit the free flow of goods between England and foreign parts may all suggest that the government was inclined to look unfavourably on change. This may be a false impression. Every government's role, if it does not want a revolution on its hands, must be to control factors which lead to social instability. Much of the restrictive legislation was directed principally to this end. Moreover, given a situation in which there was limited technological advance, regulations limiting the size of units, preventing masters from taking too many apprentices for fear they should find themselves lacking employment in later life, maintaining adequate standards of quality, all have an integrated and defensible rationale. A master, making a fair but not excessive profit, should not be able to expand his business more than a certain amount. If he does it must either be that he is exploiting cheap labour (in the form of apprentices) who may be unable to find work later, or that he is skimping on the product. If he is keeping to himself the profit that might have supported a second master as well, by obliging that man to work for him as a journeyman, thus increasing his personal profit without adding one iota to the output, he is not benefiting the commonwealth. It is therefore in the wider interest that his activities should be curtailed.

Where it is possible to argue that idle men are put to work by the employment of capital, as in the wire drawing or pin making works, the government's attitude is quite different. It was the suggestion that the principal objectives were maximum quality output for a minimum input of labour and raw materials, to the benefit of all by a reduction in costs, that enabled the monopolists to make their proposals respectable. The government, in fact, showed a fairly constant, if often naive and over-optimistic, interest in promoting industrial development. If many of its efforts went astray, wasting capital resources and disrupting trade, it is as well to remember that there were plenty of bankruptcy cases and impediments to trade in the eighteenth and nineteenth centuries. As often happened, the idea was right but the execution defective.

The situation may not have been a total loss. By encouraging an atmosphere in which effort was well received, and in which certain standards were expected, the government may have been assisting development more than it knew. After all, one of the most important aspects of a flourishing market was and is a confidence in the probity of the merchants' dealings and in the reliability of the goods they offer. This was one thing which the government never tired of repeating, whenever pronouncements were made on the importance to the kingdom of a flourishing trade: the following is a commonplace government admonition.

'Whereas trade and commerce was an especial means of the flourishing estate both of this our kingdom and every other commonwealth, and that the true and honest dealing of every man in his trade is a great occasion that trade doth prosper and flourish. The uttering of false and deceitful wares tendeth to the prejudice both of us and our subjects, and apparently to the over throw of trade.'[97]

(iii) *Government influence through control of the money supply*
Possibly the single most important way in which the central government directly influenced the economy, however, was in its control over and regulation of the money supply. Unfortunately, although there is some evidence that the royal ministers appreciated the importance of and need for an adequate and also a respectable money supply, there is no evidence that they even aimed for any detailed control over the total in circulation or that there was any mechanism whereby they could have varied the supply to influence market conditions, shifts in prices and short-term demand. A currency in which precious metal is the main circulating medium is not well suited to such things. They attempted to keep the currency in the realm by prohibiting its export, though even here success may have been limited.[98] Since England had no really significant internal source of silver, a favourable balance of trade was necessary for an inward flow of bullion to supplement existing stocks, and the government paid some attention to this. Merchants continued to strike base tokens for their workmen to supply the need of a small value coin,[99] but there is no real evidence of an overall shortage. More important to the economy may have been the by-products of the monarchs' early tampering with the coinage. Debasement in the last years of Henry VIII's reign and the earlier years of Edward VI was the highly profitable last resort of a government running in perpetual deficit. Its economic effects were debatable since an increase in the coin supply – if the coins were acceptable – might actually improve the workings of the economy by providing sufficient circulating medium for it to function smoothly. If in addition it made the country's goods cheaper in terms of outside currency and outside goods it might stimulate an export boom. On the other hand the uncertainty and disruption of trade and the loss of confidence attending upon frequent

debasements might have adverse effects, throwing the economy into recession. Historians are not agreed upon the effects of this debasement.

During this time prices rose fairly markedly, and there has been much debate about the extent to which this was due to the debasement.[100] On the whole, opinion seems to be agreed that the coincidence in time and extent between debasement and price rise is too imperfect for the one to be the effect purely and simply of the other, and that debasement could only in its final eighteen months have been responsible for the boom in cloth exports.[101] Dr Challis, in fact, thinks that so acute was England's need for an increase in the total coinage, which he believes was about £1.3m. in 1545, that it absorbed most of the increase from debasement, which brought the total up to approximately £2.5m., without the prices of goods being affected to anything like the same degree. It would be rash to conclude from this that debasement had no impact on prices at all. In 1551, the debased coins were 'called down', that is, made to circulate below their face values, but this did not bring prices down. After some attempts at recoinage which were not carried through, the coins were ultimately recoined in 1561, and thereafter the English monarchs refrained from drastic tampering with the coins.

The government's continuing interest in the problem, however, is demonstrated by the debates over the shortage and scarcity of coin in James's reign, and by the marked resistance of the business community itself, despite Thomas Mun's persuasive pen, to the East India Company's taking silver from the realm to trade in India. Mun argued that the re-export of goods brought back more than the East India Company could take out, but proof of this claim is harder to come by.

Whether the government's maintenance of a currency in which merchants and others could have confidence was important in promoting economic enterprise is a problem which does not lend itself to conclusive proof or disproof – but the fact that contemporary writers judged it important may be in itself an indicator. Recent scholarship, however, is tending to support Nef's general recognition of the significance of the role of government for reasons other than those Nef himself alleged.

THE CONTINUING PROBLEM OF MEASUREMENT

If one considers Nef's thesis in the light of this brief indication of economic concepts one can see that Nef has been subject to criticisms which range from errors of method to errors of interpretation and errors of omission. The criticism, however, has yet to result in an adequate alternative formulation. One reason for this is the very real difficulty of putting the evidence into a usable shape. An economic historian must deal with figures, numbers of units, volume, value ,and so on. These figures must relate to a standard agreed norm. In the sixteenth century this comparability is almost impossible to achieve. Almost every industry had its own individual measure of size, weight or volume, and the measure might differ from one part of the country to another. Even for common commodities like grain or cloth, the measure varied from town to town: local measures might be greater or smaller than the Winchester bushel, which could make a considerable difference to the price. Even attempts to introduce standard measures could result in confusion being worse confounded (Doc. 1). Nef's general practice was to convert his measures into a modern ton, but he had difficulties with this even with coal because of the difference between the Newcastle chaldron and that of London, and some who have used his work doubt his conversion. Beveridge's work on prices, weights and measures has provided more recent historians with a much-needed basis for calculations and a much keener appreciation of the pitfalls.[102] It is clear, for example, that isolated prices are virtually meaningless; valuation depends on intended use, quality, local demand and supply, and a variety of other factors. These can be seen but not assessed even in a single source. In Document 2, which shows wood sales from the Middleton estate in 1571, 1587 and 1613, the accountant has no need to explain why the value of 'two oaks' may differ between one lot and another. The absence of differentiations makes a precise comparison between years impossible – only an impression of an overall upward creep in prices is possible and this does not in itself give any clue as to the likely explanation.

It is therefore dangerous simply to average isolated prices (as Thorold Rogers did)[103] and impossible to construct price indexes which meet any of the requirements of the modern statistician[104] (namely, that all price information should be rigidly defined and each price used should be obtained under exactly similar conditions with goods of exactly similar quality), let alone to 'weight' an index which includes more than one commodity in terms of its proportion of the total consumption or production, since this is by definition unknowable. Various attempts at price indexes have been made, but all are open to grave objections.

Historians are now very wary of comparing prices unless they come from series known to be internally consistent. Document 1 gives a clear idea of the problems – even if one assumes that the variations which took place from year to year in the size of the Caernarvon bushel, though vexatious for the local consumer, were not sufficiently great to make a substantial difference to price comparisons.

Moreover Document 1 underlines the problem of establishing not only the quantity being measured but the nature of the price. Ideally, prices should only be compared in identical circumstances. Coal at the pithead in Newcastle might be only 2s a ton while the price on the London market might be as much as 15s for the identical ton, the difference representing transport costs and middleman's profits. Prices at source must be distinguished from market prices; wholesale and retail prices should not be confused.

In practice this is hard to establish, particularly when endeavouring to cost industrial enterprises. Efficient bookkeepers might 'impute' a price to commodities which were available to the owner on his own estates – fuel for example – but many did not bother. The alternative 'sale-value' of the goods involved, however, needs to be taken into account by the historian as it diminishes the apparent profit from the enterprise itself. The interests of the owner in calculating 'profit' may be as well served by including the effective 'bonus' of 'free' fuel. Nef can be criticised for an over-willingness to accept calculations of profit at their face value. He may also be criticised for a tendency to assume that costs which may be known for one operation can be safely transferred to another. Further research, particularly in the mining industry, has tended to show very different cost structures for different areas depending on such items as the relative yield of the ores and the local availability of fuel or other necessary supplies. Nef's calculation of the capital costs in establishing a new works frequently suffers from a tendency to distinguish insufficiently between different elements in the cost structure – between the cost of the physical building and the costs of getting the works into operation. Nef, however, showed some appreciation of the relative crudity of available price information and the need to weight the component parts of a single price. The significance which he tried to draw from this exercise was, perhaps characteristically, more than it could bear.

Nef tried to argue that the price of bread and more particularly of beer had possibly not risen as fast as the price of wheat and barley. To the extent that labour costs must be included in the price of the commodities, he has some reason; the question remains, however, whether one can establish what percentage of the total cost was likely to be affected by such considerations. Nef takes the price of wheat for 1619–20 (years which exercise a curious fascination on the economic historian) and the manufacturing costs allowed that year for the assize of bread to estimate that the costs of milling and baking represented one-third of total costs. This, however, is a percentage which decreases in years when the cost of grain is higher: and in most years at that time it seems that the cost of grain was higher. As the price of firewood, which was one of the baking costs, rose perhaps faster than the cost of grain, the fraction of the baking costs which it represents must be allowed. In a year when the price of grain was nearer the average, the maximum difference which labour cost could make, on Nef's own terms, was 8 per cent, and the actual difference would be nearer 5.

The possibility that the costs of beer had not risen in the same way, because of large-scale production in London and the use of hops to reduce the amount of malt needed, may be better taken, though the possibility that the food value had also decreased must not be overlooked. Whether the labourer could afford to buy intrinsically dearer meats, whose price was not rising as fast as that of bread, or whether the price was not rising as fast because they were out of reach of the mass market, is a question which awaits further evidence.

Until the likely effect on prices of manufactured goods of factors such as those Nef suggests have been more carefully assessed it is difficult to estimate the degree of significance which they may have either for the economy or for the assessment of the well-being of the poorer classes.

CONCLUSION

Clearly, in our current state of knowledge it would be rash to offer firm conclusions about the growth of the industrial sector in the wider economic matrix. Some tentative hypotheses may, however, be put forward. The demographic upswing, although it was by no means without its problems, was absorbed by the economy, despite some digestive upsets, and without the reduction of the poorest of the poor to a level of misery and ignorance which would be a positive social check on development. This suggests, again, that however 'barely' agricultural output was keeping pace with the rise in population it was nevertheless not losing the race entirely. Famine was by no means an unimaginable disaster but it did not become a commonplace of social existence to be met with fatalism or stoic philosophy. Instead, major organisational efforts apparently ensured an improved chain of distribution so that no town need starve when fifty miles away there was food and to spare. This, then, may imply that advance over a wide front, however jerky and imperfect, however quantitatively small compared to a later 'take-off', may be envisaged.

The co-ordination of advances in different areas, however, was poor or non-existent, damping or destroying a flow-on of effects. Nevertheless, the advances were there. Improved techniques, new or improved economic institutions, continuing government interest, even, arguably, the right socio-intellectual framework for industrious self-interest, created a matrix in which economic growth might take root.

Notes

1 For a general theoretical study of the problems involved in assessing economic growth cf. J. D. Gould, *Economic Growth in History: Survey and Analysis* (London, 1972) and J. R. Hicks, *A Theory of Economic History* (Oxford, 1969).

2 D. C. North and R. P. Thomas, *The Rise of the Western World: A New Economic History* (Cambridge, 1973). Their belief that property rights are the crucial factor and that all significant technological change is induced, not autonomous, has been criticised in reviews, especially by J. R. Hicks in the *Economic History Review*, 2nd ser., XXVII (1974), pp. 692–4.

3 J. U. Nef, 'Industry and Government in France and England, 1540–1640', *Memoirs of the American Philosophical Society*, XV (1940), p. 1.

4 J. U. Nef, 'A Comparison of Industrial Growth in France and England from 1540 to 1640', *Journal of Political Economy*, XLIV (1936), p. 289.

5 J. U. Nef, 'The Progress of Technology and the Growth of Large Scale Industry, 1540–1640', *Economic History Review*, orig. ser., V (1934–5), p. 4.

6 J. U. Nef, *The Rise of the British Coal Industry* (London, 1932), Vol. I, p. 14.

7 ibid., Vol. II, p. 330.

8 ibid., Vol. I, pp. 163–4.

9 ibid., Vol. I, pp. 237–8, 244–5, 255–6, 257–8.

10 ibid., Vol. I, p. 379 (repeated in several of Nef's later works).

11 ibid., Vol. II, p. 322.

12 ibid., Vol. II, p. 321.

13 *Economic History Review*, orig. ser., IV (1932–4), p. 238.

14 G. N. Clark, 'Early Capitalism and Invention', *Economic History Review*, orig. ser., VI (1935–6), p. 153.

15 *Economic History Review*, orig. ser., IV (1932–4), p. 484.

16 Nef, *Industry and Government in France and England, 1540–1640*.

17 J. U. Nef, 'War and Economic Progress, 1540–1640', *Economic History Review*, orig. ser., XII (1942), p. 25.

18 J. U. Nef, *Western Civilization Since the Renaissance* (New York, 1963), (originally published as *War and Human Progress*, Cambridge, Mass., 1950), p. 3.

19 ibid., p. 66.

20 J. U. Nef, introduction to reprint of *Industry and Government in France and England, 1540–1640* (Ithaca, 1967).

21 F. J. Fisher, 'Some Experiments in Company Organisation in the Early Seventeenth Century', *Economic History Review*, orig. ser., IV (1932–4), p. 178.

22 E.g. D. C. Coleman, 'An Innovation and Its Diffusion: The "New Draperies",' *Economic History Review*, 2nd ser., XXII (1969), pp. 417–29; 'Technology, 1500–1750', ibid., XI (1958–9), p. 506.
23 P. Deane, *The First Industrial Revolution* (Cambridge, 1965), pp. 1–2.
24 F. J. Fisher, 'Tawney's Century', in *Essays in the Economic and Social History of Tudor and Stuart England in Honour of R. H. Tawney*, ed. Fisher (Cambridge, 1961), p. 2.
25 C. Russell, *The Crisis of Parliaments: English History, 1509–1660* (London, 1971).
26 C. Wilson, *England's Apprenticeship, 1603–1763* (London, 1965), p. xii.
27 ibid., p. 66.
28 P. Ramsey, *Tudor Economic Problems* (London, 1963).
29 For a convenient summary of later statistics which shows the distribution of the labour force between the different sectors, cf. B. R. Mitchell and P. Deane, *Abstract of British Historical Statistics* (Cambridge, 1962).
30 The number, of course, fluctuated: cf. L. Stone, 'Elizabethan Overseas Trade', *Economic History Review*, 2nd ser., II (1949), pp. 30–58.
31 A. J. and R. H. Tawney, 'An Occupational Census of the Seventeenth Century', *Economic History Review*, orig. ser., V (1934–5), pp. 25–64.
32 L. A. Clarkson, *The Pre-Industrial Economy in England, 1500–1750* (London, 1971), pp. 88–90. Clarkson has produced a table of distribution by occupation for varying time periods within 1500–1750, based on a variety of sources from parish registers through freemen's rolls to muster rolls and inventories. Problems of the nature of these sources make them of variable reliability and certainly not strictly comparable: his calculation and mine for Gloucestershire do not tally. It is, however, an interesting exercise inasmuch as the highest percentage of those living in rural areas engaged in agricultural pursuits given is 78 per cent (mid-Essex from 1635 to 1749) and the other whole-county estimates are all in the 60–70 per cent range except for Gloucestershire which he reckons as 50 per cent.
33 M. W. Beresford, 'The Poll Tax and Census of Sheep in 1549', *Agricultural History Review*, I (1953), pp. 9–15.; II (1954), pp. 15–29.
34 E.g. W. W. Rostow, *The Stages of Economic Growth: a Non-Communist Manifesto* (Cambridge, 1960); S. Kuznets, *Modern Economic Growth: Rate, Structure and Spread* (New Haven, 1966); W. A. Lewis, *The Theory of Economic Growth* (London, 1957).
35 E. E. Rich, 'The Population of Elizabethan England', *Economic History Review*, 2nd ser., II (1949–50), pp. 247–65.
36 Hakluyt for example in the 1580s thought the country had been singularly free of killer diseases; S. Pollard and D. W. Crossley, *The Wealth of Britain, 1085–1966* (London, 1968), pp. 83–4, make the same suggestion.
37 C. Creighton, *A History of Epidemics in Britain* (Cambridge, 1891; London, 1965), supplemented by C. F. Mullett, *The Bubonic Plague in England* (Lexington, 1956), is still the standard work.
38 J. Godber, *History of Bedfordshire, 1066–1888* (Bedford, 1969); C. M. L. Bouch and G. P. Jones, *The Lake Counties, 1500–1830: A Social and Economic History* (Manchester, 1951), show a divergence between Westmorland and Cumberland in the seventeenth century. For divergence of patterns of growth between different areas of Bedfordshire, cf. M. Spufford, *Contrasting Communities: English Villages in the Sixteenth and Seventeenth Centuries* (Cambridge, 1974).

39 D. C. Coleman, 'Labour in the English Economy of the Seventeenth Century', *Economic History Review*, 2nd ser., VIII (1956), pp. 280–95.

40 Quoted in E. Straker, *Wealden Iron* (London, 1931; repr. Newton Abbot, 1969), p. 120.

41 North and Thomas, *The Rise of the Western World*, pp. 113–19, 146*ff*., see the sixteenth century as one of diminishing returns to labour but lend Nef significant support when they argue that in the seventeenth century 'real income *per capita* doubtless increased' in the Dutch and British economies 'despite the continued pressure of diminishing returns in agriculture' in a period of rising population. They appear to see it, however, as a seventeenth not a sixteenth century achievement, and primarily late seventeenth at that.

42 *Agriculture and Economic Growth in England, 1650–1815*, ed. E. L. Jones (London, 1967).

43 E. Kerridge, *Agrarian Problems in the Sixteenth Century and After* (London, 1969), p. 121.

44 E. Kerridge, *The Agricultural Revolution* (London, 1967), p. 209.

45 *Agrarian History of England and Wales*, Vol. IV, p. 199; J. Thirsk, 'Seventeenth Century Agriculture and Social Change', *Land, Church and People: Essays Presented to H. P. R. Finberg* (*Agricultural History Review*, 1970), pp. 152–3.

46 E.g. E. L. Jones, 'The Condition of English Agriculture, 1500–1640', *Economic History Review*, 2nd ser., XXI (1968), pp. 614–19.

47 W. G. Hoskins, 'Harvest Fluctuations and English Economic History, 1620–1759', *Agricultural History Review*, XVI (1968), pp. 15–31.

48 For a general discussion, cf. Clarkson, *The Pre-Industrial Economy in England*, pp. 45–74.

49 R. Grassby, 'The Rate of Profit in Seventeenth-Century England', *Economic History Review*, LXXXIV (1969) and R. Grassby, 'English Merchant Capitalism in the Late Seventeenth Century: The Composition of Business Fortunes', *Past and Present*, XLVI (1970).

50 G. V. Scammell, 'English Merchant Shipping at the End of the Middle Ages: Some East Coast Evidence', *Economic History Review*, 2nd ser., XIII, (1960–1), pp. 327–41.

51 They can be counted on Symondson's map.

52 G. R. Lewis, *The Stannaries: A Study of the English Tin Miner* (Cambridge, Mass., 1924), pp. 214–5; revised for the beginning of our period by J. Hatcher, *English Tin Production and Trade before 1550* (Oxford, 1973).

53 H. J. Habakkuk, 'The Long Term Rate of Interest and the Price of Land in the Seventeenth Century', *Economic History Review*, 2nd ser., V (1952–3), pp. 26–45.

54 A. Simpson, 'Thomas Cullum, Draper, 1587–1664', *Economic History Review*, 2nd ser., XI (1958–9), pp. 19–34.

55 S. Kuznets, 'Capital Formation in Modern Economic Growth and Some Implications for the Past', *Third International Conference of Economic Historians* (Paris, 1968), offers some figures based on extrapolation from modern figures which suggest a long-term rate of growth of *per capita* production no greater than 0.2 per cent a year, but this is unverifiable and estimated for purposes different from our present study.

56 North and Thomas, *The Rise of the Western World*, pp. 2–5, argue about the relationship between private benefits or costs and social benefits or

costs, and the 'free-rider' – the individual who benefits without contributing – deserves consideration here.

57 J. U. Nef, 'Silver Production in Central Europe, 1450–1618', *Journal of Political Economy*, XLIX (1941), pp. 575–91.

58 T. K. Rabb has recently emphasised the significance of this problem in the sixteenth and seventeenth centuries in quite another context – a contribution to the debate on capitalism ('The Expansion of Europe and the Spirit of Capitalism', *Historical Journal*, XVII (1974), pp. 675–89.

59 The best recent survey of the problems of inflation at this time is R. B. Outhwaite, *Inflation in Tudor and Early Stuart England* (London, 1969); the central articles have been collected together in *The Price Revolution in Sixteenth Century England*, ed. P. Ramsey (Debates in Economic History series, London, 1971).

60 W. G. Hoskins, 'The Rebuilding of Rural England', *Past and Present*, IV (1953), pp. 44–59.

61 Nicholas Breton, 'Court and Country', in *Complaint and Reform in England, 1436–1714*, ed. W. H. Dunham and S. Pargellis (New York, 1938; repr. 1968), p. 462.

62 D. W. Crossley, 'The Performance of the Glass Industry in Sixteenth-Century England', *Economic History Review*, 2nd ser., XXV (1972), p. 423.

63 D. W. Crossley, 'Some Aspects of Fieldwork in Sixteenth Century Industrial History', *History of Metallurgy Bulletin*, V (1971), p. 9.

64 L. Stone, *The Crisis of the Aristocracy 1558–1641* (Oxford, 1965), p. 68.

65 A. Simpson, *The Wealth of the Gentry, 1540–1660: East Anglian Studies* (Chicago, 1961), p. 194.

66 J. T. Cliffe, *The Yorkshire Gentry from the Reformation to the Civil War* (London, 1969), pp. 110–11.

67 R. B. Grassby, 'The Personal Wealth of the Business Community in Seventeenth Century England', *Economic History Review*, 2nd ser., XXIII (1970), p. 225.

68 M. E. Finch, *The Wealth of Five Northamptonshire Families, 1540–1640*, Northamptonshire Record Society Publication XIX (1956), p. 159.

69 V. T. H. Skipp, 'Economic and Social Change in the Forest of Arden', *Land, Church and People: Essays Presented to H. P. R. Finberg (Agricultural History Review*, 1970), p. 103.

70 *Household and Farm Inventories in Oxfordshire, 1550–1590*, ed. M. A. Havinden, Historic Manuscripts Commission (London, 1965), pp. 30–2.

71 A. Everitt, 'The Farm Labourer', *Agrarian History of England and Wales*, Vol. IV, pp. 396*ff.*

72 F. Braudel, *Capitalism and Material Life, 1400–1800*, trans. M. Kochan (London, 1973), pp. 88–92.

73 Cf. E. H. Phelps Brown and S. Hopkins, 'Seven Centuries of Building Wages', *Economica*, XXII (1955), pp. 195–206.

74 Printed in G. Unwin, *Industrial Organisation in the Sixteenth and Seventeenth Centuries* (2nd edn, Oxford, 1904; repr. London, 1957), p. 236.

75 North and Thomas, *The Rise of the Western World*, pp. 97–121.

76 F. C. Dietz, *Finances of Edward VI and Mary*, Smith College Studies in History, III (1918), p. 74, gives the revenue in 1540 as precisely £200,000, but it is not clear whence he derives the figure and, unless it included the sale of ex-monastic lands (which it should not), it is much too, high.

77 British Museum, Harleian MS. 7883. This has been edited by W. C.

Richardson as *Report on Royal Commission on Finance*, Archives of British History and Culture, Vol. III (Conference on British Studies at West Virginia University, Parson, West Virginia, McClain, 1973).

78 F. C. Dietz, *English Public Finance, 1558–1641* (New York, 1932; repr. London, 1964).

79 Cf. A. Hassell Smith, *County and Court: Government and Politics in Norfolk, 1558–1603* (Oxford, 1974).

80 Cf. R. Schofield, 'Parliamentary Lay Taxation, 1485–1547', unpublished PhD thesis (Cambridge, 1963).

81 For an analysis of the Norwich returns which make this point very clear, cf. J. F. Pound, 'The Social and Trade Structure of Norwich, 1525–1575', *Past and Present*, XXXIV (1966), p. 51.

82 For a fuller discussion, see E. Cannon, *History of Local Rates in England* (London, 1912).

83 Edward Coke, *The Reports*, ed. G. Wilson (London, 1777), pt V, pp. 67–8.

84 British Museum, Additional MS. 41137, fols 180–3.

85 *Victoria County History of East Riding of Yorkshire*, Vol. I, p. 99.

86 Cf. Hassell Smith, *County and Court*.

87 Cf. M. Oppenheim, *History of the Administration of the Royal Navy & of Merchant Shipping in Relation to the Navy; from 1507 to 1660* (London, 1896; repr. 1961).

88 Elizabeth in an unprogressive way complained of the flavour which seacoal gave the beer and inhibited her brewers from using it. (*Calendar of State Papers, Domestic, 1547–1580*, p. 612, item 68.)

89 A. Woodward, 'Purveyance for the Royal Household in the Reign of Queen Elizabeth', *American Philosophical Society Transactions*, new ser., XXXV (1946); G. Aylmer, 'The Last Years of Purveyance', *Economic History Review*, 2nd ser., X (1957–8), pp. 81–93; B. Pearce, 'Elizabethan Food Policy and the Armed Forces', ibid., orig. ser., XII (1942), pp. 39–46; C. S. L. Davies, 'Provisions for Armies, 1509–50', ibid., 2nd ser., XVII (1964–5), pp. 234–48; F. J. Fisher, 'The Development of the London Food Market, 1540–1640', ibid., orig. ser., VII (1936–7), repr. in *Essays in Economic History*, ed. E. Carus-Wilson, Vol. I (London, 1954), pp. 135–51.

90 S. T. Bindoff, 'The Making of the Statute of Artificers', *Elizabethan Government and Society*, ed. Bindoff *et al.* (London, 1961).

91 H. Miller, 'London and Parliament in the Reign of Henry VIII', *Bulletin of Institute of Historical Research*, XXXV (1962), pp. 128–49.

92 E. Kerridge, 'The Returns of the Inquisitions of Depopulation', *English Historical Review*, LXX (1955), pp. 212–28.

93 M. W. Beresford, 'The Common Informer, the Penal Statutes and Economic Regulation', *Economic History Review*, 2nd ser., X (1957–8), pp. 221–38; G. R. Elton, 'Informing for Profit', *Cambridge Historical Journal*, IX (1954), pp. 149–67.

94 Cf. Hassell Smith, *County and Court*.

95 For a general discussion, see Clarkson, *The Pre-Industrial Economy in England*, pp. 159–209.

96 Folger Library, Bagot MS. L.a. 973.

97 Public Record Office, Exchequer, E 159/471, fol. 42.

98 R. Hitchcock in *A Pollitique Platt* (London, 1580; repr. New York, 1971) assumed that the export of bullion to France was common knowledge.

99 P. Grierson, 'The Monetary Pattern of the Sixteenth-Century Coinage', *Transactions of Royal Historical Society*, 5th ser., XXI (1971), p. 51.
100 J. D. Gould, *The Great Debasement* (Oxford, 1970), esp. pp. 1–7; cf. A. Feavearyear, *The Pound Sterling* (2nd edn, Oxford, 1963), for a chapter so entitled.
101 C. E. Challis, 'The Circulating Medium and the Movement in Prices in Mid-Tudor England', *The Price Revolution in Sixteenth-Century England*, ed. P. H. Ramsey (London, 1971), pp. 117–47.
102 W. Beveridge, 'A Statistical Crime of the Seventeenth Century', *Journal of Economic and Business History*, I (1928–9), pp. 503–33.
103 J. E. Thorold Rogers, *A History of Agriculture & Prices in England from . . . 1259 to . . . 1793* (Oxford, 1866–1902). Volume IV covers the period with which we are concerned.
104 P. Bowden's appendixes A and B in *The Agrarian History of England and Wales, Vol. IV, 1540–1640*, ed. J. Thirsk (Cambridge, 1967), pp. 814–68, are a valiant but probably misguided attempt to achieve such an index in the face of impossible problems.

2

A Re-examination of Development and Change in Sixteenth and Seventeenth Century English Industries

In the narrowest sense, current assessment of Nef's thesis must still stand or fall by the strength of his case touching the industrial and technological developments of the period. In the last analysis, if it can be shown that there was a marked surge forward in a number of different areas within the industrial sector, all coinciding in the same period of time over a wide front, it would become plausible to argue that here indeed was an industrial revolution 'aborted', and the nature and cause of that abortion would then deserve extremely careful consideration because it would shed considerable light on the nature of the development at other times and the factors critical for its success.

It would also discredit some of the more recent attempts at an overall explanation of the rise of the modern Western economy; although North and Thomas, for example, claim to have built on the work of Nef and Heckscher, they have done so only selectively – using the arguments about the role of government and the growth in productive capacity but rejecting technology as a significant factor and stressing the efficiency of the market structure as critical in a way which Nef had not envisaged.[1]

Nef was particularly interested in new or rapidly growing industries. The sector, however, must be considered as a whole, and due weight given to the relative importance of the industry in question. A notable development in the making of clay pipes, important though it may have been to the comfort and well-being of the many smokers of the time, is hardly important enough on a national level to carry a revolution.

The technique of piling up instances of change significant within the particular industry without any attempt to consider the order of magnitude of the development makes perhaps a good *prima facie* case, but does not clinch the argument. To consider Nef's thesis seriously it is necessary to review, briefly, the whole range of industries and to assess the relative importance of each.

THE EXTRACTIVE INDUSTRIES

Since it was the one closest to Nef's heart, the first area to be considered should perhaps be the extractive industries: the digging up of coal, iron ore, copper ore, tin, lead, calamine and other basic raw materials. There was also extensive quarrying in many areas for local building stone, and some areas already had a reputation which enabled them to export stone to the rest of the country: Purbeck marble, for example, was in demand and being located near the sea was carried long distances. Demand for millstones also led to considerable quarrying in the Derbyshire peak area from which came the stones for grinding barley, and on Tyneside. In Cornwall quarrying for roofing slate was a commercial undertaking,[2] and slate was extensively exported from Wales in the sixteenth century. In 1587 100,000 slates were sent to Ireland alone.[3]

Nef's own subject was the coal industry, and no one has seriously questioned his conclusion that total production of coal multiplied five-fold in the period, and that in the Newcastle-upon-Tyne area, and to a lesser extent elsewhere,[4] this increase resulted in deeper mines, more elaborate organisation and a greater expenditure of capital. It has, however, been suggested that Nef underestimated the volume of the coal trade before 1550, which would of course affect his estimates of the rate of growth since these are mainly based on the records of the coal trade rather than on direct estimates of mine production.[5] In itself, however, the need to invest more capital is no great advance – rather the reverse – unless it is accompanied by a rise in productivity per head of the labourers employed, and Nef made no direct claims for techno-logical change of the sort that might increase productivity, though that might ensue if the deeper mines offered thicker seams of better coal which were easier to work.

The coal mines in Beaudesert Park and Cannock Wood were profit-able enough to make the expenditure of about £60 and some £20 a year on a sough profitable in the late 1570s. The accounts for the pits were kept in such a way that one can see from day to day how much the miners were bringing in gross over and above their wages. Except at very poor times the gross profit over and above the wages was about three times the wages, but against that had to be set expenditure on candles, on tools, on timber and timbermen to saw it, on tree trunks to carry away the water, on various devices to cure fire damp and on the sough (Doc. 8). This took at least as much again as the wages, but still in a normal year left a handsome 'profit' of at least one-third of the gross yield. The pits were thought to be deep, but where figures are given they are given in ells, and unless these were a very different length from the standard, the pits were rarely more than fifty to a hundred yards deep.[6]

An increased demand for coal, however, is not necessarily an indication of industrial growth, since coal, unlike other ores, can enter directly into domestic consumption. Nef's own tentative estimate suggested that in 1700 two-thirds of the output was for domestic consumption, and he made no attempt to give any earlier indication of the different rates at which domestic and industrial demand may have grown. Moreover, if the percentage distribution is at all the same in 1640 or 1600 one must recognise that only a fraction of Nef's total growth is going to promote industrial development. Since so much of the coal from the Durham coalfields was shipped coastwise to London, mainly for domestic use, the percentage of coal used in industry may earlier, indeed, have been less than the one-third it had become by 1700. After all, the advantage of coal lay in its comparative cheapness, and Nef knew well that the price of coal in London was considerably more than double its pit-head price,[7] so that most industries which sought to use coal tended to move close to the source of the fuel. Coal, moreover, was not a new product but a substitute for wood fuel, and by stressing declining use of wood Nef decreased the growth in total demand for a source of power supply. Coal was, it is true, exported in increasing quantity, but although this was of definite significance in some localities such as Wales,[8] it did not matter greatly at a national level.

Nef not only stressed the significance of demand for coal: he also saw the ultimate slowing down of industrial growth in terms of the failure of key extractive industries to solve the technological problems related to the substitution. It took another hundred years – if Dud Dudley's claims were dismissed – for coke to be used in iron smelting. Recent research, however, has tended to play down the shortage of charcoal, to stress the 'farming' of supplies and the technological improvements which cut down on demand for fuel.[9] This argument has been largely conducted in relation to the iron industry.

Iron extraction is the area we know least about. Iron was available in small quantities near the surface in many parts of England, and there are no signs in this period that any elaboration of the existing extraction techniques was felt to be worth considering at existing prices. The lord of the soil was paid 1d a load in 1540, the miner was paid 7½d for digging it, and 1,500 loads a year from one area was a not uncommon rate, yielding the landlord a comfortable but not princely return.

In the midlands readily available supplies of ore were showing signs of being exhausted in the 1570s. Willoughby's official warned him, when he was contemplating setting up a mill, that 'it is hard to come by for it is daily laid for by my lord Paget, but he cannot take nor purchase as I am credibly informed by honest men'.[10] Eventually both Paget and Willoughby were getting their supplies of ore principally from Walsall, which was more convenient for Paget than for Willoughby but involved a fair expenditure on carriage for both. Prices were rising, but not enough to justify the inordinate expense of deeper mines, though by 1600 an iron mine could be let for a down payment of £26 4s 2d on a payment of 14d on every load of iron.[11] Technically, the normal iron mine at this period remained the bell-shaped pit requiring little capital which had been used throughout the Middle Ages and beyond.

Much more valuable, because much more rare, were the lead mines in Derbyshire, the West Riding of Yorkshire and the Mendips. Demand for lead was evidently on the increase, for the Swaledale mines were reopened and by the end of the sixteenth century were being widely worked, though on a small and individual scale.[12] Another area newly opened was in Wales, near Aberystwyth, though in this case it was the silver content of the lead which made it attractive. Changes in the methods of mining, however, were slow to develop and generally seem to have been forced on to the miners by worsening conditions. The actual digging of the ore had long been in the hands of numerous 'free miners', who, once they had a licence to dig from the lord of the field, could explore, find a promising area, stake a claim and have a fixed area measured and registered by the barmaster (the official in charge) and set to work subject to the rental payment of one pan in every so many (agreed number) to the lord.[13]

Most mining was still carried out in open trenches or meres, with primitive tools, and using fire and water to create cracks in an unyielding surface. It was reckoned that in this way two miners could raise a ton of ore in a week or 40 tons a year, since twelve weeks had to be allowed for time when the wet made work impossible.[14] In fact, the estimate may be over-optimistic since Myddelton in Wales had 150 men working and producing only 20 tons, though some of them were probably smelters and the like. There were no fundamental changes in technique before 1640, though in Wales Myddelton had to use pumps, and in 1629 a sough was started to drain the Dovegang mine.[15] There seems no evidence that output per miner increased, though the number of miners probably did; on the contrary, the only important innovation was the use of a simple buddle which retained smaller pieces of ore that had previously been lost. The fact that the miners began to obtain ore from this 'smitham' – though they claimed it gave a lower yield – points if anything to the possibility that the ore was becoming harder to win, as the surface seams were exhausted.[16]

By 1631 it was claimed that there were 4,000 miners in the Peak and Wirksworth area.[17] In 1635 a muster of 'able men' in Derbyshire produced 15,672 names,[18] which suggests that the county – when lead, coal and iron miners were added together – was one of the few already heavily dependent on industry.

The copper mines were less important and much harder to work. For most of the period they were exploited by foreign workmen. The report on the Cumberland copper mines in 1602 shows that they were deep and expensive to run.[19] The cost of the construction described in Document 9 was £301. There were at that moment eight pickmen getting 20 kibles of ore a week (at 8d a kible to the miner and 6d to the drawing and other work) at a total cost of 4s 2d a kible. Though they hoped soon to increase the output to 30 kibles, reducing the unit cost thereby to under 4s (since the overheads remained steady any increase in output reduced the average cost), it is clear that only a mineral for which an irreducible minimum of people were prepared to pay a high price could afford overheads of this size. In fact the industry never established itself as a fully viable concern and after 1640 virtually died out for forty years. Nef explained the failure away by claiming that Keswick ran out of wood, but Hammersley thinks this unlikely, offering instead an explanation in terms of lack of demand and competition from richer (and so cheaper) continental ores. Only the skill of the German managers, he thinks, kept it going as long as it did.[20]

Similar competition and problems may have affected tin mining, which was quantitatively very much more important to the English economy. The costs of mining tin were rising with the increasing depth of the mines and the change from stream to lode mining, but owing to continental competition from French and Flemish pewter the demand for tin was rising little if at all, and the price of tin was not keeping pace with other prices. The effect of this was to squeeze many of the 'free miners' to the point at which they turned to husbandry and other employment, and capital turned to more profitable ventures. The prosperity of the mines was destroyed for a hundred years and more. Dr Lewis, in fact, describes the end of the sixteenth century as a period of 'extraordinarily severe depression throughout the stannaries' and considers that the reason was in part the absolute failure of the existing drainage works. 'The mines had been deepened to a point where the drainage engines of the time failed to keep out the water.'[21] Nor was this, like the copper industry, one which employed at most 100 men. Owing to the administrative machinery set up by the government we know that contemporaries were accurate when they talked of the mining community as numbering up to 10,000 or 12,000. Production, however, had dwindled very severely though tin was still mentioned as a very important export in 1638 by Lewes Roberts. The tin industry's fortune was not to revive until the Restoration period, a decline which must be set against the rises elsewhere. Throughout the early seventeenth century production was kept down to 500 tons. James I sent £17,000 at one point to buy up all the tin, in the hopes of improving the miners' lot.

TECHNOLOGICAL DEVELOPMENTS IN THE IRON INDUSTRY

In all these fields, however, it is clear that any significant developments at this time were occurring not at the extractive stage but in the smelting of the metal. The need to expend capital on mining works at this time was more a sign of a worsening capital output ratio than of significant new advances, so that while a solution of technical problems, where it was achieved, was important for the future, its immediate impact was limited.

The industry which in the period 1540–1640 saw the most notable technological change was undoubtedly the iron industry. The gradual substitution of the 'indirect' method of production from blast furnace and forge for the direct method whereby in one single process a 'bloom' of wrought iron was produced undoubtedly increased output dramatically in the period.

The best contemporary description of the indirect process is probably that published just after our period by John Ray.[22] According to Ray, one of the ironmaster's skills lay in mixing together the ores of different types so that the metal melted to advantage. The ore had first to be roasted or calcined with charcoal so that it could be beaten in pieces with a sledge hammer before it was put into the furnace. The furnace was filled with charcoal and heated for a day or two before they first added the treated iron ore and began to blow, using the bellows to increase the heat by degrees until after ten weeks or so the heat was at maximum. The ore was heated with the coals and every six days or so they would have a 'foundday' when they tapped the hearth and let the molten metal run out into the moulds. More ore was then added. The art of the blast furnace was to 'blow' for as long as possible without having to let the fire out; the longer the run the more metal could be smelted in the six days, because the hearth grew wider with the force of the fire – but eventually the hearth would wear out. In the early days they could rarely 'blow' for more than twelve to fourteen weeks, but by Ray's time a blow of forty was not uncommon. Ray gives the proportions as one load, that is 11 quarters, of fuel to one load, that is 18 bushels, of ore, and said that from 24 loads of coal they expected 8 tons of iron, but the proportions at the beginning seem to have been rather different.

The iron obtained in this way had a high carbon content and was therefore very brittle – suitable for casting cooking pots or firebacks but not for instruments which needed tensile strength. The sows were therefore taken to the forge where they were reheated and beaten until the carbon was almost totally removed, and the material was then wrought iron, suitable for horseshoes, locks, hinges, axes and the like. The forge had two fires, the 'finery' and the 'chafery', and the refining of the metal consumed another three to four loads of coals per ton of iron produced (which demanded rather more than a ton of pig). Both forge and furnace had to be situated near a good supply of running water to drive the bellows at the furnace and the hammer at the forge, both of which were powered by a water wheel, while water was needed at various other stages for tempering.

Ironically, if steel were required some of the carbon extracted earlier had to be painfully returned to the metal, but not until the second half of the nineteenth century was it at last possible to make steel directly. Attempts to make commercially viable steel in England met with very little success at this period. The process in use was the surface cementation process, and not all ores were suitable for this. When Sir Henry Sidney and his associates started a steel works at Robertsbridge (and at Boxhurst in Sandhurst parish, then Hawkhurst) the German workmen they imported were dissatisfied with the local ores, and the first iron was therefore imported to the works from South Wales. The costs of establishing the enterprise were considerable: over £1,900 was spent in 1565/6 alone, and the results were not entirely satisfactory. Sidney found that his product could not compete for price or quality with the imported steel, and although the works continued they did not become a major enterprise.[23] In about 1600 the price of steel started to rise, and in 1614 William Elliott and Mathew Meysey patented a new method of making steel. This was the manufacture of blister steel, by enclosing the iron in a sealed pot with a flux. Complaints came quickly about the quality of the steel produced in this way; however, though its production continued, its use was confined to coarser goods.

Though steel was essential for such things as surgeons' tools and swords, the price of making it was such that it was very narrowly confined to the absolute necessities, and its production was therefore never on a scale to make much impact on the level of total demand.

Iron, however, was becoming more widely used, and the blast furnace made steady progress. The advantage it offered over the bloomery was twofold. A bloomery yield of 33 per cent could become a yield of 46 per cent in the more efficient blast furnace which extracted more metal from the ore. At the same time a blast furnace processed much more in the time: even at first it was seven times greater, and this increased still more as time went on.[24]

David Crossley speaks of these developments as being one of 'a number of interesting case-studies in the interrelation of technology and the market' and comments on the major savings in costs – particularly fuel costs – consequent on changes in furnace design.[25] Unlike Nef, however, he holds rather that the growth of market demand encouraged technological change than that autonomous technological change enabled more of a virtually limitless consumer demand to be satisfied. Certainly his view is more consonant with the patchy geographical adoption of the new techniques.

Bloomeries were not ousted very rapidly; they were not actually introduced into the Forest of Dean until the early seventeenth century, though they had been established on its borders twenty years before.[26] This was partly because whereas bloomeries demanded relatively little capital expenditure, the costs of building a furnace and forge were quite high, the fuel costs, initially may have been higher,[27] and, what is probably most significant of all, the availability of men skilled in the new techniques was even more limited than the capital. It certainly appears that when the landowning classes sought in the 1550s to exploit their iron resources, they did not instinctively think in terms of blast furnaces. In 1541 Rutland estimated that one seam, or six blooms, could be made in a week by one bloomsmith – the amount producing half a ton of forged iron.[28] The calculations in 1553 are on the same basis. In 1571 the Willoughbys were still interested in bloomsmithies, and their calculations suggest that the bloomsmithy was becoming more efficient. Willoughby's official estimated that 'stone' (ore) cost 4s a load and that a load cost 3s to transport to the bloomeries. From one load of 'stone', a bloom could be made in twelve hours at a cost of 16d. From the bloom two brands would be made at a cost of 6d each, taking four hours to make, the whole process consuming eight loads of coals at 6s 8d a load for the eight blooms which were thought to make a ton. Total costs therefore came to just under £6 for a ton which was reckoned at £7, while Rutland's official thought twelve blooms would go to the ton, each bloom worth 14s. 12 x 14 = 168/- /8 8/-

The distinction between a bloomsmithy and a blast furnace may not always have been as clear to contemporaries as we like to think.

However, if bloomsmithies were becoming more efficient, blast furnaces from the start could produce 2–3 tons a week while they were in blast; this rose to 1 ton every twenty-four hours by the 1590s, and in the early seventeenth century in some furnaces to 2 tons in twenty-four hours. Just before the period starts there is an estimate of the costs of the new method from Newbridge iron mills in Sussex. This estimates that fourteen loads of ore make one ton of metal, at a cost of 1d a load for the ore and 8d for digging, that is, 10s 6d in all plus 4s 8d carriage. Eleven loads of charcoal at 3s a load was enough for 1 ton at the furnace; another five were required to make it into wrought iron at the forge, so charcoal, in all, cost 48s. The cost of casting the iron at the furnace was reckoned to be 3s 4d and the wages of the finer and hammerman 13s 4d; so they calculated the costs per ton at £4 1s 8d in all. Capital costs were not directly included, but as repairs were reckoned at 40s a year, in which time a production of 80 tons of metal was expected, they come to 6d a ton. Carriage to London, however, cost 6s 8d a load, and as iron was then selling for £5–6 the profit – somewhere between 10s and 30s – was not enormous.[29] The price, of course, depended very much on the 'goodness' of the metal: amongst the Middleton mss. there is a note 'The price of a ton [of iron] is according to the goodness thereof, in some places it is sold for £10.10.0, in other at £11.00.0 or £12.00.0 and at Cannock £13.00.0.'[30] Profits, however, might always be consumed by the unexpected need for more coals – at Newbridge it was noted that consumption might vary between 1,200 and 1,500 loads – or they might disappear because the price of iron had fallen because there were no buyers.

Setting up and running a furnace and forge, moreover, demanded a great deal of preparation and organisation, as may be seen from Document 10. Since it was important to 'blow' as long as possible, and that mainly in the winter months when transport of materials was difficult if not impossible, large quantities of materials had to be laid in in advance so that there should be no risk of shutting down at an inconvenient moment. Since much might depend on the skill and honesty of the charcoal burner, trials had to be held to determine who should be employed; trials of the foundryman and of the ore had to be

made to determine the yield to be expected, and much money laid out
before there was any prospect of starting to recoup.[31]

Estimates of costs and profits are therefore bound to vary from
furnace to furnace, in accordance with the source of the ore, the distance
from the furnace of ore, and of the markets for the metal, local costs of
wood, and so on. It is also important to notice that the cost of simply
erecting the mill is a small percentage of the total. When estimates of
£1,000 or £3,000 are given, it is clear that what people had in mind
was not the cost of building, but the total costs of establishing a mill –
that is, the amount of money which would have to be laid out in all
before any returns started coming in.

Document 11 gives a reasonably informed estimate of establishing a
blast furnace and forge, probably in the late 1580s or early 1590s. The
costs of building a hammer were given as £120, which may be compared
with £79 6s 1d paid at Worth, Sussex, in 1547, and the costs of building
a furnace as £50 – a small percentage of the total costs. At Middleton
an accountant calculated that the costs of erecting and equipping a
forge and furnace should not have exceeded £500.[32] His profits he
calculated in a conservative way on the basis of the furnace being
twenty-four weeks in blast, producing an average of 8 tons a week. It
is worth noticing that the Willoughby's officials expected to be in
blast for thirty weeks but only to get 180 tons in the time – an amount,
however, over double that expected at Newbridge fifty years earlier.
Unfortunately neither estimate reveals whether this was to be a single
'campaign' or not. The length of time which a furnace could be kept in
blast before it had to be allowed to go out, so that the accumulated slag
could be removed and the hearth rebuilt, varied considerably and
although, if you had a short campaign, you could have more than one
in a year, there were inevitably extra costs in fuel and time. Furnaces
were only thought profitable if they were in blast for at least twenty to
thirty weeks in the year, but early in the sixteenth century this consisted
of a number of shorter firings while towards the end of the century a
single campaign might continue twenty, twenty-five or even thirty
weeks. The organisation required to keep a steady inflow of ore and
fuel for this was naturally considerable.

The relationship between furnace and forge depended on the type
of output that was envisaged. A furnace specialising in cast iron ordnance
might need to be a double furnace in order to yield enough ore at a
single tapping for the size of the guns, in which case there might be no
forge at all attached. At the other extreme, if all the output was to be
turned into wrought iron, as seems to have been the case with the
Middleton works, one forge (since it worked more slowly than the

furnace) might barely keep up with the output of one furnace, so that one occasionally finds two forges to a furnace. Where some of the output of the furnace went into more domestic cast iron goods such as firebacks, cooking pots, salt pans and the like, the ratio of one forge to one furnace was easier to maintain. Dr Schubert considers that in general the ratio is five forges to four furnaces.

A single iron works employed a large number of people, though it is hard to estimate these in terms of units of full-time employment since most of the common labourers were employed on a day-to-day basis, and one generally knows of the miners, cutters of wood and charcoal burners only on the basis of their overall sales, which may or may not represent full-time work in this employment. There were probably, however, from ten to twelve miners and as many as fifty woodcutters[33] and burners kept going; at least four carters as well as carpenters (one full-time was the usual estimate for a forge and furnace), and work for perhaps one full-time common labourer on average. The aristocrats, however, were the founders at the furnace and the hammermen and finers at the forge, who were all paid by the ton of iron produced. The founder might expect to earn, at 3s/4s a ton, some £30 a year, and the finer and hammerman the same, or perhaps slightly more.

There are various accounts for periods of years from different forges which give some idea of the ordinary running costs of an established forge and foundry, but they rarely include costs of fuel or sows produced, because these were not the accountants' concern. Inventories of costs are better but the profit given is not always a true profit for often all the costs prior to those at the forge are not taken into account. The historian is left to calculate the true profit if he can by adding in known or estimated costs of earlier work, or making allowance for expenses which do not properly relate to the works. Often the accounts kept do not permit this, as Document 12 illustrates. This, while frustrating for the historian, does very aptly illustrate the extent to which even large-scale industrial enterprises were still embedded in the matrix of ordinary country life. They estimated, however, that the furnace at Oakamoor produced 6 tons of rough iron a week from 16 loads of coals at 12s a load and 16 loads of stone at 5s a load or £13 12s in all, the founder's wages at 4s a ton coming to 24s and repairs to 8s. At the forge 30 hundredweight of rough iron would give 1 ton of wrought iron, consuming 3½ dozen of coals in the process (costing, as the accountant put it, 52s and 20d). The workmen received £1 and 6s 8d went on repairs, coming in all to £7 9s 2d a ton.[34] The forge made 120 tons a year. If this was sold at £11 or £12 a ton the forge was making a reasonable but not an excessive profit.

The sale books make it clear that most of the iron from these midland forges was being consumed locally, and the Middleton records suggest that for a time at least, when it was newly established, they were selling directly to the iron workers on a fairly small retail basis – possibly because they found the need to stimulate sales. The profitability of a new furnace and forge, after all, depended very much on the capacity of the market to absorb the additional output without a drop in price, and the effective area of that market was limited by the additions to the price which carriage any distance created. Demand for the manufactures of the Birmingham and Dudley regions – for nails, horseshoes, bits, cutlery, locks and keys, hinges, files, axes and the like – had to keep pace with additional output of the metal in the area.

OUTPUT OF THE IRON INDUSTRY

It is important at this point, therefore, to see whether any general indication of output on a national basis can be obtained. In 1936 Nef produced a short article in which he attempted to calculate the progress of iron production in England in the period. In doing so he based himself on Straker's book on the Wealden area and Rhys Jenkins. He also made use of a persistent contemporary figure of 800 works, which first appears in a petition of 1611 and was repeated subsequently by a number of people including Lewes Roberts and the unreliable Dud Dudley. He came to the conclusion that on the eve of the Civil War there were 'not less than 100 nor more than 150 furnaces in blast and that the average output per furnace was between 200 and 250 tons, the annual output of pig iron would have been not less than 20,000 nor more than 43,000 tons'.[35] He goes on to estimate the output of bar iron at 15,000–33,000 tons, and to suggest that national output was greater than in the early eighteenth century when a reasonable estimate was 25,000 pig and 18,000 bar iron, though he concedes that output in the 1630s may have been lower than in the 1620s.

His figures are, however, optimistic. For one thing, when contemporary estimates can be pinned down the 'unit' involved can often be shown to be something less than the 'unit' Nef was envisaging – a separate count of hammers and fineries, for example. Dr Schubert spent a long time attempting to identify sites and periods of operation of blast furnaces. He undoubtedly missed some, but his evidence is more reliable than that used by Nef. The figures refer to blast furnaces only, and some allowance must be made for the number of bloomeries in operation at any given time – which are harder to identify and even when they are identified, it is harder to know when they were functioning. It must, however, be recognised that while the figures are thus lower than the total production, they probably overstate the rate of increase, since it is generally accepted that the blast furnace was steadily driving out the bloomery, so that the opening of a new blast furnace meant the end of some bloomeries. Schubert thought that the years from 1625 to 1635 saw total production at about 26,000 tons, 'the highest annual output . . . in the English charcoal iron industry'.

Recently Dr Hammersley, who has recalculated the figures for the number of occupied blast furnaces by decade,[36] has shown a sharp rise in number up to the end of the 1570s and then to 1720 at least a stable oscillation around seventy-nine operative furnaces – the decline of the Wealden works being offset by growth elsewhere. Total output, however, requires a multiplier, and this clearly must increase as larger furnaces and longer blows become normal.[37] Hammersley estimates 5,000 tons in the 1550s and about 15,000 tons in the 1580s – a satisfying growth rate. Thereafter, however, output grew slowly – by 1600–10 to perhaps 17,000–18,000 tons, 19,000 tons in the 1620s, and perhaps 20,000 tons in the 1630s. The reasons for the dramatic slowing down are still not wholly clear. Hammersley demonstrates that wood supplies were adequate for this level of production, and that the rate of return per acre on wood did not make it an attractive substitute for grain growing or pastoral use of land. He also suggests that imports from Sweden were both better and cheaper – for reasons unconnected with technology. The sharp early rise may be due to the production of ordnance (much in demand) in the Weald. When in the late 1570s the government began to fear that the export of ordnance was a threat to national security, it started to take steps to prevent unlicensed exports. It is uncertain how effective this was: one founder suggested that 2,500 tons of ordnance were cast – which would amount to one-third of the total cast iron produced – and 1,600 tons were secretly smuggled out,[38] and smuggling is hardly surprising when one considers that ordnance that sold at £12 a ton in England sold for £40, £60 or £80 on the Continent.[39] Production in the Weald was severely checked, nonetheless, and as the output of ordnance had accounted for over half of the growth rate in the area, growth slowed.[40] Perhaps significantly the domestic price of ordnance appears to have dropped between 1565 and 1600 from £10–12 to £9–10 a ton. There is scattered evidence that the Sussex founders found it necessary to diversify into other types of goods. The national rate of growth in the industry then seems to have dropped back to under 1 per cent a year, or less if the bloomeries were going out of business.

Had the matter been simply a crisis in the availability of wood for fuel, particularly in the Wealden area, one would have expected some sort of price rise, making it profitable for furnaces to be opened in more favoured areas and to export their products farther afield; but despite the periodic outcries about woods, the Wealden furnaces apparently managed to maintain their existing level of output down to the Civil War, and growth elsewhere was only moderate. The decline in the midlands may be more apparent than real, for Richard Foley, who introduced a slitting mill into the area in the 1620s, also apparently set out to rationalise production there, so that he owned, in various partnerships, a string of works stretching across three counties. Even if one makes allowance for this, however, Nef's optimism seems unfounded. Iron production may have trebled in the period, but a growth rate across a century which can scarcely have averaged 2 per cent a year would not in itself generate an industrial revolution.

Demand for iron at the existing price might have been increasing only slowly, and it might be argued that successful cutting of costs by the use of coal might have sharply increased demand. Nef himself was inclined to stress the introduction of coal as a fuel at the chafery stage, but, as can be seen from Document 10, the value of iron made in this way was 20 per cent lower; the saving on fuel costs hardly compensated for such a drop, particularly when domestic production had always to compete with overseas products in quality as well as in price. Certainly, there is no evidence in the form of exorbitant rates of profit that demand was being in any way held back at the end of the period; indeed, the higher level of integration introduced into the field by the Foley partnership in the 1620s suggests that profits may have been reaped at this period only from a high level of marginal efficiency. The other extractive industries are little more encouraging.

CHANGE IN THE LEAD INDUSTRY

Lead smelting was also undergoing a slow technological change. In the Middle Ages lead had been smelted in the open in great hills known as bole hills (with alternate layers of ore and fuel) from which the molten metal had flowed out into pits, but which left so much metal behind that the eighteenth-century masters found it profitable to rework the slag. By the mid-sixteenth century the ore was beginning to be smelted in charcoal-fired furnaces with water-driven bellows which were able to smelt three to four fodders a week per furnace – a considerable improvement on the bole hill, it was also reckoned a 50 per cent saving on fuel. In 1564 William Humphrey had taken out a patent for the introduction of this 'new' method, but, as with so many ideas which were in fact borrowed from the Continent at this time, it had almost certainly been introduced earlier. The new method, or open hearth method as it was called, effected no change in the organisation of the smelting which had long been in the hands of the gentlemen or merchants of the area, who bought the ore from the free miners and sold the metal to their agents in London. Production of lead was probably rising, but since control of the limited areas from which it came was already firmly pre-empted, we learn about its progress only in the fringe areas where entrepreneurs were seeking to open up new sources. Early in the seventeenth century experiments were being made with reverberatory furnaces, in which fuel other than wood – which was short in the areas – might be used. The disputes over the Mines Royal in 1623 show clearly that attempts were being made to use sea coal or peat in such furnaces, though as yet with indifferent success. The furnaces had not taken over from the open hearth method by the end of the period.

It is hard to know what the output was in the period. In the Welsh trials in 1623 3 tons of ore yielded in two long days' smelting 1 ton, 2 hundredweight, 1 quarter and 3 pounds of lead using 31 hogsheads of white coal and 5 barrels of pit coal costing 16s, for the colliers had agreed on 10s for the charcoal needed for 1 ton of lead, and pit coal cost them about 10s the ton weight.[41] If this is an accurate guide, then the estimate made in Charles I's reign of an output of 12,600 fodders[42] would suggest that either the output of a Derbyshire mining community of 4,000-odd plus others in the Mendips and elsewhere was lower than the suggested 20 tons of ore a head, or that it was underemployed. It is of course difficult to establish a fixed relationship between fodder and ton. Raistrick and Jennings, after an exhaustive argument, conclude that a fodder would be '1,560, 1,872, or 2,184 pounds weight' and that one cartload was roughly equal to a fodder.[43] Twelve weys generally went to a fodder, but the wey was 15 stone in Yorkshire and only 14 in Swaledale, to go no deeper into the complexities. If the ton was standard avoirdupois it would tend to be more than a fodder, but one cannot be certain that it was, and a 40 per cent range of difference for the weight of the fodder makes it quite impossible to come to fine conclusions of any sort. Exports of lead in the early seventeenth century were running around 4,000 fodders a year, so that the overseas demand, which was not rising, played an important part in the whole, if the estimate for 1636 is at all accurate.

In any case, it is clear that the volume and the value of the lead which sold in 1600 for around £7 13s 4d a fodder was not far short of the volume and value of iron production, and though output was undoubtedly rising there is nothing to suggest that contemporaries found the industry a field particularly worth exploiting except when there was the possibility of a high silver content. It was this which attracted the Mines Royal to the Welsh ore, and encouraged them to use the expensive, fuel-consuming, old-fashioned process of cupellation to extract the silver from the lead. It seems unlikely that the silver did more than pay for the cost of extraction, but without that will-o'-the-wisp, lead production would presumably have been even lower.

GOVERNMENT-FOSTERED DEVELOPMENT: THE COPPER AND CALAMINE INDUSTRIES

While lead was both an important industry and an important export, we have paradoxically far more information at our disposal about the copper and calamine industry which was neither. The government had its own reasons for encouraging the search for and production of the minerals, and copper was in itself, ton for ton, the most valuable of the base metals, but it is doubtful whether the output ever justified the money put into the venture, even in the government's eyes. The mining flourished briefly in the middle of Elizabeth's reign, languished again at the end of the sixteenth century but was taken up again and continued until the Civil War, though always, it would seem, at a loss to those who undertook it. At the height of the boom less than 150 workmen were employed, and they were mainly Germans. Receipts over a six-year period totalled £23,658 19s 5½d or approximately £6,000 a year, and this cannot all have been from copper production as the income from copper even in a good year rarely exceeded £4,000.[44]

The German machines, the import of which gave the excuse for the patent of monopoly, were certainly effective: they were also, as we have seen, very expensive. The smelting of copper also presented greater technical difficulties than the smelting of iron, tin or lead, particularly if it was intended to extract the silver from the copper as well. Output of copper from the furnace was relatively slow: in eighteen weeks and five days Hochstetter reckoned to get 70 centners of copper. This may be pessimistic: Nedham wrote more optimistically that one furnace could smelt 16 hundredweight of ore a day, so that in 282 working days he could smelt 27,072 centners.[45] In fact in 1568 450 tons of ore were worked with two furnaces in forty weeks. The technical developments after 1579 may have improved output: the two Welsh furnaces could now apparently smelt 560 tons in forty weeks as well as producing a useful by-product,[46] but other difficulties arose to impede growth. Output for the first eighteen years for Keswick oscillated as follows:

Year	Cwt
1567	10
1568	293
1569	791
1570	1,248
1571	1,023
1572	1,197
1573	1,200
1574	532
1575	105
1576	574
1577	285
1578	60
1579	360
1580	150
1581	660
1582	—
1583	810
1584	1,050
total	10,348 cwt (av. 610 p.a.)

This amount, less the queen's share, left total income from sales in the period at £34,000. Copper sold at about £3 a hundredweight, so that the value of the copper even in a good year rarely exceeded £4,000, while the value of silver extracted in the period was about £1,167 or £80 p.a., about 4 per cent of the total income. By the end of 1600 sales had grossed £68,103 but as the costs of mining and smelting came to £2 14s 8d a hundredweight or 91 per cent of receipts, without any allowance for amortising capital outlay, it was not an outstandingly profitable undertaking, and there seems no evidence that the shareholders benefited.[47]

Expenditure on getting the mines and smelting houses going before any return was seen came to £18,612 by 1568: 39·3 per cent was spent on the mines, 31·7 per cent on smelting and 29 per cent on travelling and other general costs. By 1576 total expenditure had risen to £51,615 (though in the three previous years outlay had settled down to just over £2,000 a year) and even on running costs alone the venture was still making a loss. The debit balance at that point was £32,091. In 1572 a balance sheet suggested that realisable assets at that point were £8,165 15s 4½d (against a debit of £28,861 laid out); the assets, plus an estimated value of £3,888 15s 6d, suggest that at this point the company's loss might be about £16,000. In the 1580s when the mines were leased the costs seem to have settled down and the lessees were able to report a modest profit of £1,300, but by the late 1580s the yield was declining and the lessee once again made a loss, this time of about £1,200. The losses continued into the 1590s when in seven and a half years another £1,200 was lost, and although the mines were kept going until the Civil War it was again at a further loss.[48]

There is no reason to argue that it was unreasonable of the venturers to undertake the development of copper mining: copper mines were potentially very profitable if the ore was found in abundance and in an easily workable form, and no one could know in advance what the supplies would be like. Nor is the initial heavy outlay without return, or the building up of sizeable material assets, surprising: these are the costs which anyone attempting to establish a new venture must expect. The failure of the enterprise to bring in a fortune was always a possibility with an undertaking of this sort; it does not mark its undertakers as fools or rogues, but neither does it lend much support to the idea of the vigorously expanding demand for raw materials which one would expect to accompany an industrial revolution. On the contrary, the problem seems to have been that with costs, particularly wages, at an irreducible minimum, the price was at a level where the enterprise was barely profitable; a lower price might have stimulated demand, but was not possible in the absence of major technological improvements. Nef asserted that Keswick ran out of wood for fuel, but Hammersley thinks that the Keswick smelter at a maximum output of about 50 tons a year would use only the produce of 90 acres of woodland or the annual increment of 4,000–5,000 acres, and considers that with weak demand Hochstetter did well to keep going.[49] Copper at this stage was used for coinage, for the manufacture of copper containers such as brewing vessels, for wire, and as a component of brass manufacturing, and in many of these things the use of iron was cheaper though the product was less durable. Any benefits which came from the establishment of copper mining at this period were at best very long term.

SMALL-SCALE INDUSTRIES: SUCCESSES AND FAILURES

It is possible, certainly, to point to industries enjoying successful growth but these must mainly be classified as useful but small scale. The manufacture of gunpowder was one which had strategic rather than great economic significance. Gunpowder is a mixture of six parts of saltpetre (potassium nitrate) with one part each of sulphur and charcoal. Potassium nitrate was not found naturally in Western Europe, but by the mid-sixteenth century knowledge of how to manufacture it artificially was well established on the Continent, and in March 1561 a German captain named Gerard Henrick undertook for £300 to instruct the English in the art. It was one of the more immediately successful promotions. In 1562 five powder mills had been established, and three Englishmen, in return for the right to take the necessary raw materials, undertook to supply the queen with 100 lasts of gunpowder at £3 15s 0d a hundredweight (where 24 cwt = one last and 100 lb. = one cwt) and 100 lasts of serpentine powder at £2 16s 8d, a contract worth £15,000-odd.

Limitations on the production of gunpowder, in facts seem to have come from the raw material side. To obtain saltpetre one needed earth saturated with animal excrement (pigeon dung seems to have been particularly suitable) which had to be left in piles exposed to the air and wetted at intervals with urine until the saltpetre crystallised; the patentees found difficulties in obtaining enough, despite their licence to take it where they pleased, which was understandably unpopular. Production fell short of requirements, in fact, to the extent that imports of foreign powder were necessary, even though it was dearer.[50]

Another minor industry referred to by Nef, which was successfully established at this period, was the manufacture of copperas, which was established, amongst other places, at Queenborough and Whitstable. The process was slow, but not technically difficult. Iron pyrites was piled in layers and dissolved by exposure to rain (over a period of up to five years), and the resultant liquid was then boiled with pieces of old iron in iron or lead pans until it crystallised. Although this was useful, it was not a very major industry even on a local basis, as Document 13 may make clear.

The establishment of an alum industry was potentially more critical, since alum was the mordant most commonly used to fix the colour when dyeing cloth; it was argued that with an assured home supply of the mordant English cloth manufacturers would be in a better position to challenge the hold which the Dutch had over the dyeing end of the cloth industry. Alum, however, was a rare commodity: Europe, indeed, had imported most of its alum from the East until the discovery of alum mines in the papal states near Tolfa enabled European production to be established in the fifteenth century. Sixteenth-century searches for alum in England had proved unsuccessful, and it was not until 1600 that alum was found in the parish of Skelton near Guisborough in north-east Yorkshire.

Subsequent discoveries made the area a workable proposition, and an enticing field for a monopolist. Once again, local knowledge was not enough to exploit the discovery successfully, and twelve foreign workmen were imported. Like so many of these ventures which the government and monopolists embarked upon, it was planned from the start as a very large-scale enterprise into which a lot of capital was poured, and Dr Gough is undoubtedly right in condemning it as 'financially unsound, indeed, extravagant'.[51]

The plan was to prohibit imports of alum and to start domestic production at once at the level of the whole existing domestic consumption which was reckoned at 1,000 tons a year, developing production very rapidly until there was another 1,000 tons to export. To achieve this, they immediately built five 'houses' at Slape Wath, Belamn bank and Newgate bank near Guisborough and at Sandsend and Assholme Mulgrave wood near Whitby. Each house cost at least £1,000 to build and equip and needed sixty workmen, who were not, of course, skilled in the work. The result of this precipitate behaviour was the running up of large and increasing losses amounting after one year to £20,000, after two to £30,000 and after five or six to £36,000. Moreover, the debts were thus limited only because the price of the inferior English alum was artificially maintained at a much higher price than the £15 which consumers had been paying for superior imported alum, so that there was not unnaturally a wave of protest, and a flourishing smuggling trade developed. Estimates in the 1610s, however, continued to be made on the basis of production of 2,000 tons, the residue of which was to be exported – though no one seems to have wondered how it was to be sold at more than the existing foreign price which was lower than the English. The problem did not in practice arise, since output did not exceed 600 tons at this period.

In 1612 losses amounted to £19 on every ton so far produced. Gradually the position improved, even though liabilities continued to mount and profits were as far away as ever. Output increased to 1,200 tons and running costs began to be lowered. Even so, it was not until the late 1630s that the situation really began to improve. The cost to the nation in terms of government assistance, to the cloth industry in terms of additional costs, to the entrepreneurs in terms of the opportunity cost of the capital invested in establishing the industry, is unlikely to have been offset by the employment provided for a few hundred workmen and the import saving. The possible ultimate benefit of establishing the industry made no contribution in the period with which we are concerned.[52] (See Document 14.)

Though Nef constantly refers to these industries to bolster his arguments, particularly since he felt that large-scale investment was in itself significant, he rested his argument in the last analysis on three industries: salt, ship building and glass. It is these to which we should therefore pay particular attention. He was especially interested in them because the development of all three was associated with the coal industry.

THE SALT INDUSTRY: A CASE OF MODERATE GROWTH?

England's dependence on imported salt was a development of the later Middle Ages. Before that, she had obtained most of her salt from salt pans around the coast, and from the brine pits in Cheshire and Worcestershire. Exploitation of the brine pits continued, though it is hard to establish how much they produced. Nef considers that the Cheshire and Worcestershire wiches produced 20,000 tons or more. He treats his evidence ambiguously, however, especially since he accepts Hughes' conclusion that consumption in Henry VIII's reign was 40,000 tons, without explaining how the Cheshire output fits the idea that 40,000 tons were imported. The output of the seaside works he considers to have been only a few hundred tons in 1540. In fact, Nef had not noticed that Harrison was copying Leland and that the observations were therefore forty years old; Harrison, moreover, had returned the manuscript to its owner before he wrote the passage up and had therefore muddled his notes, attributing to Droitwich things which Leland had written of Nantwich. Leland's comments are in fact very revealing (Doc. 15): at Droitwich, he points out, there are now 400 furnaces, each of which should yield four loads of salt in the six months of the year in which salt is made. Nef had assumed they worked for forty-eight weeks in the year. Leland conjectures that the restriction was due to a desire to keep up the price or to control the consumption of wood, but Hughes may also have pointed to a reason in his comment that 'a brine pit might not be equal to regular and heavy drawings off all the year round'.[53] Droitwich's output therefore would hardly have exceeded 1,600 loads, which were probably about a ton each. Leland's comment on the Cheshire salt towns, Nantwich, Middlewich and Northwich, accords with Collins in according pre-eminence to Nantwich which he said had 300 salters. He says nothing about the length of time for which the salters operated, but it may have been more continuous than at Droitwich. The number of wich houses was, however, limited, and the price at which such houses changed hands not excessive. In the 1590s a double wich house changed hands at £170 and three and a half houses at Nantwich somewhat earlier realised only £136. It would therefore be unrealistic to assume that the owner of such a house expected a clear profit of much more than £10, and probably unrealistic to think that a house would produce much more than double the yield of a single house at Droitwich. If a single salter therefore produced eight to ten loads a year, the total output of the three Cheshire wiches is unlikely to have exceeded 6,000–7,000 tons – a total, in all, of under 10,000 for the brine pits, most of which was almost certainly sold and consumed locally, especially since the price of salt in Leland's time seems to have been higher here than in the coastal regions. Output may have increased in the period, but if so, it only kept pace with local consumption for there is no evidence that it was sold farther afield.[54]

Certainly, the furnaces which produced salt from sea water were the ones on which contemporaries fastened as lending themselves to rapid expansion and exploitation. Whether or not the queen was thinking in terms of establishing a *gabelle*, it is clear that her ministers dreamt of the prospect of making £60,000 yearly in profit if they could control and monopolise the production of salt for domestic consumption, and equally clear that the entrepreneurs whom they sought to interest were less sanguine about the prospect. The reason for this may perhaps be discerned in Collins. Salt produced by boiling sea water was not good quality white salt. Collins considered that Newcastle salt was unsuitable for a preservative – a point the Cinque ports had made in the 1630s.[55] The way in which the best salt was made on the east coast, in fact, was by taking the imported solar salt – that is the salt which had been evaporated in salt pans in the more southerly latitudes of France and Spain, solely (and therefore cheaply) by the heat of the sun, and improve the quality and remove dirt, sand and bittern by boiling it up again in a solution of sea water. This was the method of making salt on salt, and it is quite clear from the fracas about the seventeenth century attempts at monopoly in Charles' reign that this was what a large number of the salters around the East Anglian coast were engaged in doing. Merchants writing about commerce at this period, like Lewes Roberts, took it for granted that salt was a commodity which England imported because it was a product of warmer climes. It was one of Tobias Gentleman's complaints in 'The Trades Increase' that the salt trade had passed into the hands of the Dutch. Speaking of the diminution, in his view, of the trade with Lisbon, Andalusia and Portugal, he wrote of the loss to Aldeburgh of employment for thirty to forty sail of some 200 tons by the Dutch monopoly of the trade in salt for the fishing industry.[56]

The south coast certainly got most of its salt from France and Portugal, and even then it was short of salt for the cod fisheries. The ships set out for Newfoundland with half their lading of salt, or not less than 7,000 tons, and bought additional supplies if they could from foreigners on their arrival.[57] Expansion of the cod fisheries, in fact, depended on the accessibility of further supplies of salt, and it was partly for this reason that the fishermen began to think in terms of a shore settlement.

In a sense, indeed, it could be argued that the interest of a native salt industry and the interests of the shipping industry were mutually incompatible, for salt was an important and bulky element in trade (Doc. 29).

This is not to say that the English industry had not undergone an important expansion. Nef may, however, have underestimated the size of the industry in 1540. There had been salt pans at Shields by that time for more than fifty years, and it is clear from the letter Mount wrote to Cecil in connection with the establishment of the monopoly in the 1560s that the industry was also an established one in Yorkshire.[58]

In Hughes' opinion, the real stimulus to English salt production came with the civil disturbances in France and the Netherlands and the embargoes on English shipping which accompanied the troubles. At any rate, it appears that prominent local people began to see the industry as a potential source of profit: in 1585 Thomas Wilkes, Clerk of the Privy Council, was granted a new salt patent, and the speed with which it was sold to a local syndicate suggests that the deal had been set up in advance. Perhaps the main object of the syndicate was to keep out, or at least regulate, the import of Scottish salt, which was cheaper than the home produced variety. Two of the syndicate, Anderson and Bowes, had an interest in the manufacturing end. Bowes had been using Crown money from the Berwick garrison to speculate in the acquisition of coal mines and salt pans, and it was the collapse of this house of cards which revealed the size of the works at Sutherland. Bowes himself claimed that the capital invested in the works amounted to £4,000, and one of his servants, writing to Burghley, spoke of the stopping up of a water gate which had cost £2,000. For a time at least, Bowes' mines were drowned, but Burghley finally managed to lease the whole unit of mines and pans for £800 a year which suggests that the level of production must have been at least 1,000 tons a year. In 1605 it appears that there were 153 pans in operation in Northumberland and Durham, each of them consuming on average 160 Newcastle chalders of coals and probably producing about 8,000–9,000 tons of salt – not much more than that freighted by the cod fishing fleet alone.

In fact, despite Bowes' venture, the patentees seem in the 1590s to have decided that the profit lay rather in the monopoly of the sale of salt than in any attention to attempts to produce it, and the small independent producers on the Tyne found themselves undercut by the prices which the Scots were prepared to accept. The local producer, in fact, had to be protected by the Lords by an agreement made during the time of the 1593 Parliament, after the local knights and burgesses had raised a protest. By this the patentees, in return for permission to refuse to take Scottish salt, agreed to pay 1s a bushel for 'Such reasonable quantities of white salt as should be agreed on between them to be brought by them to the ports aforesaid'.[59] The union of the crowns clearly made the exclusion of Scottish salt more difficult, but demand for salt was evidently buoyant enough to keep the northern salt manufacturies growing. In exceptional years like 1630, Newcastle salt might suddenly all be bought up for sale on the Continent, and it is clear that the industry was able to stand without protection at its existing, fairly modest level. There may even have been sense in the government's argument, when preferring a corporation claiming to manufacture salt to a contract for its free importation (which was favoured by the London saltmongers and fishmongers), with a higher custom on the commodity that 'strangers . . . will sell at their pleasure [that is, at what price they like] . . . when the English salt pans shall be laid down'. In Shields at this time there were evidently about 200 pans in operation, which suggests that output might have risen to 12,000–13,000 tons or more, if productivity had risen in the previous thirty years.

The description which William Brereton has left us of the pans on the Tyne at this time is worth careful consideration, as it is, like Leland's descriptions, the result of direct observation, and not, as in the case of so many writers, the more or less accurate reportage of what may be inaccurate or out-of-date information. His description of the new type of pan, as well as his estimates of the number of workmen, their not inconsiderable wages and the capital costs involved, are all very enlightening. It is clear, however, that the older style of pit had only one man to tend it.[60] (See Document 16.) Brereton's figures give a comfortable gross profit of 33 per cent, but it is not clear how much of this actually accrued to the salt makers.

In 1630, when the dearth of salt had produced the usual scheme of monopoly solution, the Tyneside salters entered a very interesting protest. They claimed that the monopolists' plan to supply salt to all England for 2s a bushel, or 16s a quarter, would give them a grossly inflated rate of profit. They claimed that they had for a long time sold salt on Tyneside for only 9d a bushel and had recently raised their prices only by 1d. The shortage, they suggested, was artificially created by the merchants, who declined to come to buy the salt at Shields in the hope of putting prices up in the country and down at Shields. The Essex salters added their own protest in similar terms. The salters estimated that the monopolists' profit would amount to £100,000.[61] Now 10d a bushel is the cost net of transport costs, as the salters and the government were well aware; £100,000 would represent the gross receipts from the sale of 25,000 tons at £4 a ton or 2s a bushel. It therefore seems likely that the salters considered that annual consumption in the east coast areas and London alone in which the proposed patent would be operating was in the region of 100,000 tons[62] or more. When Brereton reckoned the number of pans on the Tyne as 250 he may have exaggerated. Their output was probably about 16 quarters a week each, or something under 700 a year. When the pans came briefly into royal hands there were 220, which may be a more realistic number, though they estimated the annual output of the Tyne saltpans at 2,087,000 bushels or 52,175 wey in 1630,[63] which would certainly take 250 pans working full time. At 5 quarters to the ton, however, Nef's estimate of 15,000–20,000 tons is quite possibly low. Indeed the Yarmouth salter Nicholas Munford reckoned the whole production of England at 80,000 weys,[64] but this has to be offset against a much larger total consumption than he envisaged. In 1597, when salt was scarce and dear, London received seven shiploads of Scottish salt in a month. The salt industry may have been expanding, but it was in all probability hardly maintaining much more than its original share of the market.

THE GLASS INDUSTRY: TECHNICAL CHANGE AND MONOPOLY

The history of the glass industry is a less straightforward one because of the discontinuities which technological change and monopolistic interference introduced into its development. It is a subject which has aroused a great deal of archaeological and artistic interest, and the careful investigation of surviving products and identification of glass furnace sites enables the student to be in some ways more precise than is possible for industries which were economically more important. At the beginning of the period glass was a luxury item, most people making do with leather bottles, wooden plates, pewter or, increasingly, pottery ware and only the rich having window or broad glass in their houses. In the course of the sixteenth century the price of glass fell and demand rose, but not to the extent of making it a material of vital importance to the economy.[65] Excavation has made the normal size of the woodland furnace reasonably clear, and it is sensible to suppose that a single furnace or team of two to three glass makers might make at least 400 cases or 40 tons of glass a year because both the archaeological and the historical evidence suggest this.[66] (See Document 17.) Crossley thinks that if the furnaces operated for 30 weeks in the year, allowing for rebuilding time, 1,000 cases might be a pessimistic estimate and the 'profit' of a furnace £200 a year. At that time there were at least fifteen or sixteen furnaces, making green drinking vessels and apothecaries' wares, operating at any one time, and about as many making window glass, so that the total gross return may have been in the region of £20,000 a year. Even allowing for the crystal glass works in London which had been omitted from this calculation, the industry, though a flourishing and a profitable one, was economically not of major significance, whatever its artistic merits may have been. It demanded very highly skilled labour, but did not employ a very large fringe of unskilled labour, though the labour involved in the cutting of wood and the digging of sand must not be forgotten. Although the successful adaptation to coal firing about 1612 probably meant that the furnace grew in size,[67] and total output per furnace may have increased proportionately, the resultant relocation of the industry probably caused at least a temporary setback to total output.

Glass had been made in England, in fact, throughout the Middle Ages, though in small quantities and of poor quality – the coarser type of bottle glass, which corroded easily. In the 1560s, therefore, Cecil was prepared to listen favourably to suggestions that the quality, and probably the quantity, could be improved if patentees were given the encouragement of a monopoly to bring over to England families of skilled glass workers who knew more of the 'mystery' than the native English, and who in the current unsettled state of the Continent were only too happy to come. There seems no doubt that this was one of the more successful patents. Analysis of surviving fragments of glass makes it clear that the quality of the later forest glass made in England after the 1567 patent was superior to the earlier product, while it lends no support to the hypothesis that all that was involved was the importation of soda from Spain to act as a flux. The analysis concluded that 'a whole range of technological aspects was involved in moving from the earlier glass to the later'.[68]

It is therefore understandable that the highest cost in glass making was the wages paid to the workman. Carre at the outset in 1568 is said to have paid his principal man 18s a *day*; with such rates, it is not surprising that the workmen claimed, and were permitted, to entitle themselves gentleman. Eighteen shillings a day was the wage paid for an output of three cases a day, but this output was apparently not normally achieved, and it seems likely that normally the wage was paid at a rate of 2s or 3s per case, and possibly a share of the profits. This was still very high.[69]

The cost of building the furnace was apparently negligible: £12–20 in all, and the main cost apart from wages was fuel, for sand and lime could be had more or less for the taking, though the right sort of clay and firing for the pots in which the glass was to be melted at first caused some trouble. An ordinary furnace, however, consumed about thirty cords of wood every ten days, and the total bill for fuel at the Knole furnace for seven months in 1585–6 was £146.[70] Once fuel and wages and other incidental expenses were paid, the profit from a single furnace may have been in the region of £200 a year, which was comfortable but not excessive.

Expansion of total production in the sixteenth century in this industry may indeed have been limited by the availability of fuel, for not only was wood becoming scarcer in the Weald, where competition for its use was severe, but for technical reasons the glass makers sought beech for preference, and the area in which beech grows is even more restricted. By the early seventeenth century, therefore, the Wealden glass manufacturers had reached, if not passed, their maximum.

The London glaziers – who found their supplies inelastic – complained of the artificial scarcity created by the hard-headed man who was then the leading glass maker, Bongar, but it is unlikely that very much more could have been produced there. Glass had also been made for many years in Staffordshire at Abbots Bromley, Wolsely near Rugeley, Eccleshall, Cheswardine and elsewhere, but transport was a greater problem.[71] One of the advantages mentioned in the proposal to set up works at Wollaton is its nearness to the water. Forest glass works were also open in the north and west.

Technological change included improved furnace design to cut down fuel consumption and lead to an improved produce, but coal-fired furnaces were undoubtedly the breakthrough of greatest significance for the industry.[72] The first patent granting a monopoly of coal-fired furnaces came in 1612, and furnaces began to be set up very shortly thereafter, though they experienced all the usual teething troubles which afflict such breakthroughs. One of the major difficulties was that an essential ingredient of the glass itself was pure wood ash, which the glass makers had always previously had available from the firing, but which, purchased commercially at so much the bushel, nearly always turned out to be contaminated with other fuels such as peat. On 19 January 1615, Sir Robert Mansell obtained sole possession of the patent, and on 23 May 1615 James proclaimed that henceforth glass was to be made with coal fuel only.

The Wealden glass makers did not yield without a struggle, but Mansell had the position and the money to enforce what became, by this, his legal rights, and by the end of 1618 virtually all the wood-fired Wealden glass works were shut down.[73] Glass making migrated to Newcastle-upon-Tyne and to a lesser extent to Staffordshire and to Stourbridge in Worcestershire.[74] The émigré families, who were still the principal glassmen, since they guarded their secrets well, seem for the most part to have accepted Mansell, but although, once the new process had settled down and new furnaces had opened up, the English glass makers may have been ahead of their continental rivals in some points of technique, there is no evidence of a spectacular rise in output, and glass did not become an important English export. Fine glass ware continued to be imported.

SHIP BUILDING: THE COMPLICATIONS OF DEMAND

The fortunes of a ship-building industry depend very much on the demand for ships for transport of goods or for fishing or for defence. It is rare for a nation to be able to build up an industry on the export of ships alone; on the other hand, it is possible that a large number of ships used in England and by Englishmen were not built in England. Contemporaries certainly saw the merits of a strong fleet, if few of them wrote in quite such ecstatic terms as Tobias Gentleman: 'They are our weapons, they are our ornaments, they are our strength, they are our pleasures, they are our defence, they are our profit; the subject by them is made rich; the kingdom through them strong; the prince in them mighty.'[75] The development of a domestic ship-building industry was therefore desirable, but to see what the potential demand for ships was like it is perhaps better to look first at the fishing and transport industry.

THE FISHING INDUSTRY: THE PROBLEM OF FOREIGN COMPETITION

In the period there were three basic fishing grounds to which organised fleets sailed. These were the Iceland fishing, the herring fishing and the Newfoundland fishing for cod, or as it was then usually called, staple fish. To each of these fishings the boats were organised as a fleet, with an admiral appointed from amongst the boats as leader.[76]

The Newfoundland fishing may be dealt with first, because its story is the simplest and, despite inevitable setbacks, is one of reasonably straightforward, satisfactory growth. The ports which benefited from this expansion were mainly the west country ones like Exeter. The vessels involved were for their time reasonably substantial, for they had to cross the Atlantic and be able to carry provisions for a fair length of time. The pattern was for the ships to set out early in the year and for them to have a number of smaller boats with them to do the actual fishing; these were then left on shore in Newfoundland and picked up again the following year, repaired if necessary on the spot, and reused. The fishermen needed these shore settlements particularly if, through shortage of salt, they intended to preserve the cod by smoking them, and there was much dispute between the various nations which sent fleets to the fishing about the choice of sites for these temporary lodgings, the theft and destruction of the structures which were set up, and the overwintering of men.

By the end of the century England was established on the Avalon peninsula. The expansion of the market for salted dry fish had helped in the expansion of the fleet. This had grown from nothing at the beginning of the period. In 1578 Hakluyt tells us that there had been an increase in the number of fishing vessels in Newfoundland from thirty to fifty, though there were more in some years than in others. In 1594 there were 100 sail and some time thereafter, Tobias Gentleman thought, 150. By 1615 there were 250 fishing boats of 15,000 tons with 5,000 men employed. In 1620 an optimistic estimate said 300 and it may have been as high as 500 in the 1630s. In 1634 the western ports were thought to supply 26,700 tons of shipping and 10,680 men. Even so, some of the western ports, Fowey for example, decayed. In general, however, it is the most unambiguous success story of the period, though the costs of engaging in the industry were not low.[77] Document 18 shows the breakdown of the costs involved. Whitbourn argued that a 100-ton ship with forty men would cost £420 1s 4d to provision. It would have eight to ten three-man fishing boats subsidiary to it, which would catch an average of 25,000 fish a boat, worth, with the oil arising from them, £100–120. This gave a total catch of 200,000 cod. This was assumed to be a load for a 100-ton ship, though some of the fishing boats sold part of their catch to traders who came out to buy. The load weighed 2,200 quintals, which at 12s a quintal would bring £1,320 and at 16s £1,760; in addition, there were 12 tons of cod oil which could be sold in Newfoundland at £10 a ton or £120 in all. To this he added 10,000 large green fish at £10 per 1,000 to produce a grand total of £2,250. Of this the master and the ship's company were entitled to one-third, the owners one-third and the victuallers one-third. The profit left after deducting £420 1s 4d from £750 was comfortable, and there seems no doubt that profits of this order were made.

Another fishery off the shores of North America which developed in the early seventeenth century was the New England fishery. The number of vessels engaged in this rose from a handful in 1616 to fifty in 1624, and the ships made a good profit. In 1619 a 200-ton ship left Plymouth and earned for each sailor a profit of £16 10s seven months later. The following year three ships reported £20 a share. Even if these profits were the cream, it looks as though the milk would have produced far more than the common labourer's earnings.[78]

The Iceland trade, on the other hand, was less flourishing. In 1517 there were supposed to be 300 ships in the trade, but this figure was probably out of date. Hull had ceased to send ships to the Iceland fishing by 1520s, and the numbers dwindled to 100 or 120 by 1600. Though Tobias Gentleman thought that one-quarter of all seamen were employed in the Iceland trade, he was clearly ill-informed about the Newfoundland trade and exclusively preoccupied with the east coast ports and the threat from the Dutch (Doc. 19). The number of ships sailing to Iceland does not seem to have varied much in the next thirty years – in the early years of Charles I's reign Coke was still writing of a hundred boats, fifty of which sailed from Yarmouth, and of an estimated tonnage of 50–150 tons each boat.[79]

There were minor ventures which flourished for a time: both the Muscovy company (which considered it had a monopoly) and the sailors of Hull embarked upon the whaling business, but this, as Ralph Davis remarks, was 'picturesque but never very important';[80] the crucial fishing over which the government and pamphleteers agonised was the herring fishing.

There were a number of attempts to increase the fishing trade. The first idea was to increase consumption of fish by adding additional days to the number on which meat was not to be consumed. This, however, was as likely to promote importation of fish as fishing, and in 1580–1 an additional act was passed (23 Eliz. c. 7) prohibiting the import of foreign fish by Englishmen, though exempting such fish as came from Iceland, the Shetlands and Newfoundland. The consequences of this, as reported by the act repealing it (39 Eliz. c. 10), were not quite those intended. The preamble claimed that

'the navigation of this land is no whit bettered by the means of that act, nor any mariners increased nor like to be increased by it; but, contrari-wise, the natural subjects of this realm, not being able to furnish the tenth part of the same with salted fish of their own taking, the chief provisions and victualling thereof with fish and herring hath ever since the making of the same statute been in the power and disposition of aliens and strangers'.

Though this pronouncement must be taken in the context of the continuing divergence of interest between manufacturers and merchants, it must be recognised that, in the late sixteenth century, the English did not supply themselves with their total domestic consumption of fish. Sir George Peckham wrote in 1584 that despite the recent drive to build ships specifically for the fishing trade 'yet notwithstanding, the fish which is taken and brought into England by the English navy

of fishermen will not suffice for the expense of this realm four months
if there were none else brought of strangers'.[81]

It was not unreasonable, therefore, for Robert Hitchcock to put
forward a plan to the English Parliament in 1576 (finally printed in
1580–1) suggesting that the solution to a lot of English problems at
once would be for money to be raised by the government on loan to
finance the building of 400 fishing busses of 70 tons each. He thought
that this would cost £200 a ship fully rigged and ready, and that the
costs of setting the ships forth for the fourteen to fifteen weeks of the
herring fishing season and of providing them with tackle, salt and other
necessaries would come to as much again. Each ship should employ
forty men and boys, some skilled, others initially from the unemployed
vagrant class. He thought that each ship should fill 50 last (or 600
barrels) of fish worth £10 a last, besides 20,000 wet and 10,000 dry
fish worth in all £500.

The whole of England, Hitchcock thought, would be supplied with
120,000 barrels of salted fish (at 16s 8d a barrel) and there would be
as much again left for export. The sailors, he hoped, would make £20
a year clear from two voyages, presumably working on the share basis
which operated in the cod fishing.

Hitchcock's figures may have been optimistic, but since the plan was
taken seriously they must have been tempered with plausibility, and
individual figures of prices and outlay seem compatible with other
evidence. The actual fleet was of smaller boats. In 1528, 222 ships took
part in the herring fishing – 110 from the Cinque ports. In the early
seventeenth century 300 small boats joined the herring fleet, but it was
not enough and they arrived only when the season was half over.[82]
The supply of fresh fish was a minor aspect of the fishing industry.
Analysis of the lists which were produced by all the ports of England
in response to the government's military anxiety at various dates in the
1560s and 1570s and again in the 1620s suggests that there was some
increase in the total tonnage of shipping, but not particularly linked to
fishing. The lists seem to have been taken with some thoroughness and
in some cases shed light on ownership and manning as well as on size,
yet the total impression is of the small number of both ships and sailors
(Doc. 20). Kent, an important maritime county, had shipping totalling
5,188 tons, and 202 masters and 782 mariners: just under 1,000 men for
a populous county, certainly under 2 per cent of the population. Despite
this, towns like Rye were said to get their chief living by fishing.

On the other hand, Ralph Davis makes the total tonnage of English
ships in the 1560s not more than 50,000 tons – so Kent had one-tenth
of England's total. If Dr Scammell is right in assuming that one sailor

to every 8 tons was an average proportion, then the total number of seamen in England may not have exceeded 7,000 and it is small wonder that in 1545 it was hard to raise 5,000 for the fleet. Many of these fishermen and mariners, moreover, were fairly poor men, unlikely to get together sums of money large enough to transform the industry rapidly.[83] Growth of some sort there probably was – in 1582 it was estimated that there were 1,488 masters, 11,515 seamen and 2,299 fishermen plus 957 London watermen available for service with the navy – a doubling of our earlier estimate.

THE MERCHANT MARINE

The fishing industry, however, if the proportions are even approximately right, was of far less significance than the merchant marine. The growth of the merchant marine, however, unless the country develops as a carrier of goods for other nations, which England certainly did not do before the 1630s, is not a stimulus in itself to industrial growth. Rather, it is an indicator of such growth since it is governed by the growth in the volume of goods to be transported. Nef, of course, particularly relied on the increasing need for colliers to carry coals from Newcastle, but if Keymer was right in claiming that 600 foreign ships were engaging in carrying coal to the Continent, these ships were by no means certainly English owned, let alone English built. A distinction must be made, too, between the transporting of trade goods in English merchants' hands, and their use of English ships for the purpose – the correlation, while it exists, is by no means perfect.[84]

In 1540 the English merchant fleet had a very low tonnage which was not adequate for its own trade. The small size of the vessels is partly attributable to the economy of a quick turn-around in small ports with few facilities and slow trade,[85] but in the port of Hull the percentage of English-owned ships entering declined from 75 in the 1520s to 50 in the 1540s and was to remain at that level until well into the seventeenth century.[86] Though English owned does not mean English built, since Elizabeth, on the grounds of preserving English woods, had prohibited the export of ships on 23 August 1559,[87] it undoubtedly defines the upper limit except perhaps in times of war when the figures are complicated by the capture of prizes.

The government was certainly concerned to promote the construction and use of ships, particularly large ones. Acts in 1541 and 1563 controlled the shipping of goods in English ships and in 1563 prohibited the coastwise trade to foreigners. A bounty of 5s a ton on ships over 100 tons (perhaps one-sixth of the total cost of building in 1540) was a positive encouragement. Even this took only slow effect – indeed the growing trend to larger ships may have quite other causes.

The troubles from 1570 on gave England an opportunity to break into the long-distance trades with the Mediterranean and Levant and, at least for a time, the Baltic.[88] The real upsurge, however, dates only from the 1630s.

By 1583 tonnage had risen to 67,000 tons and the number of ships over 100 tons to 173.[89] The disruption of trade and growth of privateering after 1585 saw a boom in the construction of large ships.[90] Once the Dutch could reassert themselves these gains seemed precarious. The shift of interest to long-distance trade with its need for heavy capitalisation had its critics. The loss of the *Trade's Increase*, the one merchant ship built in the period with a tonnage which on some calculations exceeded 1,000 tons, increased their number. The building of the *Sovereign of the Seas* brought a protest from Trinity House which suggested that large ships were both dangerous and impractical (Doc. 21). Such ships denuded the country's timber and rarely lasted more than three or four voyages, so hard was the travel on the structure. England should emulate the Dutch and build capacious (if slow) undefended merchantmen for bulk transport. Tonnage continued to increase: in 1629 it was estimated at 115,000 tons with 145 ships over 200 tons and 178 more over 100. This represents an average annual rise of 1·5 per cent since 1582, and the following years saw a further ship-building boom.[91] Such a growth rate was satisfactory, given the conditions of the time, and undoubtedly important in making the merchant fleet a viable entity, but it was hardly revolutionary. The geographical redistribution which accompanied it must have caused local upset and unemployment as geology, geography, economics and the effects of war on the narrow seas caused a decline in most of the Kentish and some Sussex ports which no pier building could arrest.[92] Elsewhere ships were getting larger, but not necessarily more numerous. Aldeburgh and Orford in 1577 had fifty-four vessels, nine over 100 tons; in 1629 they had thirty-four ships over 300 tons, four over 200, and more than fourteen over 100.[93]

While Kent, Sussex and, to a lesser extent, Dorset and even Hampshire were struggling, the western ports and those of the farther north-east were growing – Hull and Newcastle in a spectacular way.[94] Shipping, however, was growing at this period all over Europe, and England's increases are outclassed by those of the Low Countries and even North Germany.

SHIP BUILDING: EVIDENCE OF GROWTH BUT ALSO OF TRADITIONALISM

Not all this tonnage was necessarily English built but there is evidence to suggest that English ship-building yards were becoming larger in scale and more efficient, and furthermore to show that royal concern over the navy played an important part in this.

Owing to the interest that there has always been in Drake's navy, we are rather better informed about the building of the royal ships and large merchantmen than we might otherwise be. It is clear that at the beginning of the period large ship-building yards hardly existed. Such yards would have to provide sufficiently continuous employment for shipwrights of all sorts to encourage them to settle in the neighbourhood. This would reduce costs per unit by eliminating the discontinuities of *ad hoc* arrangements and by providing a team with experience of working together. Without continuous demand, however, such teams would tend to scatter to points at which there was enough demand to keep a smaller team going, or even to become peripatetic. When Henry VIII wanted to build the *Henry Grace à Dieu* he had to press men from all over England to assemble the yard force necessary, and the list of places from which they were brought may serve as a rough guide to ship-building centres as they then existed: Plymouth, Dartmouth, Bere Regis, Exeter, Saltash, Bradford, Bristol, Southampton, Exmouth, Poole, Ipswich, Brightlingsea, Yarmouth, Hull, Beverley and York predominate.[95] Not the least useful aspect of the Tudors' decision to keep a more or less permanent number of royal ships was possibly the fact that thereby they kept a permanent royal shipyard in being, and the royal dockyards at Woolwich, Deptford and Greenwich, and later at Chatham, provided a nucleus of skilled workers for non-naval yards, so that ship building on the Thames increased and some traditions of building developed. In this, as in other matters, the passing on of knowledge tended to be almost a family affair, and although in the Pett family there seems to have been open hostility between some of the members,[96] Phineas Pett's autobiography shows how important the passing of knowledge between master and servant was to the training of apprentices, even in this art. Moreover, the men who were the king's master ship builders also ran private yards, which meant that designs became widely used.

It is hard to tell how many men were employed in a single yard, and how long a large ship took to build at the beginning of the period. In 1559 there were some 550 men at work repairing, rebuilding and building twenty-two ships at Dartford, Woolwich and Portsmouth, but this was a moment of pressure.[97] The largest ships throughout the period seem to have taken about nine months to a year from the moment of laying the keel to the launch, but smaller ones were probably quicker, though not necessarily proportionately so.

Despite the attention which has been lavished on the great ships, however, we are still remarkably ignorant about any technical advances there may have been in the period. There are endless lists of the names of the royal ships and the merchants' ships which could be pressed to join them, and some of the lists give dimensions, but the technical details are obscure. There are one or two detailed woodcuts of the *Henry Grace à Dieu* and the *Ark Royal*, and a treatise on ship building written around 1620-5 casts a fitful light on the problem; but otherwise the evidence is incidental and indirect.[98] It seems generally agreed that the design of the English man-of-war in the 1580s was superior in sailing power to the Spanish, and possible that in 1586 and 1587 the two royal shipwrights Pett and Mathew Baker were experimenting with new designs.[99] This is somewhat surprising, since neither before nor subsequently, if the protests over Phineas Pett's designs were simply guided by prejudice as he alleges, did the English shipwright show much sign of being ready to adopt the novel.[100]

Even the appearance of the smaller ships is hard to pinpoint. One is forced to rely on the (possibly fanciful) representation of them on early maps such as Saxton's or the various views of London, tantalisingly vague verbal description and occasional excavations: the early Whitby collier was a shallow draught bark with a blunt bow and a broad stern, while the hoy was a bluff-bowed ship which sometimes had a trapdoor at the stern.[101] They suggest that these earlier boats were simpler than the earliest models of small boats now preserved in the Science Museum, but not perhaps basically different in concept. Ralph Davis considers that any competent carpenter could have built such vessels, but it is likely that the men who built them specialised in boat building, and that small yards therefore existed wherever there was enough business demand from local boat users. Few remains are likely for most if not all such sites were temporary. Ships of this size could be built on suitable beaches with space for a sawpit, sheds and forges.

There is evidence of new ship-building yards opening on the east coast and in Pembrokeshire in the 1600s and again in the 1630s,[102] but nothing to suggest what sort of demand they existed to meet and it is hard to discover how many yards there were at this time.

Some may have concentrated on repair work. It was clear that the royal ships had to be repaired substantially every ten years or so, and probably replaced after twenty-five. In the 1580s, when the merchant fleet numbered around 1,300-1,400, this would have meant that at any one time over a hundred might need major repair in any one year, with another fifty or so being built to maintain numbers. Cost per ton of building is based, for the most part, on equally scrappy information. Scammell calculated that in the 1540s cost per ton was about 25s to 30s for a vessel of 50 tons or more. In 1580 Hitchcock suggests a cost for a 70-tonner which works out at approximately £3 a ton. In the early 1600s payment was being made at a rate of £5 per ton for the large royal ships. In the early 1620s costs of ship building had risen again (Doc. 19). Phineas Pett contracted with London merchants to build two pinnaces, one of 120 tons and one of 80, for £1,270, which works out at £6 a ton, and he eventually built 500 tons for about £3,000.[103]

If tonnage in 1580 was 67,000[104] there would need to be ships on the stocks with a tonnage of 2,700, costing about £8,000 to build, to keep the size of the merchant fleet at par, and perhaps another 1,000 tons to allow for growth. Even allowing for depreciation such as that shown in Document 22, the total capital investment represented by English shipping was not less than £140,000, and in 1628-9, when costs had doubled, the shipping may have represented £462,000. Dr Scammell thinks that investment in shipping in the 1540s absorbed a high, if not the highest, proportion of the kingdom's industrial capital and that shipping was one of the biggest employers of wage labour. If the cloth industry is included this is clearly not so; shipping must undoubtedly rank fairly high otherwise – but this was high-risk capital.[105]

Apart from seamen, the building of ships was labour intensive. The number of men employed in building any one royal ship was rarely much under 200, and ship-building trades in east London may have employed 3,000–4,000. Keymer thought the building of one buss and her three subsidiary sloops would employ 30 different trades and 400 people.

The satisfactory overall growth of the shipping industry, therefore, must not blind us to the precarious nature of the gain, and the many potential setbacks which it had to face.

THE CLOTH INDUSTRY: THE COMPLICATED COLOSSUS THAT DOMINATED THE ENGLISH ECONOMY

Moreover, whatever the percentage of fixed capital in shipping, it should not disguise the fact that the country's single most important industry throughout the period was, and remained, the cloth industry. Much of Nef's thesis must turn on growth in this industry. Apart from some minor exportation of minerals it alone accounted for almost all of

England's exports and was undoubtedly England's major employer of industrial labour. Its fortunes in the period were somewhat mixed, and it is important to realise that the cloth industry was composed of a number of different branches, not all of which enjoyed the same fortunes at the same time. As a broad generalisation it may be suggested that after the first ten years of the period, during which the sale of broadcloths boomed, the production of broadcloths, which had been England's staple, found itself unable to expand and thereafter lost importance to the lighter and cheaper cloths. Since production of the different types of cloth was concentrated in specific local areas (thus Wiltshire made the older broadcloths in an area concentrated in the western half of the country, where there was clear water, fuller's earth and a drive for the mills[106] the regional impact of the changes varied considerably. At the other end of the country Yorkshire, particularly the West Riding, was flourishing on the manufacture of cheap kerseys and was posing such a threat to the older fabrics by the end of the sixteenth century that the London clothiers actually complained to the government that the northern kerseys were being too well made.[107]

Some idea of the scope of the industry can be obtained from the fact that in 1561 there were no less than 353 clothiers from all over the country brought before the Exchequer for false making of cloth alone.[108] Not all these clothiers would have operated on the same scale, however. The inventory of Peter Courtopp (Doc. 23) shows that at his death he had fifteen cloths in hand, and wool in various stages of readiness for another fifty or more. This may represent his annual turnover, for the process of production was a long, slow business in which the capitalist at any one time had a large amount of money tied up in inventory. It almost certainly took the better part of a year before the wool which left the sheep's back reached the market in the form of cloth. The man who became the clothier was generally the dyer, because dyeing was the process which demanded the highest level of skill and judgement and the most expensive input. Thus evidently Peter Courtopp was a dyer, or kept the dyeing process under his eye, for while he did not have spindles or looms he had wood ash (from which they obtained potash for the dyeing process), alum (the mordant for many dyes), copperas, which is amongst other things a dye, and pipes of oil, as well as eight pairs of shears. The long list of debts also makes it clear that the cloth industry operated on very extensive use of credit. Courtopp, however, was probably wealthier than most of the clothiers who may have operated on a much smaller scale, perhaps dealing with as few as six or seven cloths a year.

The spinning and weaving was put out to men and women who were technically independent, though in some cases their looms might already belong to, or have been acquired with credit lent by, the clothier. A loom, however, was not an impossibly expensive piece of equipment – most of those valued are estimated at between £1 and £3 – so that the weaver, particularly if he was an expert in fine cloths or complex patterns, still had a fair degree of freedom. Plain weaving might be easily learned, but the more complex was an art, and paid and valued accordingly.

It is possible to get some idea of the number of people whose work went to a loom. Each Cranbrook loom is said to have employed two men and one quill winder. These kept busy fourteen scribblers, two sorters and two scourers, two dyers and four 'clothworkers', and eighteen women to spin. The loom is also said to have 'consumed' 90 pounds of wool a week.[109] If this is so (and it agrees with other information, such as the order that every woman in the poor house should spin 6 pounds a week) it explains why then, since the Kentish cloth when finished was supposed to weigh 90 pounds, one may assume that a loom could produce a cloth in a week. Modern workers on hand looms take forty to fifty hours however, and there is the setting up of the loom to consider which for a complex pattern may have taken as much time again, so it would perhaps be rash to assume that one week's work of forty-five workers produced one cloth.

In any case, it is hard to tell how many cloths were produced in the country. Figures for exports of 'short cloths' show that after a fairly rapid rise in the first part of the century, and a slump in the mid century, figures for exports settled down at an average of just under 100,000 cloths. This, however, makes no allowance for smuggling – and the cheaper kerseys were apparently being smuggled in their thousands by the 1550s[110] – nor does it distinguish between the genuine broadcloths and the 'notional' cloth for customs purposes. Even if the total gave an approximate guide, there is little evidence of the percentage of total output represented by exports. In the 1570s or 1580s one estimate made by a would-be patentee put the total output at 200,000 cloths, 40,000 kersies, 10,000 dozens and 20,000 bays.[111] Too much weight should not be placed on this, though it would probably have seemed a not unreasonable assumption to contemporaries. The gross value of such a total cannot in any case be determined, since so much depended on the type of cloth and whether it was dyed or white, and if dyed what sort of dyeing and weaving process it had undergone. One might however say, taking the most conservative figures, and purely for the purpose of giving some basis of comparison for the other industries, that the gross value of the cloth industry's annual output cannot have been much less than £1·5 million and may well have been considerably more. A change of 10 per cent in the output of an industry of this magnitude would therefore have more impact on the economy than virtually the whole output of the iron industry at the time. In the crisis of 1622 it was estimated that 8,000 people were unemployed because of the slump in the cloth industry, and two years earlier when matters were not so acute the Quarter Sessions records spoke of 130 looms standing idle.[112] If every loom employed forty-odd people, such figures are not impossible, and they cast considerable light on the total number of people probably engaged in the industry.

There is, however, little evidence that the cloth industry saw any major improvements in productivity per head in the period. Professor Coleman argues that 'sustained population increase' provided 'a massive bonus to clothiers', because falling real labour costs in a labour-intensive industry, combined with additional demand for the product and government approval, meant increased profits as well as the continuous emergence of 'new products' – new fabrics, new designs, different colours, different finishes – which was the clothier's answer to the threat of stagnation.[113] In this, if in anything, growth in the textile industry consisted. Technical innovations were, significantly, mostly to be found in the area of cloth finishing. The introduction of gig mills to raise the nap of the cloth was notoriously prohibited by law on the grounds that they reduced the quality of the cloth. Despite this, they seem to have been widely used by the seventeenth century, but this was a minor element in the costs. The spinning wheel, which improved the spinners' output, did spread at the period, but for the very finest thread, the distaff and spindle were still indispensable, in fact, as Coleman has pointed out,[114] the new draperies were retrogressive and labour intensive, since the worsted yarn they used had to be spun on a spindle and distaff. The change indeed meant that more people could be employed in the woollen industry and, it was alleged, live better by it and be their own masters,[115] a vital consideration for the time, but one which fits uncomfortably into the sort of 'revolution' Nef was postulating. The stocking knitters alone may have numbered between 90,000 and 110,000 people – more than any non-woollen industry.[116]

The Protestant refugees from the Continent did bring some modified forms of looms, and the looms on which the 'new' draperies were woven were sufficiently different in type from the old broadcloth loom to make the change a significant one for the weaver, but their difference did not make much of a change in output. The minor modifications that were probably introduced at this period did not speed up the process. It was, and remained, a slow, labour-intensive business.

Was the clothing industry as a whole significantly increasing its output in a way likely to promote further change? The question turns upon the output of the new draperies, since the older product was running into increasing competition and the clothiers were caught in a scissors situation where, since wages could be squeezed no further, the quality of the cloth was likely to suffer. Everyone was aware that English cloth makers did not have a monopoly of skills, indeed, perhaps that the comparative advantage which they enjoyed depended on the fact that the Dutch could make an even higher profit on certain other businesses – provided English prices remained low.

The squeeze on the clothiers' accustomed profits, however, meant that they continually had an envious eye on the profits which the Dutch were said to make by finishing the cloth. One estimate made as part of a campaign against the selling of white cloth divided up the total value of the finished cloth amongst the inputs as follows:[117]

raw materials	10
combing	6
spinning	2
weaving	7
fulling	5
dyeing	47
miscellaneous	10
'profit'	13
	100

Most of the concern expressed in the 1620s and again in 1640 by commissions of inquiry, however, was concentrated on the traditional cloths; though most of the causes alleged would apply equally well to the lighter stuffs it seems that they did not (Doc. 24).[118] Lower-priced cloth could tap the demand of poorer consumers and open up a whole new area for trade.

In 1594–5 there were exported from London 10,976 bays, 4,256 says, 33,455 worsted and 1,593 woollen stockings, and 168,065 'cottons', mainly Welsh, northern and Manchester.[119] This is a guide to total exports, though the northern ports and the Kentish ports exported comparatively more of the cheaper cloths: in particular they exported them illicitly to towns which were not the staple towns to which the merchant adventurers, whose monopoly it was supposed to be, exported.

This, of course, was one of the hotly contested issues between clothiers and merchants in the debates over 'free' trade (that is un-regulated trade, not custom-free trade) in the early years of James I's reign.[120] The clothiers felt that more cloth could be sold if it was carried to a wider variety of ports by a greater number of merchants, and the merchants felt that this would only depress the price obtained per unit. The early years of James's reign were, however, comparatively good ones for the industry; it was in the 1620s, earlier for some areas and later for others, that the real crisis of readjustment occurred.

Despite the comparative success of the new draperies, nothing that we know about the industry at this period suggests that after the 1540s it was growing in any 'boom' fashion; rather it was doing little more than painfully readjust its level and type of output to changing circum-stances. Presumably domestic consumption of cloth rose to some extent proportionately to the rise in population, but there is nothing to suggest that consumption of cloth *per capita* increased. The sumptuary laws would imply that those with money were turning to silks and apeing their betters rather than using warm cloths in greater abundance.

SILK, COTTON, LINEN: A GROWTH AREA

The importance of the silk industry as a part of the whole clothing industry has perhaps been overlooked because it was so much in the hands of the Huguenot immigrants. But because James I's efforts to promote the art of sericulture, by distributing the mulberry trees on which the grubs fed as well as instructions about the methods used to rear the worms and wind off the silk, were unsuccessful, it does not mean that the manufacture of woven silk was either unimportant or not expanding. In fact, all the evidence is that it was expanding rapidly. In 1559–60 imports of raw silk were valued at £9,920.[121] If this repre-sents a value of 15s to the pound weight as the valuations after the 1563 book of rates do, England imported about 12,000 pounds of raw silk that year. In 1592–3 she was importing 51,697 pounds.[122] By 1620–1 this had leapt up to 168,611 pounds and in 1632–3 it was, incredibly, 691,816 pounds. After that it dropped back to 322,168 pounds and in 1639–40 218,403 pounds.[123] The silk weavers at this stage were mainly settled in Canterbury, Sandwich and other east coast towns, and London. In 1594 the silks were woven white at Sandwich and carried to London to be sold and dyed, and it seems likely that the Canterbury weavers did the same. The calculation made in 1594 suggested that 10,000 grograins and mackadoes might have been made in Sandwich at that point, each piece being 22 yards long and weighing 6 pounds. Probably the actual number was rather less, since not so much raw silk was imported. The staggering rise in imports by 1620 suggests that many of the criticisms of the frivolity of the court and the 'uselessness' of the imports, made by contemporary writers, had some justification. Some of the silk, however, was part of the growing East India Company imports which were later re-exported. Mun, with perhaps some exaggeration, thought the total employed had risen from 300 to 14,000.

Early in Charles I's reign, moreover, there is an illuminating case of fraud which was heard in the Exchequer. Two merchants, Richard Hull and John Clutterbuck, had decided to make an additional profit on their business by using methods of dyeing which did not decrease the weight of the cloth so much as those which were normally accepted, at the price, it was alleged, of making the finished cloth less serviceable and long lasting. They persuaded a number of silk dyers to co-operate in this scheme by paying them 50 per cent more per raw pound than the normal rate: 2s instead of 1s 4d. In the course of five years it was claimed that they had had 200,000 pounds (weight) of raw silk dyed in this way, for which they were heavily fined.[124] Figures of this sort make it unsurprising that the industry could maintain 126 master weavers in Canterbury alone, and possibly at the height of the boom 590 looms there. The goods they produced were sent up to London by factors who dealt with the London merchants, for the weavers became involved in a dispute with the common carrier over the arrangement.[125] From the gross value of the goods produced the substantial costs of the imported silk must be deducted; nevertheless, if around 40,000 pieces of grograin were produced in 1639, which would not be impossible on the figures given, the value added to the product may have been in the region of £200,000.

Other clothing industries which were beginning to grow at this time included the very early manufacture of cotton cloth. This seems to have started in 1600, and imports of cotton wool were reaching the 1 million pound mark in some years by 1620. The manufacture had from the start centred on Lancashire, and the thread was at first used in combination with other types of fibre. Estimates of its value are therefore hard to come by, but it should not be wholly forgotten.[126]

Linen was also manufactured in Lancashire, but the manufacture of linen cloth in the country, despite the provisions made for it, never met the demand, and substantial quantities were imported.[127] Much the same is true of the manufacture of canvas and other hempen goods such as ropes. Nevertheless, English domestic production was on the increase, particularly in the hinterland of Hull and other east coast ports, near the shipyards.

LEATHER: THE HIDDEN GIANT?

More important than these rising manufactures, however, was probably the leather industry, which, it has been suggested, was second only to the cloth industry in importance in the sixteenth and seventeenth centuries.[128] Though there is no reason to doubt that it was, at the least, a very important and essential industry, we are still singularly ill-informed about the volume and value of its product. The widespread demand for leather can be seen in large numbers of different accounts, from those of the iron forge and furnace to those of the farmer and pastoralist. From the king and nobleman to the peasant, leather had a role to play. Apart from boots and shoes, belts and straps, jackets and trousers, purses and bags, bottles and flasks, it was used for saddles and harness, thongs and loops, hinges and ties, buckets and bellows and the like. The number of leather workers amongst those prominent in city affairs in provincial towns like Leicester, Northampton, Birmingham and elsewhere underlines the importance of the trade.[129]

Tanning is a lengthy process. The act of 1563 stipulated a twelve-month minimum period for the processing of the hide. It therefore demands, like cloth, a relatively higher investment of movable capital, as well as the outlay on land for the vats and the various ingredients in which the hides are to steep. It does not demand the large quantities of labour which cloth takes up, which may in part explain why we hear so little of the production of the leather beside the organisation of leather workers, but it does require experience and judgement to know when the hides should be moved from one process to the next.

One might, therefore, have expected to find tanners relatively wealthier than the surviving tanners' inventories suggest. The wealthiest man Dr Clarkson could find was John Neal of Horncastle, whose property was worth more than £1,300 when he died, and Clarkson comments that there were not many like him. Certainly, this represented wealth for a man in the provinces, but it is surprising, and perhaps unlikely, that the owners of the eighty London tanneries (mainly in Bermondsey and Southwark), whose intake from the London shambles must potentially have run into thousands a week, could apparently do no better.

Tanning was not the only way to process leather: a more supple, if less hard-wearing material was produced by 'dressing' the hide with train oil, or tawing it with alum. This was also a faster process, and the resultant leather was used for gloves and other fine-wearing garments.

The value of hides was modest initially, and varied seasonally (Doc. 25) so that tanners, banished to the outskirts of towns because of the noxious fumes, may not have needed excessive capital.

England exported hides in some numbers but little in the way of finished leather products, suggesting that domestic leather workers were confined to the utilitarian trades. Much of the use of leather was in any case made or shaped for the particular job or individual, since a horse collar, for example, to be efficient must fit the particular horse perfectly.

THE LESSER INDUSTRIES: THE SIGNIFICANCE OF DIVERSIFICATION

Leather workers are not the only hidden industry. One of considerable local importance, which was not to be significant nationally or inter-nationally until the eighteenth century, was the making of pottery. The excavation of kilns and domestic sites from the period is adding now, belatedly, to our knowledge of an industry little referred to in written records. Experts can identify regional products which sometimes spread far afield unobtrusively. Wrotham slip ware, which flourished between 1612 and 1700, for example, is highly regarded, and the Staffordshire areas which were later notorious as the Potteries already had local potters of some importance. It was certainly less valuable than glass but equally more widespread, and Italian treatises from the period whose technical advice seems to have been known in England show advances in kiln design and practices.[130] Many other minor industries flourished; clay pipe making became a good living for a few; the Sheldons' tapestry-making industry did well for a time; in the heyday of English dominance in the musical world there seems to have been some local manufacturing of instruments.

The problem remains: does this diversification imply revolutionary change or even solid advance? Does a wide range of local manufactures indicate a sophisticated economy, or a bastardised imitation of an import which can no longer be afforded? Local paper production, for example, seems to fit the latter category. Despite increased consumption of good-quality paper by an ever-widening band of printers printing ever more numerous editions of more and more different titles,[131] most local paper was poor-quality stuff. The reason for this was basically the hold which the French and Italians had on the market which enabled them to undercut the local producer whose experience, command of raw materials and other resources, and entry to the market were not good enough to enable him to match the foreigners' price without loss. The first good-quality venture to succeed as commercially viable was Henry Spilman's. He had a monopoly, and also in theory a monopoly to collect the rags and broken linen which formed the basic raw material, to aid him. It is not, however, clear whether white paper was manu-factured continuously in England after Spilman's death, though the manufacture of paper continued. It made little impression on the foreign production which dominated the scene. In 1637 a petition from three paper makers complained that their mills had been shut because of contagion and that with their families this left 120 people without means of support.[132] If, as seems likely, this was the Dartford mill initially opened by Spilman, it casts some light on the truth of Churchyard's laudatory poem which has been so often quoted in this context, and suggests that since no more than three or four mills were operating at that time the paper industry was a negligible employer of idle labour.

On the other hand, the building industry, with its dependent subsidiary the brick-making industry, seems to point conclusively to growing affluence. Certainly it is possible to show, as Nef did, that brick making, once the kilns could be fired with coal, increased considerably. It is, however, harder to establish that this was anything more than the substitution of one building material for another which might be dearer or less convenient or both. Moreover, it is always a borderline question as to whether a building is a 'consumer durable' or an investment: whether a better home is simply a form of more than usually conspicuous consumption, or whether it has the same sort of functional use as a mill, a loom shed, a granary, a pigsty, or some other industrially or agriculturally oriented structure. A well-built house which excludes the rain and most draughts, and is potentially light (to lengthen the usable day) and comfortable, may effectively preserve and lengthen the lives of those who live in it. In this respect some prominence may well be given to the development of the chimney which was a necessary concomitant of the domestic use of coal for fuel, and a desirable one even without it. Whether the great house fulfilled the role more efficiently than the humble thatched cottage in proportion to the extra expense involved is, of course, doubtful, but if, for the sake of convenience, one classifies all such expenditure as investment, it is still hard to say whether there was a marked increase in building activity in the period.

It is true that from 1570 to 1620 there was a noticeable spurt of great house building when aristocrats and gentry, sometimes to their own undoing, built themselves stately homes to replace their more austere fortified manor houses or baronial halls. Other sorts of expenditure on building had more or less ceased, however. The glories of late Perpendicular stonework embellishing the last cathedral and monastic building had demanded skills now out of fashion and not to be afforded by a suddenly impoverished Church. The great royal castle-building era, after a last pale flicker in the 1540s, when the gun-dominated castles along the south coast and especially Kent and Sussex were completed, passed finally with the fall of Calais, except for the occasional hurried refurbishing at the time of the Armada and other, lesser scares.[133] The royal palaces, once Hampton Court and Nonsuch were finished, were for the most part limited to minor extensions and repairs. There was, it is true, generally something major in progress, particularly around London – Somerset House for Northumberland, Mansion House, the Royal Exchange – but against this must be set the unbuilding – the steady destruction of the ex-monastic buildings which, unless they served to house the new owners, were pulled down and the stone sold. Malmesbury was converted for a time to a 'useful' purpose by William Stumpe. Even that experiment, however, did not last long. It seems possible, in fact, that the 1560s and 1570s were times of depression for the skilled free mason and the carvers in stone.

Not all building, of course, was done at this level: the smaller house and barn, forge and furnace, were built modestly by local men out of local materials (Doc. 26). But it is usually difficult to date a surviving house precisely enough for the economist's purpose, and impossible to calculate from the chance of lesser or greater survival how vigorous building for the lower classes may have been at any one time, so that the real size of the building industry is hard to estimate. The constant need for repairs to structures both domestic and industrial is another factor involved (Docs 27 and 28).

THE CONSUMPTION INDUSTRIES

All the industries which we have considered so far belong to the category which Nef considered significant. He largely excluded from his vision of industry those activities which relate directly to agriculture – the daily grinding of flour to make bread, for example, and the making of drink. Yet the partial mechanising of the former in the Middle Ages released significant amounts of labour, while the production of malt and the brewing of beer were industries which lent themselves to large-scale production once consumption was conveniently concentrated. The various acts which attempted to ensure that malt was properly made also suggest that it was best made on a fairly large scale, and there is evidence that in 1590 at least one provincial maltster, Hugh Evance of Thetford, had capital of £260 and more invested in his malting house and kiln.[134] Even so, whenever in time of dearth a proclamation was issued to restrain the excessive making of malt, the returns from the justices suggest that the ordinary maltster was a fairly small-scale operator.

Similarly, the size of individual brewing businesses in London in

Elizabeth's reign with capital of £10,000 involved is evidence that the industry could in favourable conditions cut costs by producing in greater bulk. The London brewers, however, were an incorporated body with a monopoly within 2 miles of London, and although the outward spread of London may have provided them with competition from brewers operating on the fringe of their area, it is probable that this gave them greater control over the licensed inns and alehouses. It is not clear whether they were able to prevent or merely to discourage such people from brewing themselves. Probably a London innkeeper in any case had other things to do.

Control of the retail outlets – what was later to be called the tied-house system – was a crucial factor in establishing large-scale production, and outside London there does not seem to be much evidence that such control was even beginning to encroach on the independent innkeeper. The sixteenth-century court rolls for Burton-on-Trent give long lists of brewers amerced for petty offences, more than one might have thought the town itself was well able to support; it may be that Burton beer already had a reputation which made it saleable outside the vicinity, but the very length of the list argues against any very large individual units.

When Charles I started to seek profits from monopolies in earnest there were not lacking people who saw that profit could be made from controlling production of beer, and a patent was duly issued to a group whose leading spirit was a member of a family which had been king's brewers and knew about large-scale production. The proposal was to prohibit brewing except by a select group of men who were to be incorporated and pay licence and rent to the king. This was to be done on a county and borough basis, and the justices were dragged in to give information. The argument for restricting brewing to a few was that this was more economical on malt and that it would be better for the poor because more small beer would be brewed.[135] There was no shortage of men in the provinces willing to take up such a licence with its promise of profit and by 1638 there were incorporated bodies of brewers in nearly every county. A list drawn up at the time which covers most counties names 643 brewers and 132 maltsters, but Essex alone had 71.[136]

It soon became clear that London experience was no guide to the success of a design in the rest of the country. Innumerable petitions were directed to the king both by aggrieved brewers who found it impossible to oblige innkeepers to purchase their beer and by innkeepers who complained of hardship and offered to pay a fee rather than be obliged to buy.[137]

The country innkeeper's economy was evidently differently organised from his London fellows'; by brewing his own beer he not only obtained beer, but yeast to bake his bread and mush to feed his pigs, and the loss of these commodities, as well as the cost of 15s a barrel, was playing havoc with his profits.[138]

Even the London brewhouses were not as large as they were to become: 18 tons of beer at a brewing or 5,616 a year was clearly a good output.[139] Total output for London brewers might be calculated on this basis, but output for the rest of the country can hardly be known; so many people must have brewed their own that it is also hard to say whether output was increasing, or merely passing from the housewife's orbit to the commercial brewers.

Soap making, though it was a crucial industry, especially for hygiene, was another industry where part at least of the output must have been produced in the home by farmers' wives using the tallow from their husbands' beasts and home-produced wood ash. Commercial production was confined to the towns and was commoner in places like Bristol which had easy access to the sea for the sorts of oils used in better-quality soaps. Again, Charles saw in soap a potentially profitable monopoly, and his patentees estimated that between 5,000 and 10,000 tons might be annually brought under their control, 5,000 being made in London alone. There was an excuse for the monopoly in the introduction of new methods – the use of new ingredients such as rape-oil. The Bristol manufacturers, however, fought a bitter rearguard action to preserve their livelihood, and the case was hardly settled before the Civil War.[140] The value of the total commercial production at the rate of 3d a pound for fine and 2d for coarse soap was hardly critical for the economy, and even allowing for domestic production one is driven to the assumption that consumption per head of the population was so low that most washing must have been done without it.

THE ROLE OF SECONDARY INDUSTRIES

Nef's reason for concentrating on industries manufacturing wholesale rather than on the secondary industries which turned the undifferentiated iron (for example) into nails, locks, hinges, files, axeheads, knives, ploughshares, fire irons and other tools, was of course that which has prompted economic historians of all periods – the fact that the raw material is to a large extent the measure of growth. The total amount of iron, or leather, or cloth, to some extent controls the number of tailors, saddlers, lorrimers, glovers, haberdashers, bowyers and fletchers.

Nevertheless, the skills and the diversification of these secondary industries are not without their significance, and technological changes could transform this aspect of industry as well as any other. For this period, however, it is even harder to establish information about change in secondary than in basic industries. There is nothing to suggest any widespread or significant technical changes, but a certain amount which suggests that increased specialisation and perhaps efficiency (education) were showing at least modest increases in productivity. It is possible that this impression is illusory, derived from the increasingly informative nature of the material. The various categories of carpenter, for example, from the jobbing man who did small repairs, the house builder, ship's carpenter (aboard for repairs), ship's carpenter (for shipyards), craftsman furniture maker, and so on, can be more fully demonstrated for Charles I's reign than for Henry VIII's, yet some of the distinctions must have existed, like the blacksmiths concealed under a blanket term. Nevertheless, some increased output and improved quality seem likely.

The tendency to concentrate in certain well-defined regions near to an important source of supply can be observed in the manufacture of small iron wares, which were settling around the Dudley and Birmingham area where wood, coal and iron could all be readily had, and where the relative infertility of the local soil made conflict with settled agricultural interests less likely; this is another indication of increasing structural sophistication. Apart from this, however, and the growth of London (which, the more it became the normal source for luxury goods, the more it attracted manufactures of such goods, from cutlery to silks, to work near at hand), there seems to have been little change in the scattered nature of secondary production. This again tends to confirm the probability that the expansion of the secondary industries can be measured by the expansion of the primary industries on which they depended. The two went hand in hand. Demand for leather or iron goods may ultimately have governed the output of the basic raw material, but the output is still a good measure of the growth of the secondary industries where that material did not enter into foreign trade.

This, however, tells us neither how much value the secondary industries added to the original price of the basic material in any given industry, nor how many people were employed in secondary industries, which would be necessary if the percentage of the population engaged in industrial pursuits was to be estimated. One writer claimed that there were 3,000 shoe makers in London, but this leaves unanswered how many shoe makers were there in Bristol and York, in Shrewsbury and Stafford, in Northampton and Coventry, and how many village cobblers. And if the question could be laboriously answered, what of all the other crafts ? The question might be answered for the major towns, which are relatively well documented, but could it be answered for the rural craftsmen, the village blacksmith, the thatcher, the carpenter ? It should not be forgotten that our ignorance, and therefore our assumption that little or no significant change took place, may conceal important structural development.

CONCLUSIONS

This re-examination of the basic industries of the period, however, leaves us in general with little confidence that important physical growth had occurred over a wide spectrum of industries in a concentrated period of time. Rather, it demonstrates sporadic growth in specific and unrelated industries at diverse points of time. Technological developments show the same discontinuous pattern, while the investment of large lumps of capital seems frequently either misguided and fruitless optimism or a response to worsening conditions. Significant change may have been structural, that is, concerned with a growing integration of industry, rather than with large-scale growth in itself. What was occurring concerned the changes which are necessary before revolution can come rather than revolution itself.

Notes

1 North and Thomas, *The Rise of the Western World*, pp. 151–5.
2 R. Carew, *The Survey of Cornwall*, 1811 edn, p. 20.
3 *The Welsh Port Books (1550–1603)*, ed. E. A. Lewis, Cymmrodorion Record Series, XII (1927), p. xxvi.
4 The technological improvements were by no means new; and by no means English inventions, despite appearances. Adits, pumps and soughs were well known in continental Europe by at least the fifteenth century and the claims made by Jeffrey Fox for his devices at the mine in Warwickshire were exaggerated ('a horse mill with engines thereupon belonging which before were never invented'); Nef, *The Rise of the British Coal Industry*, Vol. I, p. 355.
5 G. V. Scammell, 'English Merchant Shipping 1450–1550', *Economic History Review*, 2nd ser., XIII (1961), p. 327.
6 Stafford County Record Office, Anglesey MSS, D (W) 1734/3/3/256, 257.
7 Nef, *The Rise of the British Coal Industry*, Vol. I, p. 348.
8 Exports of coal to France were important for local shipping and the loca balance of payments (Lewis, *Welsh Port Books*, pp. xviii–xix).

9 G. Hammersley, 'The Crown Woods and Their Exploitation in the Sixteenth and Seventeenth Centuries', *Bulletin of Institute of Historical Research*, XXX (1957), pp. 154–9; 'The Charcoal Iron Industry and Its Fuel, 1540–1750', *Economic History Review*, 2nd ser., XXVI (1973), pp. 593–613.

10 Nottingham University Library, Middleton MSS, 5/165/82, 92.

11 ibid., 92.

12 A. Raistrick and B. Jennings, *A History of Lead Mining in the Pennines* (London, 1965), p. 57.

13 *Mendip Mining Laws and Forest Bounds*, ed. J. W. Gough, Somerset Record Society, XLV (1931), p. 11. This sort of free mining tends to come into existence wherever the ore can be mined in adequate quantities at little capital outlay. It was typical of the early gold rush days and can be found to this day on the Australian opal-mining fields.

14 J. W. Gough, *Sir Hugh Myddelton, Entrepreneur and Engineer* (Oxford 1964), pp. 105–7, 118*ff*.

15 Raistrick and Jennings, *Lead Mining in the Pennines*, p. 187.

16 *Victoria County History of Derbyshire*, Vol. II, p. 331.

17 ibid., p. 341.

18 ibid., p. 184.

19 M. B. Donald, *Elizabethan Copper* (London, 1955), p. 216.

20 G. Hammersley, 'Technique or Economy? The Rise and Decline of the Early English Copper Industry, c. 1550–1660', *Business History*, XV (1973), pp. 1–31.

21 G. R. Lewis, *The Stannaries*, pp. 47, 217. Hatcher, in *English Tin Production and Trade*, does not entirely agree with Lewis's explanation, but since his book ends at 1550, he offers no detailed alternative for the later period.

22 For a transcription of this see Straker, *Wealden Iron*, pp. 44–6.

23 ibid., pp. 313–15; H. R. Schubert, *History of the British Iron and Steel Industry from c. 450 BC to AD 1775* (London, 1957), pp. 317–19. *Note*: this paragraph was written before the author had available D. W. Crossley's RHS Camden series volume on the Sydney Ironworks.

24 ibid., pp. 148*ff*, 161.

25 D. W. Crossley, 'Some Aspects of Fieldwork in Sixteenth Century Industrial History', *History of Metallurgy Bulletin*, V (1971), pp. 9–11. Dr Crossley's edition of *Sydney Ironworks Accounts 1541–1573*, Camden 4th series, Vol. XV (Royal Historical Society, 1975) arrived too late for its illuminating introduction to be used in this account.

26 H. R. Schubert, 'The King's Ironworks in the Forest of Dean, 1612–1674', *Journal of Iron and Steel Institute*, CLXXIII (1953), pp. 153*ff*.

27 Straker thinks a bloomery used less fuel, while Schubert claims a lower consumption per unit of output. Possibly initially the blast furnace used more, because fuel saving would be allied to length of blow.

28 Schubert, *History of British Iron and Steel Industry*, pp. 396–7; National Library of Wales, Wynnstay Doc. 117. (I am grateful to Dr J. Lawson for lending me a photocopy of this document.)

29 Straker, *Wealden Iron*, pp. 249–50.

30 Nottingham University Library, Middleton MSS, 5/165/92 III. For a detailed account of Willoughby's iron works see R. S. Smith, 'Sir Francis Willoughby's Ironworks, 1570–1610', *Renaissance and Modern Studies*, XI (1967), pp. 90–140.

31 Nottingham University Library, Middleton MSS, 5/165/92 III.
32 ibid., 92 II.
33 At Panningbridge furnace in 1546, 3,360 cords were used, which employed fifty-three woodcutters in all paid mainly at 3d a cord: this was probably not their only source of income. If the same situation applied as at Middleton, some apparently worked full time and others only intermittently. The cost of £78 18s 10½d to turn these cords into charcoal suggests a number of charcoal burners. The output from this furnace, if 14 loads of ore made a ton, was around 110 tons which suggests that output may initially have risen rather steeply – though as fifty-two and a half founddays (one foundday every six days) are paid, the account may cover rather more than a year.
34 ibid.
35 J. U. Nef, 'A Note on the Progress of Iron Production in England, 1540–1640', *Journal of Political Economy*, XLIV (1936), pp. 398–403.
36 Hammersley, 'The Charcoal Iron Industry', *Economic History Review*, 2nd ser., XXVI (1973), pp. 593–613.
37 Hammersley takes into account local variations.
38 Cf. Oppenheim, *History of the Administration of the Royal Navy*, p. 159.
39 P. Muskett, 'Smuggling in the Cinque Ports in the Sixteenth Century', *Cantium*, II (1970).
40 C. S. Catell, 'An Evaluation of the Loseley List of Ironworks within the Weald in the Year 1588', *Archaeologia Cantiana*, LXXXVI (1971), pp. 85–92.
41 Gough, *Sir Hugh Myddelton*, pp. 108–9.
42 Public Record Office, State Papers, Domestic, Charles I, SP 16/341 No. 130.
43 Raistrick and Jennings, *A History of Lead Mining in the Pennines*, pp. 42–5.
44 Donald, *Elizabethan Copper*, pp. 3, 166.
45 ibid., p. 216.
46 ibid., pp. 213–15.
47 ibid., pp. 216, 225–7, 354; W. Rees, *Industry Before the Industrial Revolution*, Vol. II (Cardiff, 1968), pp. 403–24.
48 H. Hamilton, *The English Brass and Copper Industries* (London, 1926), pp. 30–2.
49 Hammersley, 'Technique or Economy?', *Business History*, XV (1973), pp. 1–31.
50 For a fuller account, cf. J. W. Gough, *The Rise of the Entrepreneur* (London, 1969), pp. 204ff.
51 ibid., pp. 179–85; for fuller details of early developments, cf. R. B. Turton, *The Alum Farm* (Whitby, 1938).
52 *Victoria County History of the East Riding of Yorkshire*, Vol. II, pp. 384–6.
53 E. Hughes, *Studies in Administration and Finance* (Manchester, 1934), p. 21.
54 Nef relied on Collins for his figures, but Collins is a suspect and biased source.
55 J. Collins, *Salt and Fisheries* (London, 1682), pp. 2ff.
56 T. Gentleman, 'The Trades Increase', *Harleian Miscellany*, IV (1745), p. 215.
57 H. A. Innis, *The Cod Fisheries* (New Haven and Toronto, 1940), pp. 35–60.
58 Quoted *in extenso* in E. Hughes, 'English Monopoly of Salt', *English Historical Review*, XL (1925), p. 339.

59 Hughes, *Studies in Administration and Finance*, p. 63.

60 Nef in various places has taken the four men needed for the new-style pans to be a common multiplier for old and new: e.g. 'Progress of Technology and Growth of Large Scale Industry in Great Britain 1540–1640', *Economic History Review*, V (1934–5), p. 19; *Coal Industry*, p. 404. Brereton's account is partly printed in *Seventeenth-Century Economic Documents*, ed. J. Thirsk and J. P. Cooper (Oxford, 1972), pp. 235–6.

61 Public Record Office, SP 16/177 No. 71, 186 No. 81.

62 The ton of salt was perhaps less than one thinks; it takes today 108 pounds of salt to cure 1,000 herrings. A last of herrings was 10,000 (by the long hundred) so that it would take nearly 7 tons to cure 1 last. A. R. Bridbury, *England and the Salt Trade in the Later Middle Ages* (Oxford, 1955), Appx. B, p. 160.

salt: 1 barrel – 1 hod

    2 hods – 8 bushels – 1 quarter (28 pounds)
    $2\frac{1}{2}$ quarters – 1 mew (70 pounds)
    4 quarters – 1 hundredweight (112 pounds)
    2 mew – 1 ton or dolium (140 pounds)
    5 quarters – 1 charge, wey or dolium (140 pounds)
    4 Yarmouth quarters – 1 thousandweight or 'custom hundred' (1,120 pounds)

63 W. R. Scott, *The Constitution and Finance of English, Scottish, and Irish Joint Stock Companies* (Cambridge, 1910–12), Vol. I, p. 209.

64 ibid., p. 211; Hughes, op. cit., p. 65.

65 D. W. Crossley, 'The Performance of the Glass Industry in Sixteenth-Century England', *Economic History Review*, 2nd ser., XXV (1972), pp. 421–33.

66 G. Kenyon, *The Glass Industry of the Weald* (Leicester, 1967), p. 79. A team could make three cases a day, so that maximum theoretical output would be higher.

67 The one currently being excavated by Pilkington in Manchester is proving much larger than expected. *Newsletter of the Australian Society for Historical Archaeology*, II, No. 3 (1972).

68 Kenyon, *Glass Industry of Weald*, pp. 36–41.

69 ibid., pp. 110–11.

70 T. Lennard Barrett, 'Glass Making at Knole, Kent', *The Antiquary*, XLI (1905), pp. 127–9. The Sussex cord was about 2 tons. The price per cord seems low and may not represent the full 'sale' value.

71 T. Pape, 'Medieval Glassworkers in North Staffordshire', *Transactions of North Staffordshire Field Club* (1934); D. W. Crossley, 'Glassmaking in Bagot's Park, Staffordshire, in the Sixteenth Century', *Post-Medieval Archaeology*, I (1967), pp. 44–83. Fuel was much easier, however. When the Mansell patent was introduced in 1615 Bagot's main complaint was of the lack of alternative use for his woods.

72 D. W. Crossley and F. Aberg, 'Sixteenth-Century Glassmaking in Yorkshire: Excavations at Furnaces at Hutton and Rosedale, North Riding, 1968–1971', *Post Medieval Archaeology*, VI (1972), pp. 107–59.

73 Kenyon, *Glass Industry of Weald*, pp. 133–5.

74 Water transport was the key to Newcastle and Stourbridge success.

75 Gentleman, 'The Trades Increase', *Harleian Miscellany*, IV, p. 212.

76 *Welsh Port Books* (*1550-1603*), ed. Lewis, p. 309; Innis, *The Cod Fisheries* pp. 56, 87.

77 ibid., pp. 69-70; *Victoria County History of Cornwall*, Vol. I, pp. 491-6; Public Record Office, SP 16/103 No. 43.

78 Innis, *The Cod Fisheries*, p. 72.

79 J. R. Elder, *The Royal Fisheries Company of the Seventeenth Century* (Glasgow, 1912), p. 25.

80 R. Davis, *The Trade and Shipping of Hull, 1500-1700*, East Yorkshire Local History Society Publication 17 (1964), p. 11; *Victoria County History of East Riding of Yorkshire*, Vol. I, p. 136.

81 Quoted in Innis, *The Cod Fisheries*, p. 31.

82 Elder, *The Royal Fisheries Company*, p. 29. The Dutch dominated the fishing because they were more efficient and could sell more cheaply.

83 *Kentish Sources: Aspects of Agriculture and Industry*, ed. E. Melling, pp. 236-7.

84 For a general account of overseas trade, see R. Davis, *English Overseas Trade, 1500-1700* (London, 1973).

85 G. V. Scammell, 'Shipowning in England, *circa* 1450-1550', *Transactions of the Royal Historical Society*, 5th ser., XII (1962), pp. 105-22; 'English Merchant Shipping at the End of the Middle Ages: Some East Coast Evidence', *Economic History Review*, XIII (1960-1), pp. 327-41.

86 Davis, *Trade and Shipping of Hull*, pp. 4-5.

87 *Tudor Royal Proclamations*, ed. Hughes and Larkins, Vol. II, No. 463.

88 R. Davis, *The Rise of the English Shipping Industry in the Seventeenth and Eighteenth Centuries* (London, 1962), p. 5.

89 Public Record Office, State Papers, Domestic, Elizabeth, SP 12/156, No. 45.

90 Davis, *Rise of English Shipping Industry*, p. 7; K. R. Andrews, *Elizabethan Privateering: English Privateering during the Spanish War, 1585-1603* (Cambridge, 1964).

91 Public Record Office, SP 16/155 Nos 31, 103; H. Taylor, 'Trade, Neutrality and the "English Road"', 1630-1648', *Economic History Review*, 2nd ser. XXV (1972), pp. 236-60.

92 For a detailed examination of the geological changes, cf. *The Wealden District*, ed. R. W. Gallows, British Regional Geology (London, 1965); J. H. Farrant, 'The Evolution of Newhaven Harbour and the Lower Ouse before 1800', *Sussex Archaeological Collections*, CX (1972), pp. 41ff.; P. F. Brandon, 'The Origin of Newhaven and the Drainage of the Lewes and Laughton Levels', ibid., CIX (1971), pp. 94-106.

93 Public Record Office, SP 12/120 No. 1, 196 fols 267ff.; SP 16/155 No. 31.

94 *Victoria County History of East Riding of Yorkshire*, Vol. I, p. 134; Scammell, 'English Merchant Shipping', *Economic History Review*, 2nd ser., XIII (1961), p. 332.

95 Oppenheim, *History of the Administration of the Royal Navy*, p. 72.

96 See *The Autobiography of Phineas Pett*, ed. W. G. Perrin, Navy Records Society Publication LI (1918).

97 Oppenheim, *History of the Administration of the Royal Navy*, p. 119.

98 W. Salisbury, 'List of Dimensions', *Mariners' Mirror*, XLVI (1960), pp. 224-5; *Nautical Research Occasional Publications*, VII (London, 1959); R. C. Anderson, 'A List of Royal Ships in 1590-1', *Mariners' Mirror*, XLIII (1957), p. 322; G. Robinson, *The Elizabethan Ship* (London, 1956);

A. J. Holland, *Ships of British Oak: The Rise and Decline of Wooden Shipbuilding in Hampshire* (Newton Abbot, 1971).

99 T. Glasgow Jr, 'The Shape of the Ships that Defeated the Spanish Armada', *Mariners' Mirror*, L (1964), pp. 184–5.

100 Davis, *Rise of English Shipping Industry*, pp. 49–51.

101 Captain Lovegrove, 'Notes on Sixteenth-Century Boats in Rye Harbour', *Mariners' Mirror*, XXXIII (1947), pp. 190*ff.*; Glasgow, 'Shape of Ships', ibid., L (1964), pp. 115*ff.*

102 *Victoria County History of the East Riding of Yorkshire*, Vol. I, p. 148; *Welsh Port Books (1550–1603)*, ed. Lewis, p. xxv.

103 Phineas Pett, *Autobiography*, pp. lxvii, lxxxiv–lxxxv, 122, 211; G. V. Scammell, 'Shipowning and the Economy in Early Modern England', *Historical Journal*, XV (1972), pp. 385–407.

104 Methods of estimating tonnage differed according to the purpose for which the information was required. The merchant, concerned with carrying capacity, varied from the ship builder who used a rule at this time that

$$\frac{\text{length} \times \text{breadth} \times \text{depth}}{94} = \text{tonnage}.$$

The divisor 94 is geared to the particular shape of the sixteenth-century ship's hull and is not universally applicable.

105 In May 1628 Poole was said to have lost twenty ships with a tonnage of 1,465 worth £13,400 (£9 a ton, but this includes equipment): Public Record Office, SP 16/155 No. 31, 103 No. 43.

106 G. D. Ramsay, *The Wiltshire Woollen Industry in the Sixteenth and Seventeenth Centuries* (London, 1943 and 1965), p. 3.

107 R. Davis, *The Trade and Shipping of Hull*, East Yorkshire Local History series, No. 17 (1964), p. 20.

108 G. D. Ramsay, 'The Distribution of the Cloth Industry in 1561–2', *English Historical Review*, LVII (1942), pp. 363–7.

109 *Victoria County History of Kent*, Vol. III, pp. 403*ff.*

110 G. D. Ramsay, *English Overseas Trade during the Centuries of Emergence* (London, 1957), pp. 178–81.

111 L. Stone, 'Elizabethan Overseas Trade', *Economic History Review*, 2nd ser., II (1949), p. 45, quoting British Museum, Lansdowne MS. 114 No. 27.

112 Ramsay, *Wiltshire Woollen Industry*, pp. 74–5.

113 D. C. Coleman, 'Textile Growth' in *Textile History and Economic History: Essays in Honour of Miss Julia de Lacy Mann*, ed. N. B. Harte and K. G. Ponting (Manchester, 1973), pp. 1–21.

114 D. C. Coleman, 'An Innovation and Its Diffusion: The New Draperies', *Economic History Review*, 2nd ser., XXII (1969), p. 423.

115 T. Thirsk, 'The Fantastical Folly of Fashion' in *Textile History and Economic History*, ed. Harte and Ponting, pp. 60–1.

116 ibid., pp. 64–5.

117 Quoted in C. Wilson, *England's Apprenticeship, 1603–1763* (London, 1965), p. 68.

118 Commission printed by G. D. Ramsay, 'Report of the Royal Commission on the Clothing Industry', *English Historical Review*, LVII (1942), pp. 486*ff.*; cf. also *Seventeenth-Century Economic Documents*, ed. Thirsk and Cooper, pp. 1–48.

119 Stone, 'Elizabethan Overseas Trade', p. 44.

120 The details of this fight are not, however, relevant to the purpose of discovering what changes took place in the clothing industry, whether or not a different approach might have had different results. For some discussion of the issues involved, cf. R. Ashton, 'The Parliamentary Agitation for Free Trade in the Opening Years of the Reign of James I', *Past and Present*, XXXVIII (1967), pp. 40*ff*.

121 Public Record Office, SP 12/8/31.

122 Historical Manuscripts Commission, *Hatfield House*, IV, pp. 574–5.

123 Public Record Office, Exchequer, Port Books, E 190/42/1, 26/2, 37/4, 8, 38/1, 41/1, 42/1, 41/5, 43/5, 44/3 from A. M. Millard's analysis of the Port Books of London of which there is a photocopy on the PRO shelves.

124 Public Record Office, Exchequer, E 159/471, fol. 42.

125 *Victoria County History of Kent*, Vol. III, p. 406.

126 A. P. Wadsworth and J. de L. Mann, *The Cotton Trade and Industrial Lancashire 1600–1780* (Manchester, 1931); 'cottons' made in Lancashire in the sixteenth century were made wholly of wool. Cf. N. Lowe, *The Lancashire Textile Industry in the Sixteenth Century* (Manchester, 1972).

127 ibid., pp. 44*ff*.

128 L. A. Clarkson, 'The Organisation of the Leather Industry in the Late 16th and Early 17th Century', *Economic History Review*, 2nd ser., XIII (1961), p. 245.

129 W. G. Hoskins, 'Provincial Towns in the Early Sixteenth Century', *Transactions of Royal Historical Society*, 5th ser., VI (1956).

130 For example, Cipriano Piccolpasso, *The Three Books of the Potter's Art* (c. 1550), facs. ed. B. Rackham and A. van der Put (Victoria and Albert Museum, 1934).

131 Except for bibles, prayer books and other such privileged titles an edition was limited by the Stationers' Company to a maximum of 1,500 until the very end of the period when 2,000 was allowed.

132 *Calendar of State Papers, Domestic, 1637–1638*, p. 108.

133 Castle building, it must be observed, had disappeared not from the world, but from England and Wales. Those who would pursue the tradition must go north to Scotland or beyond to the Orkneys whose most beautiful castles are mid to late sixteenth-century creations, or to the more troubled Continent. Ralph Lane, who kept up to date with the latest thing in fort building, submitted plans for such things to Cecil, but they were never executed. H. M. Colvin, 'Castles and Government in Tudor England', *Economic History Review*, LXXXIII (1968), pp. 225–34.

134 *Tudor Royal Proclamations*, ed. Hughes and Larkins, Vol. III, No. 734.

135 *Calendar of State Papers, Domestic, 1638–1639*, p. 152.

136 Public Record Office, SP 16/377 Nos. 63, 65.

137 *Calendar of State Papers, Domestic, 1637–1638*, p. 580.

138 Public Record Office, SP 16/397 No. 31.

139 Public Record Office, SP 16/341 No. 124.

140 Scott, *Joint Stock Companies*, Vol. I, p. 211.

3

The Marketing Structure

The successful growth of large-scale manufacturing and the concentration of industries in areas which offer external economies are dependent on the existence of a trading network which can distribute the goods to the markets in which they are currently in demand without making the cost prohibitive. Local manufactures always have a measure of protection from outside competition, because even if the costs of manufacturing are greater there are no transport costs to bear and the product can be tailored to meet the precise demands of the local customer, whereas a mass-produced good is inevitably made to a more or less standard pattern. This hardly matters in the case of nails and pins, but a saddle must fit a horse and the wheels of a cart be made to the prevailing local width so that the wheels may run in the aboriginal cart track ruts.

Classical economic historians like Cunningham[1] tended to classify the period between the Middle Ages and the late eighteenth century as the period of commercial revolution – the period when English merchants developed the skills and the knowledge of the markets which enabled them to handle the goods the industrial revolution produced. North and Thomas have recently reverted to the idea that changes in market organisation in Europe at this time were of critical significance. Other authors have similarly stressed the great difference between the modern market structure and that of the sixteenth century.

Commercial transactions were already complex and sophisticated but the relative slowness and inefficiency of the means of communication created problems different from those of the nineteenth and twentieth centuries, revolving around the ability of the local authority to ensure reasonable conduct on the part of an individual rather than of his nation. Some form of internationally accepted law was necessary, together with special courts to enforce it. Credentials for a merchant's good behaviour were required, and limitations might be put upon the local merchants permitted to trade with foreigners. Since it was by no means easy in days of poor communications to catch up with a defaulting merchant and oblige him to pay his debts, the law merchant made alternative arrangements. If a merchant defaulted, it permitted the aggrieved party to recover his debt from the next merchant of the same nation who ventured into the port. Moreover, international trade entered into international politics, so it needed to be a highly organised affair. Ideally the rulers of two countries would have made a special treaty covering such problems. The merchants themselves were organised into a company which policed the behaviour of the individual members and promised to make good torts committed by their members. In order to achieve this, they preferred the trade to be kept under their eye by insisting on organised fleets sailing at fixed times of year, and acting in common on prices.

A nation which could obtain particularly favourable terms from another (the right to retail trade or to exemption from ordinary customs dues, or a monopoly of certain goods) thereby gained more than appeared on the surface, for this gave its merchants an advantage in other countries which would otherwise have themselves traded directly. The Hanse, for example, long had a virtual monopoly of Norwegian trade. There was therefore no point in English merchants shipping their goods themselves to Norway, for the Hanse, selling the same goods, could undercut them and moreover could obtain a return cargo for their ships.[2]

Local merchants could only be sure of controlling the goods that they were exporting, and as far as freight was concerned bulk was more significant than value. Cloth, however, was not a bulky export, while many of the goods England imported – lumber, pitch and tar from the Baltic – were much more bulky. A fleet able to carry all England's cloth would not therefore have been able to handle all her imports; the ships that did bring the imports were competing for freight homewards, always putting the English ships and merchants on the defensive, competing for the trade in their own goods.[3]

This was not true of all markets; the Spanish and Portuguese market, by the end of the period at least, was one in which the problem of freight worked the other way (Doc. 29), and once the merchant fleet was large enough, the problem might cease; but it added to the difficulties of getting going.

Trade flows most easily in well-established channels where the expenses and the risks are all precisely calculated and the necessary links are already in being. Costs can be cut to a minimum, and so the overthrow of an existing domination of trade cannot be accomplished in a day. It is often remarked that in the period up to 1550 the English international traders showed an obsessive devotion to the single trade channel through Antwerp, despite the fact that they themselves recognised the danger of such concentration. The reasons for it were as obvious as the dangers: the merchants had all the necessary links in Antwerp; bills of exchange, credit, factorage, insurance, facilities for debt collection all existed and, moreover, Antwerp was Europe's biggest mart. Imports could be obtained as cheaply as anywhere on the Continent. What advantage could a merchant reap by carrying his goods elsewhere? Heavier freight charges, the risks of local difficulties or lack of interest in his goods, the need for a direct home cargo (or of a bill passing through Antwerp) and, in the end, goods which his fellow had probably obtained as cheaply at Antwerp, or a sale on no more advantageous terms.

While Antwerp survived as the central market through which all goods flowed, the development of multilateral trading links was unlikely. It was the fall of Antwerp and the difficulties of the Dutch during the war with Spain which made it profitable for English merchants to begin forging their own links with other parts of the Continent.[4]

Before this, there were two main companies in existence. The merchants of the staple traded in wool, and the merchant adventurers in cloth. The merchants of the staple had a central 'staple' port at which all their wool was sold – the town of Calais, to which all the wool was shipped in organised fleets twice a year. A shipment which missed one fleet was obliged to wait for the next. Wool sales were, however, declining as the home production of cloth was increasing. Why bother to ship wool overseas when by reselling in England as good a price could be realised (Doc. 30)? It was this consideration which eventually turned the staplers primarily into domestic wool brokers, though not insignificant sums were still being exported in the mid-1560s.[5]

From the beginning of the period, London was the dominant centre of international trade, four-fifths of all overseas trade normally passing through the port. This was mainly because it offered the facilities which a merchant operating on a large scale required for his business. The London market was already a place in which specialised financial services existed. Men providing insurance for goods in transit operated on the principle of underwriters – each accepting so much of the risk on a particular venture, as he felt inclined, until the total was made up – and there were also embryo brokers. Law suits in the Court of Chancery reveal the names of some of the men involved: often it was a family business.[6]

Loans for short terms were a common feature of business life, and a clear distinction was made between the normal 'use' paid on such money and the sort of usury which informers occasionally brought before the Exchequer.[7] Payment of debts was generally made by writing a bill which was not due for payment for a set term – three months, six months or a year being normal, though longer terms were known. In this way, credit was extended from seller to buyer. If the seller's own means were stretched, however, there were people prepared to buy up the bills at a discount, equivalent to the interest they were foregoing on the money extended. Men also speculated on the exchanges by transferring money which was not to pay debts, but simply to be returned from abroad the same way. This so-called 'dry exchange' was condemned by moralists, but flourished nonetheless. The ordinary function of the exchanges was to keep the two countries involved in reasonable equilibrium. Not all merchants were both exporters and importers, and even if they were, their purchases did not always precisely balance their sales. The respective demand for money in England or Europe produced the exchange rate, which varied from week to week as the men who dealt in bills of exchange saw demand varying.[8] Since the coins of all realms at this time were made of precious metals of varying degrees of 'fineness', debts might also be settled by transfer of bullion. Government regulation, however, generally prohibited the export of coin or bullion. Nevertheless there was a point at which it was preferable to risk exporting coin. If the trade was reasonably well adjusted, these crises did not often occur. If they did they were an indication that either exports must be boosted or imports curtailed. Nineteenth- and twentieth-century pure theory saw the exchanges as self-adjusting without exchange of bullion – the increasingly low cost of goods in the one country encouraging the foreigner to buy, the increasing costs of the imports to the other eventually encouraging some local firm to set up in competition. In practice, however, especially in sixteenth- and seventeenth-century conditions, the type of goods involved often made the second an impossible short-term proposition, while an absolute lack of demand made the former impracticable.

While most English trade went to Antwerp, trade did not necessarily have to pass through a central mart, and so far as most markets were concerned trade did not have to balance bilaterally. A deficit balance with France could be offset by a credit balance elsewhere – Portugal or Spain. Providing the overall balance of imports matched exports, the country had no problems, except in the few markets which did not come within this ambit – the Indies and, arguably, the Baltic (Doc. 31).[9]

London, because it was large, and already specialised, could offer better rates for all these types of business than the other ports which therefore always had a tendency to lose business. Rates outside London were higher, but otherwise they operated in much the same way. Fishermen at Exeter, for example, who wished to go to Newfoundland fishing, could borrow from a money lender at a rate of £25 to be paid on the ship's return for £100 lent. The usury laws were avoided because the money lender was also taking a risk – he gained only if the ship did return. Having himself borrowed at 10 per cent in order to lend to the fishermen, he then laid out a further £6 on the hundred for insurance on the boat thus ensuring a profit of £9 come what may.[10] Similarly, the price of cod was agreed at Bristol before the fishermen set forth, and they then bought their needs by issuing bills recoverable from them in cod at their return at so much a last.[11] Arrangements of this sort were generally disadvantageous to the maker, since the price was set low. They were equally familiar in inland trade, however; this was the tinner's normal means of raising money, the lender in this case being the smelter.[12]

The provincial merchants were also disadvantaged because they did not have enough capital behind them. Thus Keymer reported to James I that Ipswich merchants who went to Elbing with fine dyed cloths bought them on time (that is, the seller giving the buyer credit for a period) and were obliged to sell them on time, giving up to eighteen months' credit. Shortage of capital, however, obliged them to discount the bills at a rate of 14 or 15 per cent and sometimes more on the Continent. They had thus effectively sold the cloths for less than their value. Merchants from York, Hull and Newcastle fell into similar traps, because they employed factors of little experience who in their anxiety to give the ships a fast turn-round bought on credit, and then found themselves obliged to sell their cloth cheaply to meet their debts.[13]

The factor should not be regarded too harshly. His life was by no means an enviable one. Cranfield's factors, for example, were bombarded with instructions by their master, many of which it was politically or economically impossible to fulfil, while they spent much time travelling in search of markets for the goods sent over.[14] Not all merchants could afford to maintain a permanent factor in a foreign town who would await the right moment for the sale of goods. Since a supercargo travelling with the goods and returning immediately to England with others was also in a poor position to make a good bargain, they sought instead to have some working arrangement with a foreign firm of 'correspondents'. In all these things, the London merchant had an advantage.

It is understandable, therefore, that it was the London merchants who dominated the new companies that were being established in

Elizabeth's reign to open up new markets, as the old stagnated or disappeared.[15] In this way trade was opened with Russia, with the Levant, with Africa and with the East Indies. Regulated, or in the case of the early Russia Company and the East India Company joint-stock, companies, were needed for these areas because of the distances involved, the need for the ships to be armed or to travel in an armed convoy, and to treat with the rulers of the kingdoms when they arrived. As the trade became relatively established, however, all the companies suffered from the competition of interlopers – merchants not free of the company who were to some extent benefiting from the expenditure the company had made without contributing to the costs.

Other areas nearer home which could be developed with less need of protection included the Baltic and the trade to Spain, Portugal and Italy, all of which expanded in Elizabeth's reign, while the Dutch were fully engaged in defending their liberty against the Spanish. Despite this, the total volume of goods traded in the later sixteenth century does not seem to have greatly exceeded the totals earlier. England was running hard to remain in virtually the same place, and when the Dutch were able to resume their competition the English were hard pressed even to maintain their absolute volume. Contemporaries, indeed, aided by very real difficulties experienced by certain of the companies such as the Russia Company, were sure that she was not doing even that. The number of ships that went yearly to different parts was fairly generally known, as were the commodities which they principally carried (see Doc. 19), and pessimists calculated that there were so many fewer annually to each of the different places, which argued a growing failure on England's part to meet the Dutch challenge.

Such a loss was indeed serious, since Mun calculated that 25 per cent was to be added to basic cost for the costs of freight and insurance which accrued from the merchant's activities. In fact, the English merchant does not seem to have been doing as badly as contemporaries believed. Some of the outlay in the period, especially that on establishing the colonies in America, proved to be very long term; the benefits did not accrue significantly in the period at all, and then not to the original optimistic investors or their heirs, but some of them were seen.

The East India Company, which aroused most criticism, both for its high cost in ships and for its transportation of silver out of the realm, was starting to bring in a variety of goods that were to become very important: goods for re-export. Some of the goods, such as silk were also processed in England before the re-export, bringing in additional benefits. Sugar and tobacco were also beginning to be processed. Such developments, and the ever-widening area which English merchants covered, were important diversifications of the country's interests, building up experience which was to be even more significant. Works such as Lewes Roberts' *Map of Commerce* were spreading knowledge of methods of business and areas of trade which had been unknown outside a very restricted circle.

The developments were, nevertheless, precariously based. The East India Company was nearly brought low by external attack and internal problems; government activities in the 1630s were a hindrance to merchants. For exports, despite some development of coal and beer and the new re-exports, were still painfully dependent on the export of cloth of various sorts where a fall in the continental markets because of war or blockade meant depression throughout the economy.

The absence of a bank in London was a restraint. The principles of banking were well understood by the merchants, and some banking functions were carried out, but a fully fledged bank did not exist, even where a man made most of his money from lending, as Thomas Middleton did.[16] Possibly no single English merchant house had the capital to found one. The proposal put to Elizabeth (Doc. 32) was not for a bank proper, but for a form of government finance common enough in Europe, which might hopefully develop into a lending institution. The optimism of its proposers, however, argues some naivety.

Another practice which was slow to develop was that of buying and selling on sample, which might have speeded up the process whereby goods were transferred from producer to consumer. In part this is a reflection of the small scale on which people in most industries worked, so that repetition of a cloth or other product was uncertain, and the purchaser's desire to buy more than one at a time equally unlikely. It meant however that middlemen were essential, and that from their flourishing a prosperous trade might be discerned.

Internal trade also depended to a very great degree upon the production of cloth. So far as the transfer of goods between different regions internally was concerned, the major goods were agricultural produce like grain and livestock, cloth, and metal goods and coal. To these may be added some of the minor local specialities such as bone lace and special dyes like saffron. Much of the inter-regional internal trade was also centred on London, because London was the biggest single consumer of all sorts of goods, especially foodstuffs. On their export of these goods, therefore, depended the regions' ability to pay their taxes, and to import foreign luxuries.

Much of the trade in these goods was still centred on the markets and fairs, the most convenient way of carrying on business when most of the participants are very small operators. It was generally illegal to buy up grain before it had been harvested, because the government feared the effects of cornering a market, and from time to time there was a flurry on enforcement, particularly when there had been a run of bad seasons.[17]

This sort of small market was an inefficient way to buy or sell goods, in as much as gluts or scarcities might cause sudden price shifts – to the profit of the rich merchant against the poor.[18]

But markets, probably increasingly as the period progressed, came to have goods in which they in some sense specialised over and above the purely local, goods which would be bought up and enter into inter-regional trade. By far the overwhelming majority of these specialities were the agricultural products in which the local area specialised (Doc. 33).

People who needed to amass large quantities of a particular product tended to obtain them at the fairs – annual or bi-annual events which drew produce, often of a single specific kind, from a much wider area and therefore in much larger quantities. Though fairs on the Continent had long ago become also, or even solely, places at which accounts were settled between merchants and agreements made, the evidence that the English fairs fulfilled or came to fulfil a similar function is sporadic. Certainly there is mention from time to time of accounts to be so settled, or payment made due 'on the next fair day' – it would be surprising if there were not – but evidence of a full-blown system of credit with clearance days at the fairs is hard to find. Internal financial systems were probably less highly developed. The later 'inland bill' of exchange, for example, may have existed, but lack of widespread reference to it makes it unlikely that it was common.

There remains the question of private marketing, another practice the government viewed with suspicion. The most significant element in this was probably dealings in wool. Wool was for the most part produced by large-scale farming and it was the basis of England's major industry, so this is hardly surprising. Moreover, it required sophisticated treatment because before it could be spun and woven it needed to be sorted into categories, and wools from different areas sometimes needed to be brought together. The old network by which wool had been gathered together for export therefore had never been fully disbanded, and as the export of wool dropped lower and lower many of the staplers began to turn to supplying the local clothiers and were transformed into wool brokers, combining the sorting of wool with its transport from the area of production to the area of manufacture, and sometimes with the breaking up of wool into bundles of a size which could be sold weekly on the market to the people who bought wool by the week to spin. Big clothiers preferred to bypass the middleman, obtaining their wool by direct treaty. In the course of Henry Isham's purchases of broadcloths from the Wiltshire clothiers he evidently found that his main suppliers were hampered by problems of wool supply. Isham, with his Northamptonshire connections, had no difficulties in establishing the necessary links to provide them with a regular supply of wool and himself with an acceptable side product. Finance was not directly involved, but by supplying the wool Isham saved himself the difficulties of transporting at least some currency.[19]

The problems of currency were certainly so acute that a bargain might depend upon the merchant's willingness to use the money in the city to settle the seller's debts, or to his willingness to act as a retail purchaser for his clients. This never, however, crystallised into the appearance of a formal banking system, so demand for such services was presumably not sufficiently regular. It is clear from the correspondence which has come down to us that one of the major preoccupations of the gentry, the merchant and the yeoman alike was to find a solution to the endless petty problems caused by minor time lags between the expenditure of money and its receipt. But though many people were part-time money lenders, and there was a constant need for credit due to the gap between a man's real worth and the cash he could produce at any given moment, the solutions seem to have been largely *ad hoc* until just after our period.

Men like government officials who had sums of money which they collected over a period and only disbursed at predictable intervals could therefore make a good thing out of short-term lending on the side, but this apparently did not provide an adequate income in itself. It is impossible to measure the growth of the internal market at this time, but almost beyond belief that any major change in its structure would not have been accompanied by the growth of more formal and specialised financial institutions.

For this reason it may be that the growth of London is to a very marked extent a measure of the growth of a national market and, though to a lesser extent, of inter-regional trade. London merchants could operate on better information and narrower margins than provincial merchants, kept a firm grip on trade routes of any size, and were apt to complain when local merchants developed a competitive trade.

Differences in wealth alone would tend to confirm the dominance of London in the large-scale trades. In the early seventeenth century over fifty men in London had estates which at some point were worth over £20,000, and £100,000, though exceptional, was not unknown. In the provinces a personal estate of £2,000 marked a man as wealthy, though individual examples of £40,000 can be found amongst the clothiers rather than the merchants. Moreover, wealth on this scale was confined to the few outports which were more than holding their own with London – to Exeter, Hull, Newcastle and perhaps Bristol.[20]

Notes

1 W. Cunningham, *The Growth of English Industry and Commerce* (Cambridge, 5th edn, 1910).

2 P. Dollinger, *La Hanse, xiie–xviie siècles* (Paris, 1964); *The German Hansa*, trans. and ed. D. S. Ault and S. H. Steinberg (London, 1970).

3 R. Davis, *The Trade and Shipping of Hull, 1500–1700*, East Yorkshire Local History Society Publications, 17 (1964).

4 ibid.

5 E.g. in 11–12 Elizabeth (1568–9), the mayor and staple exported 1,448 sacks of wool and 10,991 pells from London, 92½ sacks and 20,613 pells from Boston and 62 sacks and 13,546 pells from Kingston-upon-Hull, Public Record Office E 159/350, fol. 162.

6 W. J. Jones, 'Elizabethan Marine Insurance', *Business History*, II (1959), pp. 53–61.

7 Shakespeare in the *Sonnets* makes verbal play with such distinctions (e.g. Nos 4, 6, 87, 134). For cases of usury, cf. Public Record Office, E 159/355, fol. 180.

8 For an account of the Exchanges, cf. R. de Roover, *Gresham on Foreign Exchanges* (Cambridge, Mass., and London, 1949).

9 C. Wilson, 'Treasure and Trade Balances', *Economic History Review*, 2nd ser., II (1949), p. 152.

10 Hitchcock, 'A Pollitique Platt', in *Complaint and Reform in England, 1436–1714*, ed. Dunham and Pargellis, p. 289.

11 Innis, *The Cod Fisheries*, pp. 34, 40–4, 59–60.

12 Lewis, *The Stannaries*, pp. 223–6.

13 *Original Papers Regarding Trade in England and Abroad drawn up by John Keymer*, ed. M. F. Lloyd Prichard (New York, 1967), pp. 52–3.

14 R. H. Tawney, in *Business and Politics under James I: Lionel Cranfield as Merchant and Minister* (Cambridge, 1958) gives a splendidly lucid account of how the factor operated.

15 Scott, *Joint Stock Companies*, Vol. I, ii; T. S. Willan, *Studies in Elizabethan Foreign Trade* (Manchester, 1959).

16 Gough, *Sir Hugh Myddelton*, p. 7.

17 The memoranda rolls for 1554 are full of 'informations' about breaches of these laws, for example. As one informer had simply sat in the local alehouse on market day and written down the bargains struck, to a round half dozen in all, the orders must have been frequently breached or evaded.

18 Cf. A. Everitt, 'The Marketing of Agricultural Produce', *The Agrarian History of England and Wales*, Vol. IV, ed. J. Thirsk, pp. 490–552. There

were, however, usually local ordinances which gave the poor and the local man first option.

19 Finch, *The Wealth of Five Northamptonshire Families, 1540–1640*, pp. 7–9; *John Isham, Mercer and Merchant Adventurer: Two Account Books of a London Merchant in the Reign of Elizabeth I*, ed. G. D. Ramsey, Northamptonshire Record Society, XXI (1961), pp. xxiii–xxviii.

20 R. B. Grassby, 'The Personal Wealth of the Business Community in 17th Century England', *Economic History Review*, 2nd ser., XXIII (1970), pp. 220*ff.*

4

Conclusion

If one sought to establish an antithesis to Nef, one could argue, quite plausibly, that the industries on which he expends such attention were established only by the expenditure of unjustifiably large sums of money, under the protection of the State which provided monopolistic conditions within which, though without showing a magnificent profit, the entrepreneurs succeeded in selling their product at twice the price it would have cost to import them. The entrepreneurs whom Dr Gough has examined are on the whole as unconvincing a lot as one could hope to find. Scarcely one could be considered the equivalent of the nineteenth-century hard-headed business man: speculator, visionary, amateur enthusiast, patriot, peculator – these terms, or some combination of them, could be applied to most of the men who put forward schemes which were to solve the country's (and their own) economic problems overnight. To a man they underestimated the costs and overestimated the advantages.

Such a criticism would, however, be off the point. The problems of starting a country on the road to industrialisation are considerable. A careful examination of the first essays in that direction made by any country in the world would reveal much the same picture, of apparently wasted expenditure, the frustration of hopes, the degradation of ideals, the flourishing of con men and the interference of government. The problems of forecasting are ones which modern society with its considerable resources is only just beginning to tackle. Some case can be made out for the policy of monopoly with regard to what we have come to consider infant industries. The need for diversification, even where this does not lead to the maximisation of output, can sometimes be overwhelming. England's experience in the cloth industry meant that textiles were undoubtedly the most advantageous thing she could exploit in the short run, but long-term prospects may have called for capital to be turned into other channels. The idea of import replacement as a means of solving the balance-of-payments crises which periodically overtook England while she depended so heavily on a single export, even where such replacement absorbed more capital than an expansion of the existing line, must not be lightly disregarded. If, moreover, a body of native skills could be established, then there was ultimately some hope that the industry would really stand on its own feet in competition with imports. Furthermore, in an age in which population increases are creating difficulties, any expansion of industry which employs additional labour (particularly if it employs more labour than an alternative use of the capital, which is often the case) by putting money into more men's pockets stimulates demand for other local products. Unfortunately, in many of the new developments the key labour was foreign, and the spread of skills was by no means automatic or rapid, but even these gave much subsidiary employment to native labour.

The government's policy was often misguided. Some of their grants attempted, as Sir Edward Coke argued against Sir Ferdinand Gorges, to establish 'a monopoly of the wind and sun'. Charles in particular was too readily swayed by men who could persuade him that the government could, by granting patents, obtain a source of additional income not dependent on parliamentary grant, but the very interest in industry which all the Tudors and Stuarts displayed was a means of fostering development.

Examination of the economy in this way, however, provides only a crude basis for deciding the significant elements in the equation. For even a rough outline of periods of development and depression, and the factors which lay behind them, we are still heavily dependent on W. R. Scott's pioneering effort to demarcate trade cycles, and this was in turn almost wholly dependent on his analysis of international trade. The conjuncture of internal and external developments has depended to a very great extent on evidence about the harvest and on consideration of information about epidemics. There are many other elements which need to be fitted in before any final conclusions about industrial development can be made, and they are beyond a single researcher's time or scope. A rough list of queries can be drawn up and could doubtless be infinitely expanded. Professor Fisher, for example, postulated that the decline in the sale of Crown lands after the first decade of the seventeenth century may have led to the diversion of capital into schemes for land reclamation. Nef himself was given to claiming that one major stimulus to industrial development was the dissolution of the monasteries. This he felt was demonstrated by the fact that so many coal and iron mines were opened up on ex-monastic lands by their new owners. *Post hoc ergo propter hoc* is, however, a dangerous motto, and the economic advantages and disadvantages of the dissolution are more nicely balanced than he appreciated. For one thing, in many parts of England the monasteries had partially fulfilled a governmental role: they had been responsible for the defence of the region, for the upkeep of roads and sewers, for the provision of education and the maintenance of the aged. All these functions now had to be re-allocated and taken over either by the government (which found them less attractive than the lands) or supplied by other private sources. Moreover, many of the larger monasteries had been a fruitful source of loans for their neighbours, and if not loans, had provided amenities, all of which were now cut off. It is arguable that the dissolution actually set back the development of local credit facilities in the provinces.

The monasteries, moreover, had been the pivot of expenditure and consumption in some areas, on a scale which overshadowed the similar function played by the household of the gentry. A town like Battle, for example, which had virtually come into being to serve the monastery, found its economy disrupted when the abbey came to an end, and Battle was relatively speaking lucky. Battle was a staging point for travellers to London from Hastings, it had a local tannery and some other industry, and the main abbey estates did pass immediately to Anthony Brown, one of the king's esquires of the body, and about to be master of the king's horse. Although Brown for the next few years was mainly in attendance at court, he did set up his country residence at Battle and provided some alternative sources of employment in the destruction and sale of the stone from the now unwanted monastic buildings and the felling of timber (which he had a royal licence to export).[1] Neighbouring Winchelsea, however, with the loss of its monasteries and the recession of the sea, fell into great decay, and some small townships which had depended solely on the monasteries vanished entirely.

The diversion of money and expenditure from the local markets to the grasping hands of an expanding London were among the main grievances of the Pilgrimage of Grace; the importance of this can indeed still be seen a century later in Brereton's comment on the role of Newcastle in the northern economy (Doc. 34). Another factor, which may have been a stimulus to the development of a strong market economy was the growth of government expenditure in the 1540s and early 1550s when taxation, heavier than men had previously experienced, brought money into Westminster which, together with the money raised from monastic land sales, was used to equip and provision and pay large armies of men who were thus taken away from more productive pursuits. Where was the expenditure concentrated, and did it supply one of the major inflationary factors in the markets of the south and east? The stimulus to the iron industry of the Weald may be marked, and the setting up of shipyards on the Thames, but what of the less obvious effects? How much of the money was directly spent abroad – was this by transfer of bullion, or did it, by putting additional purchasing power into the hands of overseas merchants, help stimulate the export boom?

How far were the difficulties of Mary's reign due to a cut-back in government expenditure, and the comparative well-being of the sixties and seventies due to government promoted schemes of diversification, to a rise in population and the relative absence of mass epidemics – so that Hawkins could write to Burghley in 1584 claiming that 'the substance of this realm is trebled in value since her Majesty's reign'?[2] How much was due to good harvests and wages keeping their value with prices making a favourable situation for industrial growth?

How far did the building boom in the 1580s and the growth of shipping, the beginning of the expansion of coal, offset the trading difficulties as the Netherlands and then England became involved in a struggle with Spain, and the normal channels of trade were partially replaced by privateering? Is the gloom of the 1590s the illusion of an ageing queen and a run of bad harvests, in reality set off by the continuing building boom, the expansion of the production of lighter cloths, Newfoundland fishing and the like?

For the seventeenth century there is Dr Supple's study of the economy to guide us, but questions about internal markets still remain. We talk, perhaps too glibly, about the growing population of London, and all the indications are that London and its suburbs were expanding. It might, however, be appropriate to stop for a moment and consider what we are counting. Who were the Londoners? Do we mean simply those who made it their fixed abode, and, if so, what constitutes a fixed abode? Are the royal administrators, the lawyers, serjeants, justices who worked between London and Westminster, who followed the court and had a residence in the country, Londoners or countrymen? The impact on London as a market and a centre for those whom one would not on any criteria regard as Londoners must not be overlooked: in 1573–4 the mayor and council estimated that in bread corn alone the city consumed 2,571 quarters weekly in term time and but 1,409, or little more than 55 per cent, out of term.[3] The transitory population must always have been fairly large and the impact of London as a market may always have been more than the resident population would suggest. What of London as a producer and a provider of services? The concentration of industries around London at this period, the comparatively large scale of those industries, and the growth of specialised services for them, may have been very important developments in the process of industrialisation.

Too little attention has been paid so far to the significant regional developments. It is clear, from even the most superficial comparison of two dissimilar areas like the Staffordshire/Shropshire area and the south-eastern Kent/Sussex Wealden district, that the pattern and timing of development are quite different. While the Wealden iron industry flourished on the demand for ordnance and cast iron work, until it reached an upper limit set by the supply of wood (even when properly coppiced this had a maximum), the north midlands were slow to find a large-scale market for their iron and mainly supplied the local nailers and other producers of small portable goods. On the other hand, the area was largely sheltered from the fluctuations caused by changing market demands from London, or by exposure to raids and demands for defence, and therefore grew more evenly; it apparently continued to grow at a time when the Weald had begun to stagnate. The high rate of turnover in gentry families in Staffordshire, which Sir Simon Diiges lamented in the 1680s, and the obvious increase in numbers between 1600 and Diige's time, are all indicators of the growing prosperity, of an area which was later to be an important centre of industrial development. The south-east enjoyed early development partly because it was an area in which industry developed easily because of its proximity to the markets, and which therefore built up population. Staffordshire paid taxes which were never directly spent within the area, causing secondary stimulation to the economy; it was a poor region, thinly populated, but one in which industry might the more readily expand if those with the power in the area so decided.

Industry studied as an isolated unit – the coal industry, or the iron industry – can never provide the answer, because it is the combination and concentration of industries which provide the field for growth. Industries serve one another, and other institutions develop to speed up the process. This is why the phenomenon of urbanisation is so important, but an agglomeration presents other problems: it has to be fed, and housed and policed. Transport and communications have to be adequate for the first; the provision of water and sanitation sufficient for the second; the local government experienced enough for the third. London was the first big experiment in this respect, and its advance naturally created a pull on the more backward areas around it.

The pull of effective demand was probably of more importance than is generally realised. Fisher noticed, for example, that although cost-reducing innovations might be rare there was no sign that production could not be increased at roughly the same unit cost for as long as demand increased. The debate about the level of the labourers' wages may suggest that demand was hardly likely to increase – but since the percentage of the total national income which passed into the labourers' hands was initially small, their demand, as a class, was only a small motive force, easily offset by increases elsewhere if such occurred. The channels in which demand ran, however, were not always the most useful in promoting economic growth, when they ran to silks and satins, in defiance of the sumptuary laws, and to servants at the door – though even these, if they promoted a struggle to pay for them, had some function.

Nef's thesis, then, can hardly stand as simply as he initially made it. The most important industries at the time had not separated themselves from their dependence on agriculture; men had not begun to move to any town but London in the numbers which Nef once thought might be shown; growth in the economy still found its limit in agricultural growth.

Perhaps, however, too much time has been spent in stressing the relative insignificance of the industries Nef emphasised, and too little on considering what they did indeed have in common: the salt industry, the glass industry, the nascent pottery industry, the rapid growth of the silk industry, the fast, if in absolute terms still unimportant, development of Manchester as a centre for the cotton industry; all these and others were industries which had no dependence on the home agricultural market for their raw materials. That they also have in common a more than average growth suggests that, where the end product was a good which entered directly into the consumer market, if the supply of raw material at a constant price was not limited, the other inputs could be found and a growing market for the product. The rapid growth of the East India Company's trade, bringing in goods which were partially or completely processed and then re-exported, was therefore very promising for the development of capital and skill. The money poured into colonial ventures did not provide the quick return for which the optimistic investors had hoped – they had, like so many of their successors envisaged much too short a gestation period – but it proved to be an important investment for English markets in the future.

There are other signs, too, that the social and educational as well as the economic structure was adapting itself to the idea of change and growth. To run through a catalogue of scientific developments which were to be the basis of much future work would be in itself unenlightening, but it is worth noticing that the early development of the idea of calculus, which was to have so much practical application for engineering, came only at this time.

Developments with a continuous subsequent history which were to be important in the growth of the economy can be first seen in this period, insignificant in terms of measurable size or importance in the contemporary world, but present. To concentrate on measurable change, however, is to think in terms of statics not dynamics. Is the effort to move a heavy roller, once it has started to turn, greater than the effort of starting the movement from the stationary ? Before a foetus is visible to the naked eye, still more before it is independently viable, the critical features of its subsequent development have been already laid down and are immutable. The period of the 'long run up' may contain equally critical features, and the type of development to which Nef drew our attention, semantic questions apart, is worth careful attention.

Notes

1 *Calendar of Patent Rolls, 1554–1555*, p. 132.
2 Oppenheim, *History of the Administration of the Royal Navy*, p. 167.
3 N. S. B. Gras, *The Evolution of the English Corn Market* (Cambridge, Mass. and London, 1915).

SELECTED DOCUMENTS

1. Diversity of Weights and Measures

From *A Minute Account of the Social Condition of the People of Anglesea in the Reign of James I, now first printed from a contemporary manuscript*, ed. J. O. Halliwell (London, 1860).

In our late Queen's time we had ordinarily two sorts of usual measure of corn in this island, taking their denomination of the two usual markets of Beaumaris and Caernarvon, whom this country doth frequent; for the East and North part of this little island resort most commonly to Beaumaris; and the South and West part thereof frequent Caernarvon market over the water: neither of these towns had the true measure established to be the standard of England called Winchester measure, but rather a kind of measure used by custom in each of them, and taking the name of the town where it was used. And Caernarvon bushel was then wont to be bigger than Beaumaris bushel by the one eighth part or thereabouts. But the mischief was, that these measures were not permanent and settled, especially in Caernarvon, but rather almost yearly altered and changed according to the will and pleasure of the officers and clerks of those markets. And the greater mischief it was, that in each of these towns there were always divers bushels, all differing in quantity among themselves, and which is worst of all, it went for true, that in some houses especially amongst the malt women there were two several bushels, the one bigger to buy barley and the other lesser to sell malt. So that the Country did not know for their hearts what measure to send to the markets such chopping and changing, and such cogging and foisting, were there among them. This being of late years shewed and complained to the justices of the great sessions, divers good and commendable orders have been published for the establishing of the true Winchester bushel in either of these towns; much pains and some cost have been bestowed in procuring these orders to be performed. But what followed? And what good hath the country reaped thereby? ...

In Beaumaris, where there was before but the name of one measure, though divers bushels much differing in quantity went under the name of that one, now they profess two several measures, give them several names, the one they call the water measure (which is the biggest) the other is the Town measure; with the one they did use the last dear Summer to buy Corn of strangers, and with the other to sell the same to their neighbours, but in Caernarvon there is now three several measures all used to several purposes, called the greater, the lesser, and

143

the middle measure, and so many sub-divisions of those also abuses thereon depending as the iniquity of man could devise. . . .

I hold it were a good and convenient course that there were provided in the common charge of the country, one brass bushel in every Market Town stamped with the seal of the Tower of London and a good treen bushel of dry wood, to be duly and justly made by the brass bushel, to be delivered to every high constable in the country, and proclamations made to bring in all the bushels in town, and every hundred to be reformed thereafter and the rest to be broken, burnt and suppressed; and especial men to be appointed once at the least in every year to see and view all measures upon their oaths, to present all men that should buy or sell, by any other measure than the uniform bushel and parts thereof so settled. . . . The abuse is not only in measure of corn which is far more confused and out of frame than here hath been declared – but also in measures of length, in liquid measures and in weights; of each of these there are diverse sorts: and first for measures of length we have two usual yards, as commonly used, as we do our two hands; the one is the Welsh yard, the other the English. The English yard is certain and known, being reduced from a known ground and allowed by the law; the other is uncertain and unlawful, and the ground thereof (to me at least) unknown, but taken by some to be some 3½ or 2⅝ inches or much thereabouts longer than the English yard; the one is used by all merchants, mercers, pedlars, masons, carpenters, land meters, and others; the other by all tailors, weavers, fullers, housewives and such like &c. And this is one inconvenience that ariseth of the use of the two yards: let a country housewife upon the street sell a piece of cloth to a mercer by the yard, it must be measured by the Welsh yard; and let that housewife's own husband or any other follow the mercer close by the heels to the shop and there agree with him for the same piece of cloth or any part thereof by the yard, and it shall instantly be measured by the English yard.

In like manner we have in liquid measures two several gallons, the English and the Welsh gallon, and both uncertain and differing so much among themselves, especially the Welsh, as the humour and consciences of men do differ; the Welsh gallon (wherewith is usually measured butter, tallow, honey and the like) is thought to be seven quarts and a half, or as some hold eight quarts English, and of this diversity ensueth many abuses too long here to repeat.

In weights, besides the Troy weights used by goldsmiths, we have the avoirdupois weight used by merchants and mercers and withall we have another kind of pound used in this country called Pwys y garregwlan or the wool pound; by this is weighed all butter and cheese, sold in the country, all yarn, wool, hemp, flax, tallow and many other commodities; by this all our housewifes deliver their wool to the weavers. And these are so diverse and uncertain, that look how many housewifes and weavers, so many divers pounds; hereof ensueth many strifes and contentions between them, and very many actions in the base courts, and many of them determined by wilful perjury which is so common in base courts, as drunkards in the alehouse; this pound is taken by some to be 4½ pounds, by some 4¾ pounds and by others 5 pounds of the avoirdupois, but so diverse and uncertain that it would require a pretty volume to lay down in particular all the known abuses that ariseth thereof: neither would it be nothing amiss to examine the avoir du pois so much used by our merchants, mercers and pedlars, for some will not stick to say, that they are somewhat lighter than the London weights; for my own part, I cannot affirm it, because (besides report) I have no warrant for it. And yet I must uphold mine own country proverb which saieth Ni waeth cowir er ci chwilio, that is, the honest man is nothing impaired by being searched.

2. Typical Accounts of Wood Sales

These extracts from the Middleton manuscripts of typical accounts of wood sales illustrate some of the problems connected with the use of such accounts for precise indications of contemporary prices and volumes. A hagge is a wooded enclosure, a coppice; a goad is a measure, usually 15 ft but with local variations.

From Nottingham University Library, Middleton MSS, 5/165/36, 38, 44.

1571, Middleton

First sold to Hew Gorton and Robert Sykke in William Alyn's little moor 20 ash	£4
Item certain underwood sold there to Richard Hall	20s
Item more sold to Hew Gorton and Robert Sykke the moor next Drayton moor in the same ground	£9
Item to Richard Burke one hagge and 2 oaks	13s 4d
Item to John Berd 4 alders	26s 8d
Item to Edward Seale 6 runnell oaks	13s
Wood sold in Trytteley field where the hop poles were gotten	
Item to Thomas Woodshaw one hagge of 'reffis' wood	3s 4d

1587, Co. Dorset
Underwood sold in woodland.
Primus sold unto Mr. Hendry Uvydale of Morechrichell
  2 acres of wood payment at Candlemas next   £4 17s 4d
Item sold unto William Budden of Horton 32 goad of wood
  at 3d the goad   8s
Item sold unto Sir Harry Ashley of St. Giles Upwimbourne
  120 goad at 4d the goad and 20 goad of void ground   33s 4d
Item sold unto Harry Pool of Longchrichell wood standing
  in waste ground as much as comes to   10s

1613, Brandon and Knatford
A sale of ash oak and elm here at Brandon and Knatford
  about the town and in the tenants backsides. May 1613.
First sold to Clyfston men 20 dotard oaks in the standing
  wood upon the common for   £8
Item sold to Bayles of Thurleston 4 ash and 3 oak of the
  bankside against the meadow price   £2 6s 8d
Item sold to Thomas Smyth wheelwright of Wolston 4 ash
  in Worths close, they were of the best sort   £4
Item sold to Thomas Lynes of Lawford wheelwright 10
  little ash in Biggin Hills   £4
Item sold to 4 wheelwrights Thomas Smyth, Thomas Lynes,
  John Biddell and Thomas Godes 21 elms in Higgs yard
  in Knatford price   £12 4s 0d
Item sold to Percival Lapworth 11 ash 3 dotard oaks and
  1 hollow elm price   £5
Item sold to Ebenezer Losbey joiner 2 good ash in Biggin
  Hill hole price   £1 6s 8d

3. Legal Depositions Arising from a Disputed Right of Way

This is an extract from the depositions in a lawsuit concerning the right
of way over a bridge at Colton between Henry Lord Paget and William
Gresley. The bridge provided a convenient short cut for Paget's iron
works, but was making the environment more difficult for the local
tenants and farmers, as the present extract makes clear.

Paget produced a large number of old men, many of them allegedly in their eighties, to testify that the road was a common highway, that the bridge had always stood where it did and that no one had ever before been denied the use of it. Gresley produced a large number of people prepared to give specific instances proving the contrary. This witness (who is one of the fullest) gives interesting sidelights on the existence of a glass works in the vicinity and the moment at which iron and coal were first discovered in the area. The only interrogations to which he does not reply concern the actual stopping of five wains carrying iron over which the specific case has arisen, presumably because he was not an eye-witness to the event, which was not in any case itself in dispute.

From Stafford County Record Office, Anglesey MSS, D (W) 1734/1/3/7A.

Ralph Porton of Colton within the said country of Stafford husbandman of the age of 70 years tenant to Humphrey Etheraide of Worthington gentleman, which payeth for Mr. Everard to Sir William Gresley 2s 8d of chief rent, sworn and examined, to the first interrogatory sayeth that he doth know the said town of Colton and the mill called Colton mill and that the said town and mill are about half a mile distant (from the Trent) and that he hath known the same by the space of 60 years.

To the second interrogatory he sayeth that he hath known in his time two millers at the said mill of Colton at several times one after the other.

To the third interrogatory he sayeth that before 46 years past he knoweth there was no bridge over the mill stream at Colton mill but only a little bridge for footmen to pass over.

To the fourth interrogatory he sayeth that about 46 years past one Hugh Averell, farmer of the said mill, made the first bridge over the stream of planks for his own commodity for the more safety of such as should bring bags to his mill and being asked by what name the said bridge was then called sayeth that it was called the horse bridge.

To the fifth interrogatory he sayeth that Sir William Gresley knight that now is, about fourteen or fifteen years past made the first bridge over the said mill stream whereby any wains or carts might pass over for his own ease for the carrying of timber from Cannock wood for the building of Colton bridge and for carrying of coals to the bloom smithies and afore that time no wains passed that way.

To the sixth interrogatory he sayeth that all such tenants or inhabitants of Colton which did fetch coals at Wednesbury and ashes at

Cannock wood for glasses and bring the same carriages over Worsley bridge and none over the said mill stream.

To the seventh interrogatory he sayeth that the cause why the inhabitants and tenants of Colton did not come the nearest way to Colton bridge was there was no way to pass over the mill stream and therefore they were constrained to go about by Worsley bridge which is about a mile and a half about.

To the eighth interrogatory he sayeth that since the same Sir William Gresley made the said bridge it hath been commonly chained and locked so that without licence of the said Sir William and his officers no carriage might pass over for the twelve years and past of thereabouts.

To the ninth interrogatory he sayeth that afore Lyne land was amended one neighbour borrowed of another licence to go over the lands and so down the marsh by no known way but as one neighbour borrowed of another.

To the tenth interrogatory he sayeth that from Colton there was no carriage by cart or wain over the said mill stream to any market town and that the tenants and inhabitants of Colton most commonly go from Colton to Lichfield market by the high bridge.

To the eleventh interrogatory he sayeth that the tenants of Rugeley of late have passed over the said mill by licence over ploughed butts and ridges in Trent field being sown with corn to Colton.

To the thirteenth interrogatory he sayeth that Sir William Gresley and others by his appointment have stopped and stayed the carriages of William late Lord Paget from passing over the said mill bridge to his iron mills at Bromley and he knoweth that the said Lord Paget did compound and agree with the said Sir William Gresley by reason that afterwards the said Lord Paget mended the high ways there but what other recompense he knows not.

To the fourteenth he cannot depose.

To the fifteenth interrogatory he sayeth that the mill lane was amended at the only cost and charge of William late Lord Paget before his carriage would be suffered to pass that way.

To the sixteenth interrogatory he sayeth that the said Sir William Gresley had the tithes of Longdon but wherefore he was put from it he cannot tell.

To the seventeenth interrogatory he cannot depose.

To the eighteenth he sayeth that by reason of the said Lord Paget's carriage through Colton lordship the ways be so deep and foul that they cannot carry their corn out of their fields and meadows to their houses by the accustomed ways without great danger of their carriages and having more oxen than before times they were accustomed but are compelled to compound one neighbour with another to have licence to pass through their several grounds.

To the nineteenth interrogatory he sayeth that when the said William Butler did make fences for the safeguard of his corn upon his land shutting down to the said mill stream and the said George Bywater did sow his lands next adjoining to the said Butler's land there was no passage that way at all but only for horsemen and footmen.

To the twentieth interrogatory he sayeth that all the lands were ploughed thoroughly until such time as the said lord Paget compounded and that a certain state of the demesnes of the said Sir William Gresley was likewise ploughed and that the inhabitants of Colton suffered the said Lord Paget to pass that way because he compounded therefore and being askcd what the composition was said he would not tell us but as the said Lord Paget and Sir William Gresley agreed.

To the twenty-first interrogatory he sayeth that there was a glass house in Assheley hay in Colton park and that they had ashes in Cannock wood which they brought over Worsley bridge thither and that it is about 35 years since and the cause they brought the said ashes over Worsley bridge was there was no way over the mill stream and the way over Worsley bridge is a mile and a half about.

To the twenty-third interrogatory he sayeth that it is about 34 years past since the first iron smithies were builded in Cannock wood and about the same time the first coal was found in Beaudesert park and Alexander Wood deceased and Richard his son were the first that ever found coal there and afore that time no carriage passed that way over the said mill.

To the twenty-fifth interrogatory he sayeth that Calves croft doth adjoin to the said Butler's lands and that it was over the old Ring of Colton park.

To the twenty-sixth he sayeth that since the said composition made between the said Lord Paget and the said Sir William no other carriage passed over the mill stream without licence of the said Sir William and his officers.

To the twenty-seventh interrogatory he sayeth that the said Wolfe did stop the said Butler from passing over the said land of corn adjoining to the said Butler's lands shutting down to Colton mill stream and the said Butler compounded with the said Wolfe for his passage and gave him there for a hoop of corn.

4. Side-Effects of Iron Working

The establishment of iron works, the attempts to preserve the woods for charcoal burning by fencing and the use of the streams to drive the hammers all encroached in various ways on the existing use of facilities. The defendants in this case, which was fought in 1580–1, were found guilty and fined, the leading figure Thomas Adams £40 – twice as much as the others, because he was the local constable at the time of the offences. The defendants had broken down a hedge to allow their cattle pasture, and were reproved by the court for not, if they had a grievance, following the due process of law instead. The effects they complain of, however, whatever the legal rights of the case, were probably very real.

From Stafford County Record Office, Anglesey MSS, D(W) 1734/1/3/30.

The answers of Weston, Owens and three others.

To the riots, routs and unlawful assemblies and other misdemeanours they plead not guilty.

That the plaintiff is true owner of the manor of Rugeley with the royalties belonging to the same wherein the defendants, tenants of the said manor and the inhabitants of Rugeley, Cannock, Bruerton, Walton, Longdown andc. and divers other towns adjoining to Cannock wood have time out of mind had and of right ought to have common of pasture for their cattle and throughout the said wood and forest; and that the complainant had enclosed a great part of the common there from the defendants being no lawful passage into nor from the said Cannock wood as they were wont to have because the complainant hath enclosed Gadsby coppice being two miles long and Strumybrook coppice of the like compass and other coppice and many enclosures to the great hurt of the country. That the complainant hath builded upon the commons and waste grounds about the number of fifty cottages whereunto the complainant hath enclosed great part of the premises. That the complainant hath erected iron mills and forges by reason whereof the inhabitants have lost the profit of fireboot which time out of mind they have had and by means of the said iron mills her majesty's subjects receive great detriment for the tanks and pools made for supply of the iron works have wasted and decayed all the water courses which did run to divers corn mills and fulling mills which impoverish such owners of the said mills and desolation of the houses. And for that by the sudden coming down of the water of the said tanks the ways were stopped and the houses and barns drowned to the great loss of the inhabitants.

That because there is not sufficient common of pasture nor passage to the premises for the defendants and other inhabitants adjoining albeit some of them before the said months of January and February made humble suit unto the complainant for reformation of the same, and for that they were debarred of their accustomed commons and that Gadsby coppice had then been enclosed by the space of nine years and upwards and for that the defendants did perceive divers cattle to be there feeding by command of the complainant, they particularly and severally but never above two persons at one time did drive their cattle into Gadsby coppice making sufficient way for their recourse and feeding.

5. Licensing a Collection for Hastings, 1578

From *Tudor Royal Proclamations*, ed. P. L. Hughes and J. F. Larkin (New Haven, 1964–9), Vol. II, pp. 426–30.

Where of our own knowledge and certain science we do understand that our town and port of Hastings in our country of Sussex, being the ancient town of our Cinque Ports, is situated upon the main sea very near the middle of a great bay or open place lying between two points of the land which stretch forth far into the sea, called the Beachy and the Ness, distant each from the other thirty miles, right opposite to the realm of France, the ancient enemy of our country; as we are credibly informed the same town hath of long time been a place not only very well inhabited with warlike people and greatly replenished with good mariners and other men meet and serviceable for our navy, well stored with ships, barks, crayers, and boats, but also sufficiently furnished with armour and artillery of all sorts, both for sea and land, also very meet and commodious for fishing and the bay plenteously abounding with all sorts of fish according to the several seasons of the year;

By reason whereof, the same town hath of long time been by the inhabitants thereof in time of wars manfully defended against the sundry invasions and attempts of the French nation, our coast thereabouts lying very open against the French, by them often kept from spoil; our merchants and loving subjects and other travellers sailing along that coast have oftentimes by their ships and oftentimes by their harbour been saved and rescued from the fury of the enemies and the tyranny of pirates; our navy and the navy of sundry our noble progenitors, kings of this realm, the better appointed by reason of their skilful mariners and cunning seamen; also our household, our citizens of London, and our countries to the said port adjoining greatly benefited by their fishing;

And where our said town hath of long time had a pier or harbour made of timber and other things set and placed in the sea for the succour of the seamen and defence of their ships, barks, crayers, and boats against the great rage and fury of the sea, which hath been always maintained at the great and importable charges of the inhabitants of our said town of Hastings, until of late time the same pier or harbour was at a sudden by the great violence and extreme rage of the sea broken down and carried away; sithen which time the town is much decayed, the traffic of merchants thither forsaken, the fishing by reason of the dangerous landing little used, the rich and wealthy men gone thence, and the poor men yet remaining would gladly do the like if without offence of our laws, they might be elsewhere received; whereby our people are likely to perish and our said port likely to be subverted and become desolate, or else the people there by necessity driven to commit great and heinous offences to the great hindrance of the public weal unless some speedy remedy be for them provided;

And where we be informed by divers of our Privy Council and nobility and by divers artificers very cunning and skilful in that kind of faculty that a very good haven or road for the arriving and safeguard of ships, barks, crayers, and boats may near unto the said port with no great charge be made to the great relief of the inhabitants and of all merchants and travellers sailing along the Narrow Seas and to the strength of our said coast; and that the inhabitants of our said port be ready and willing to bestow their lands, goods and labours to the uttermost of their power to accomplish the same, notwithstanding of themselves very unable to finish so great a work, likely as it is thought to amount unto the sum of 4,000: . . . For the furtherance and better helping forth of the same we do commend the same good and laudable intent and purpose to the charitable and liberal contribution and benevolence of all and singular our loving subjects dwelling within any our realms and dominions.

[Two jurats of Hastings licensed to collect for this end.]

. . . And that our further pleasure is that our said justices of peace shall be their warrant call before them all and singular such persons shall refuse to give or contribute liberally towards this good work, and understand the cause of their refusal, and unto them declare our pleasure, exhorting and persuading them to conformity; which if they shall notwithstanding obstinately refuse, then to certify their names and dwelling places to us or to our Privy Council.

6. Grain in Garners in the Hundred of Toltinghoe, Kent, 1587

From Stafford County Record Office, Sutherland MSS, D 593/S/4/6/3.

The 100 of Toltinghoe 1587

A brief abstract of all kinds of grain viewed and seen in several men's garners within the said 100 by a certain jury . . . 14 Feb . . . 9 Eliz.

	wheat	barley	oats	beans	peas	malt	total
Northfleet	112	503	45	2 56	169·3	126½	1,288
Meopham	339·6	267	350	—	71	38½	1,075
Luddesdown	75·6	80	136	—	38½	22	352·2
Nursted	30	25	50	—	12	5	117
Gravesend	60	31⅓	15	—	34	61	171
Milton	148	161	9	—	23	4	345
	1,095	1,067	605	2·56	357·3	256	

A brief note of the number of acres to be sowed viz:	barley	1034 acres	grain	507 qrs
	oats	388 acres	to	184 qrs
	peas	534 acres	sow	50 qrs

Sum total of all the remainder of the several grains the season being allowed viz. 4 bu, acre of barley; 4 bu. acre of oats; 4 bu. peas	barley	550 qrs
	oats	441 qrs
	peas	307 qrs

The weekly proportion for the poor within the 100 of Shamwell. D 593/S/4/6/5.

	weekly	total
Halling	4 bu.	12 qrs
Strood	2 qrs 6 bu. 3 peck	65 qrs
Shorne	1 qr 1 peck	24 qrs

	weekly	total
Cooling	2 bu.	6 qrs 6 bu.
Cobham	12 bu. 3 peck	38 qrs
Higham	1 qr	24 qrs
Frindsbury	1½ qr	36 qr
Cuxton	3 bu. 3 peck	11 qrs or thereabouts
Cliff	1 qr 7 bu.	45 qrs
Chalk & Denton	9½ bu.	28½ qrs

The weekly proportion for the poor of Toltinghoe.

	weekly	total
Milton	1 qr	26 qrs
Gravesend	4½ bu.	14 qrs 5 bu.
Northfleet	4 qrs 3 peck	105 qrs 5½ bu.
Luddesdown	1 qr 3 peck	28 qrs 3½ bu.
Nursted	3½ bu.	11 qrs 3 bu.
Meopham	4 qrs	102 qrs
		286 qrs 8 bu.

The weekly proportion for the poor of Hoo.

Hoo	2½ bu.	7 qrs
Stoke	1 qr 3 bu.	33 qrs

Chatham and Gillingham.

Chatham	1 qr 3 bu.	34 qrs & some
Gillingham	1 qr 2½ bu. and a gallon	33 qrs & some
Grange	1 qr 3 bu.	34 qrs 3 bu.
		101 qrs 6 bu.

sum total for the poor of this division 681 qrs 5 peck

The several proportions to be sent to the market.

Rochester   114 qrs 3 bu. wheat, 14 qrs 4 bu. barley or malt, 34 qrs oats: total 161 qrs 1 bu.
Dartford   total 19 qrs 2 bu.
Maidstone   wheat 93 qrs 7 bu., barley 150 qrs 2 bu.: total 244 qrs
Sevenoaks   wheat 86 qrs 6 bu., barley 32 qrs 4 bu., oats 15 qrs: total 134 qrs 2 bu.
Gravesend   153 qrs 5 bu. wheat, 116 qrs 3½ bu. barley, 46 qrs 6 bu. oats: total 316 qrs 7 bu.
Malling   4½ qrs
Milton   8 qrs
Total   886½ qrs

[In a certificate attached to the same explaining how the calculations have been achieved it is reckoned that a reasonable allowance for one member of a family would be one peck of bread corn and one peck of beer corn weekly, plus the seed corn. Whether this was the allowance also for the poor is not so clear. The grain is to be sold to the poor at 4s a bushel for wheat and 2s 4d a bushel for barley where the prices in Gravesend market 'at this day' are]

the best	wheat	4s	10d
„	barley	2s	8d
„	rye	3s	4d
„	malt	2s	4d
„	oats		12d
„	peas	2s	4d

[the second or the worse kind being in every case 4d, 6d or 8d cheaper. Malt was to be made only by those who have no other living, millers forbidden to buy grain to resell and ministers and churchwardens given the duty of overseeing the orders at parochial level. There were also a number of licences to bakers to buy in the open market. e.g.]
Robert Martin common baker of Milton is given licence to buy 5 qr of wheat and 1 qr of barley in the open market to serve his bakery.
[In a similar way certificates were made of local dealers who were to be controlled or suppressed.]

Tonbridge. August 1590. D 593/S/4/13/12.
First Nicholas Harris buyeth barley and converteth the same into malt and selleth it. Inhabiting in Tonbridge town.
   Item Michael Blundell buyeth malt and converteth the same into meal and then selleth it in Tonbridge.
   Item Robert Palmer miller sometimes buyeth corn and converteth the same into meal and so selleth it Tonbridge mill.
   Item Herbert Ceely and Richard Mead millers do sometimes likewise buy corn and convert the same into meal and so sell the same.
   By me Nicholas Hooper curate under Mr. Stockwood, vicar of Tonbridge.
   By me Thomas Couchman, constable.

7. Commission for the Stay of Dearth of Grain in Aylesford, Kent, 1595

From Stafford County Record Office, Sutherland MSS, D 593/S/4/36/1.

Upon Wednesday the eighth of January 1594/5 William Sedley, William Lambard and John Rythers three of the commissioners within the lathe of Aylesford in the county of Kent for the execution of her Majesty's orders for the stay of the dearth of grain assembled at West Malling within the said county and lathe, to treat with such farmers and corn masters of certain hundreds within the said lathe then warned thither as had grain of any kind to spare as well for some proportion of such kind of grain as they and every of them had to spare at a charitable price for the extreme poor people as also to apportion the remain to the several markets.

And amongst others at the first entrance into this service a gent. named Richard Lee of Wrotham in the said county came before us the said commissioners of whom we entreated for some proportion of wheat for the poor at much a charitable price as other poor farmers had liberally and willingly yielded unto before him who said (when he had heard the price which others had granted before him) that it was no reason that he that had corn this year should give to the poor in the price of his corn and others that were perhaps an hundred times his betters give nothing and said with many and often repetitions that there was no reason in these orders. Mr. Lambard then said the simplest man there present would not have said that those orders being made by the wisdom of the whole realm were void of reason for if they were void of reason it is no better than madness and that if he knew what was reason himself he must needs confess that he was out of reason for said he, if her Majesty send for purveyance of wheat, who must serve her but they that have it? If she send for carriage who must do this service but they that have carts? Can wheat or carts or the like be had of him that hath none? And yet thus it pleaseth you to hear yourself talk thus fondly and perchance to say that their honours' orders are without reason, admitting nothing for reason but that which pleaseth your own foolish brain and therein show yourself to be a fool in terming her Majesty's and their honours' honourable orders to be without reason. Mr. Lee then said unto him in great heat (as all his speeching was furious) in the presence of the people with whom we were then to treat as aforesaid that he was a fool. To the evil example of the hearers at the first entrance into this service.

Upon Saturday last there came to me at Malling a gentleman of the borough of Oxenheath who is presented to have bought wheat upon the ground the remainder thereof being a pretty quantity and therefore he with the hundred of Littleford were appointed to be here before us; but because we could not dispatch all that day we attended only the remote parts of the limit and in the morning discharged all the rest until Thursday and Friday next. This gentleman came unto me (Mr. Sadler and I have divided ourselves for the more speedy dispatch) and told me that he could not attend again, therefore prayed his discharge. I told him that although we had adjourned the hundred yet I would presently take order with him and spare his attendance the next day. 'Aye, but how will you deal with me?' said he. 'As we have done and must do with all other gentlemen', said I. He then told me that we must not deal with him at all for his grain. I then said he must then show us a better, or as good a discharge as we had warrant which was her Majesty's orders advised by her honourable council and commanded to us to be put in execution which we both must and would do. He said he served an honourable lord and had for friends the Lord Keeper and the Lord Chamberlain who would exempt him from being at our dispositions. I told him that when I saw it I would give place to it: in the mean time it was not words that moved me or should cause me to cease to proceed with him as with others according to our directions, and therefore if he would be ordered now I would dispatch him if not let him keep his day with the rest. This gentleman came again to me at my house yesterday and refused directly to be ordered and bound by us saying that his case was not as other men's and that it was no reason that men's goods should be disposed otherways than as they list themselves and that he would not be bound to sell his corn at the market or in any other manner than he list himself and added further that if men were compelled to carry their corn to the market the peace of the realm would not long continue. And that he had heard divers say of late that they would go together in troops of a hundred or two hundred together with petitions to her Majesty to be at liberty to dispose and order their own goods as they list, either to the market or not as they list and that himself would kneel before her Majesty rather than be bound in any sort, with many other great words before he fell into these terms.

I offered him that he should choose his markets either Malling, Tonbridge, Sevenoaks or Rochester because he was a part of the hundred of Hoo and if his occasions were to use any sums of money I bid him give me three weeks knowledge before hand and we would apportion the market in such sort as should carry away his wheat that day by not sending in others' grain those days in such quantities as at other times but somewhat we would send of other men's lest he having the whole market those days should increase the prices which we would avoid by all means. Nothing would content this gentleman but his own liberty with many terms of scorn to be bound. But now upon his speech yesterday I thought good to acquaint you with all this long matter desiring your advice therein as that I dare not conceal it, holding the matter so dangerous as I dare not conceal it, yet loath to complain it and not knowing how deeply the concealing thereof may touch me whatsoever may ensue I thought good to import it to you both.

And for dealing with his grain I do earnestly entreat you that either you both or one of you will be with us on Thursday next at West Malling or that you will take the borough of Oxenheath to your hundred of Hoo and deal with it in your limit, wherein (if it please you) I will join with you when you deal with that hundred, and then you shall see that I desire not thus to exclude myself but I am so faintly assisted that all now doth rest upon my shoulders that am the weakest of all other. And yet it shall be well seen that in her Majesty's service I fear no man's person or friends. Let them fear whose conscience can witness against them.

This gent. is one Mr. Gastrell who married with a sister of mistress Chowne and lives in Oxenheath house.

I would have attended you myself but that I have appointed many to be with me this day which may default in this service the other days we attended the hundred they dwell in and being glad to gain time (for we have to every poor alehouse keeper a several solemn oration) I am fain to utter to you by writing what I had thought to have delivered by private speech.

Here enclosed I send unto you Thomas Payne his proportion and remainder. And also William Nicholson his rate whose remainder is great and his liberality besides, pro rata of all others.

There must soon be appointed to look to the river, otherwise will Maidstone, Aylesford and other blind seats upon the river side convey away mash barley and malt.

When we have all the remainders of each hundred within this division I will attend on you with the whole book to the end that the proportion for the market and at Hoo, may be rated by us all together. Such are my occasions as I must be at London and there stay the most part of the next week in which time I will make up books ready for your hands.

We shall be at West Malling for this service on Thursday, Friday and Saturday this week. I beseech you give me your advice concerning Mr. Gastrell and the rather for Cranbrook, although I do not hear that any one person (this gent and my blockish kinsmen excepted) be in any manner discontented with any thing that is done. But for my own security I desire to be directed. I pray you also to make a licence in both your names Mr. Sedley and mine (if it please you) for Robert Wybourne of Wrotham yeoman (being licensed to victual, bake and brew) to buy corn which is to buy on Thursday next at Maidstone market. His weekly proportion is six bushels which licence I pray you also to sign and send me by this bearer if your leisures will permit. And so with remembrance of my duty (having overtired you) I take my leave Wrotham this 19th of January 1594/5.

John Rythers

Mr. Gastrell broke out farther into these terms: if her Majesty and the Council can appoint that our goods shall be sold when and where they please then. . . . And there he rested.

8. Accounts for the Coal Mines in Beaudesert Park, 1622-3

The coal mines in Beaudesert park were sufficiently big business for it to be worth Paget's while to sink a sough at a cost of £60 or thereabouts, plus annual repair costs, to keep the mines operating. The following account, which has the usual mixture of entries, casts light on the profits from the coal pits and also upon the building costs at a house which was simply being extended.

From Stafford County Record Office, Anglesey MSS, D (W) 1734/3/3/ 260.

A declaration of the accounts of Richard Sead as well of all the sums of money by him received for the sale of pit coals and other ways as also of all sums of money by him disbursed for the use of the right honourable William Lord Paget of Beaudesert from 24 March 1622 until the 24 March 1623.

Imprimis arrears due by the said accountant upon the determination of his last account ending 24 March 1622 £35 13s 11d.

Item he is charged with money received for 130 dozen of old coals which remained on the bank in Cannock wood unsold at the last audit and now sold at 4s 0d per dozen £26.

Item he is charged with money received for 146 dozen old coals which remained on the bank in Beaudesert park at the last audit and now sold at 5s 0d the dozen £36 10s 0d.

The price of 1,558 dozen of coals sold in Cannock wood being parcel of 1,694 dozen gotten there in the time of this account whereof 5 dozen spent at Beaudesert house and 131 dozen remain on the bank yet unsold which coals sold at 4s 0d per dozen amounteth to £311 12s 0d.

The price of 1,273 dozen of coals sold in the time of this account being parcel of 1,313 dozen gotten here in the said time whereof 9 dozen spent at Beaudesert house 31 dozen remaining on the bank yet unsold which coals are sold at 5s 0d the dozen amounteth to £318 5s 0d.

Kennel coals: Item he is further charged with money received for Kennel coals gotten in Cannock Wood in the time of this account and now sold for £2 8s 0d.

Item the accountant is charged with money received of divers persons viz; for the rent of the ancient tithe hay of Longdon paid by certain tenements there 18s 0d for the rent of the Hill house and grounds besides such as are used to my Lord's use £6 8s 0d; for the rent of Parson's Fields £5; the rent of the broad hasles £3 6s 8d; for the hay of Beaudesert great park £54 9s 0d; for the rent of the little park £6 13s 4d; the rent of Alblaster hays £41; for the rent of the tithe hay of Parson's Acre in Saddlesall £4 and made of the hollies in Saymour's bailiffwick £8 18s 0d.

Foreign receipts: Item he is further charged with money received for holly tops sold £1 7s 8d; holly bark sold £1 10s 0d; for a tree sold Creswell £3 6s 8d; for a wether sold which was left of the provision at his lordship's being in the country 8s 0d; £6 12s 4d.

The wages of the said accountant for one year ending 24 March 1623 £13 6s 8d.

Paid for getting coals in Cannock wood in the time of the accountant £166 15s 3d.

Driving heads and sinking there £33 9s 7d.

Paid for getting coals in Beaudesert park in the time of the accountant £178 1s 0d.

Disbursement about the sough there £20 12s 3d.

Money disbursed by the accountant upon several titles viz: repairs about Beaudesert house £5 19s 1d.

Labourers about Beaudesert house and garden £9 1s 7d.

Work done about the wall on the court and making a new lodging there £83 11s 11½d.

For bearing, getting, hewing, setting and carrying of stone for the new gatehouse at Beaudesert being of stone got in the coppice £15 2s 0d.

For bearing, getting, hewing and carrying of stone gotten at Rugeley quarry and brought to Beaudesert £37 8s 10½d.

Carpenters' and plumbers' work done about the new lodging £12 8s 3d.

For falling, squaring and hewing of timber for the gate house £13 5s 3d.

Necessary disbursements £13 0s 4d.

Payment belonging to the Hill house and husbandry with mowing, making and carriage of hay there £3 11s 2d.

Repairs at the pale and gates in Beaudesert park £2 12s 1d.

Wheat and oats bought while my Lord lay in the country £12 14s 6d.

Cloth bought for my lady and carriage of the same to London £61 10s 10½d.

Money paid to Mr. Ilsley at several times £120.

Money paid by the said accountant viz: to Mr. Marchin at Michaelmas and our Lady day £5; and given to the midwife and nurse at the christening of a child of Mr. Stringer's per my lady's appointment £1; allowed to this accountant for the keepership of Beaudesert park £2; and for the keepership of Saymour's bailiwick £2.

Abated for coals delivered without money out of this accountant's charge as per book doth particularly appear £21 6s 4½d.

And so the said accountant hath received more than disbursed £33 16s 4d.

Examined by Thomas Oxehound auditor.

9. Technology in Copper Mines: A Report, 1602

From M. B. Donald, *Elizabethan Copper* (London, 1955), p. 216.

The course of the stream that stirs the double wheel [is] brought along the side of the mountain almost 1,200 yards in wooden troughs made of planks and from thence is carried through troughs into the mines 26 fathoms into a cistern of planks from which it falls upon the wheel of the engine, which engine serves as well to draw up the ores and deadworks when need requires as to draw the water out of the bottom of the mine through many pumps.

10. A Letter from Sylvester Smith to John Bentley Concerning Sir Francis Willoughby's Iron Works, 1592

Sylvester Smith was a servant of Willoughby (the Sir Francis of the letter).

From Nottingham University Library, Middleton MSS, 5/165/82.

To the worshipful John Bentley esquire at Wollaton 9 October 1592. Worshipful, my duty commended according to the order taken by Sir Francis, I have sent a hammerman to his worship for new mill forge and such a man as his lordship may boldly trust, but I cannot agree with him for his wages by reason he expecteth 10s 0d upon the ton and I offer but 8s 0d so as the matter is referred to yourself and his worship to determine. If he be placed there Sir Francis need be at no further charge for any to keep possession. I saw at my being at those works small provision for any winter's blowing; many things are wanting to make any great work, winter being so fast approaching. I viewed the stone mine and I find they have gotten heretofore but of the very worst sort of stone, whereas there is better by far in fetching the same deeper which I think will both make better yield and better iron also wherefore I wish the best stone may be gotten for as I am let understand his worship is to take either iron or money for his debt which, if it be so, Sir Francis is like to have but a hard bargain, for that, as I hear, they are purposed to make iron with sea coal at the chafery, which if they do they will hardly sell above £10 the ton which I hope his worship will have a regard of if he should yield £12 for the same.

As for a finer, I have heard there is one hired by Mr. Zouche or some other for him whose name is John Wilson, a man accounted both honest and an indifferent good workman. I have been to have spoken with him to see if he will be content to become Sir Francis's servant, which if he would I meant not to seek any further but as yet I cannot meet with him for that he is gone into Wales to seek workmen, but at his return I purpose to speak with him and certify your worship. As for our works at Oakmoor they go well forward, having at the place 140 dozen of coals and between 23 and 30 loads weekly to come in betwixt this and Christmas.

I have agreed since my being at Wollaton and paid some money in hand for so much stone as will keep the furnace blowing till well towards Candlemas by means whereof my charge is weekly £10 at the least, which I must either do or else I shall not make iron sufficient to keep the forge in work till I can blow again and I must now continue wood cutting for our next year's provision whereby my charge is increased. Besides I am fain to keep our Middleton furnace-men at a dead charge wherefore I beseech your worship as heretofore so now to continue your mindfulness both of me and this work and procure the residue of the money appointed for I fear all will be too little to raise so much money as this work by God's help shall yield. I think towards the end of this week to be at Wollaton, hoping to find more plenty than at my last being there, had not your worship holpen me. My founder continueth sick still to my no small loss of time and Sir Francis' hindrance, but for that he is of the mending hand I trust to blow ere I see Your Worship. Moreover, whereas my Lord and Lady of Shrewsbury granted a warrant for two trees in Alveton park; the warrant being delivered to bailiff Bale of Derby, he keepeth the same; my lady's bailiff refuseth to deliver the trees by means whereof I am not a little hindered in finishing the forge, wherefore I pray your worship to procure a letter to be sent to Mr. Dale from Sir Francis by this bearer, that he would deliver the warrant to this messenger to be given to Mr. Hatfield, otherwise Mr. Hatfield refuseth either to deliver them or to let any work at all be done on them. Thus with my humble commendation I end, Cheadle, 9th October 1592. Your worship's to command, Sylvester Smith. I am to entreat your worship to help drive a bargain betwixt Sir Francis and this bearer, if it is possible: otherwise I know not where to find a man I may so well trust both for workmanship and upright dealing, both which are not a little behoveful for that place.

11. Richard Martin's Opinions about Iron Works, c. 1580s

Most men tried to obtain estimates of costs before embarking on the expensive undertaking of iron works. Richard Martin was a goldsmith and a man much involved in the business of mills and furnaces of all sorts. This opinion was probably given in the 1580s.

From National Library of Wales, Bute MSS, 32 I 55.

Mr. Martin's opinion obout iron works

First a hammer will cost building £120

Item the building of a furnace £50   £170

Item three great loads of Earth mine will make a
    ton of sows; every load containing 12 bushels of
    Cardiff measure will cost in place: at 4s 0d load   12s   0d

Item for the limestone to a ton   12d

Item three loads of coal after 12 sacks to a load,
    every sack containing two yards and half in
    length and one yard inch broad, which will
    cost in place at 9s the load   27s

A founder's, filler's and mine-breaker's wages for a
    ton of sows after the rate of 8 tons to be made a
    week and after 28s 0d a week, is for a ton   2s 7½d

Item for a clerk's wages to attend at the furnace
    at 12d per day   12d

Item for a clerk to attend in the wood   12d

Item for carriage of three loads at 1d the load   3d

Item for three and half loads for coals to make a
    ton of wrought iron   31s   6d

Item for carrying it to the heap   3½d

Item for two clerks to attend the wood and the forge
    per day   2s

Item for the hammer-man's wages for every ton of
    wrought iron   10s   0d

Item for the finers' wages   10s   0d

Item for repairs and casual charges by day by
    estimation   2s   6d

For a carpenter to attend both furnace and forge
    by day   13d

It will require if 120 tons of wrought iron be made
    there which is worth at £10 the ton the sum of   £1,200

First of sows 180 tons which will stand in charge for
    coal of both sows and wrought iron after three loads
    to a ton of sows and three and half loads to a ton
    of wrought iron to the number of loads of coals
    960 which at 9s a load is   £432

Item in four clerks' wages by the year   £74

Item the wages of the founder, filler &c after 28s the
    week for 24 weeks   £33 12s   0d

Item for the hammerman and finers' wages   £120

Item for repairs   £46   5s   0d

Item for the heaping of the coals   £4
Item for a carpenter's wages   £20
Item for riding charges   £50
   Sum of the reprises yearly   £779 17s 0d
Whereunto is to be added for carrying of the sows
after the rate of 12d per ton for every mile, when
hammer and furnace shall be distant, arising in the
whole by estimation unto carrying them five miles
asunder   £45
   And so the whole is   £824 17s 0d
   (There is a marginal note which runs) About the cost of coals: out of
which is to be deducted £96 for the good of every load coals at two
shillings for cord to make a load of coal for that the wood is his own
and for that same is costed as so much in the aforesaid sum of £432
for the 960 loads of coals.

12. Accounting Practices

Accounts were kept for the convenience of those keeping them, not
for the instruction of historians, nor even always for the instruction of
those more nearly involved. The following exasperated contemporary
criticism shows why. See also Document 8.

From Nottingham University Library, Middleton MSS, 5/165/92.

The charges of building the furnace and forge at Middleton and Hints
could never certainly be known by reason John Tyrer his order in
keeping his book was to intermingle the payments belonging to the
workers together with the payments belonging to the house at Middleton
as for example.
To SS for hedging and labouring at the furnace . . . days the sum
   of . . .
Item to TW for threshing and working at the forge . . . days . . .
Item to TH for making of hay and going with the stone wain . . .
   days the sum of . . .
Item to TG for going to Wollaton and working at the furnace . . .
   days the sum of . . .

Item to WW for working at carpenter's work . . . days at the Hall at Middleton and at the works . . .

Item it will be proved that £500 would have sufficiently erected and stocked the said works whatsoever was there bestowed.

The price of a tun [of iron] is according to the goodness thereof: in some places it is sold for £10 in others at £11 or £12 and at Cannock at £13.

13. Agreement Concerning a Copperas Factory, 1600

Thomas Gauntlett of Whitstable, yeoman, conveys to Richard Shepman citizen and merchant tailor of London, as a security for a debt, the property set out in the schedule attached to a deed dated 23 February 1599/1600.

From *Kentish Sources III: Aspects of Agriculture and Industry*, ed. E. Melling (Maidstone, 1961), pp. 147–8.

This is the Schedule whereof mention
is made in the deed or writing whereunto
this schedule is annexed.

Imprimis the workhouse and cooling house with a cistern in the same workhouse and two bins to dry the copperas.

Item a furnace of lead with 13 bars of iron that the same furnace stands upon and iron plates that lie between the bottom of the furnace and the great bars with the two iron grates that the fire is made on with the foundation that the furnace stands on.

Item two coolers of lead for the copperas to congeal in, that stand in the cooling house.

Item three beds or racks of 'gould' stones or sulphur stones to make copperas, that lie in a field wherein the workhouse now stands, with 18 great butts that stand in the ground to receive liquor from the 'gould' stones.

14. The Manufacture of Alum

From T. Fuller *The Worthies of England*, ed. J. Freeman (London, 1952), pp. 635–6.

This was first found out nigh Guisborough in this country, some sixty years since, by that worthy and learned knight Sir Thomas Chaloner (tutor to prince Henry) on this occasion. He observed the leaves of trees thereabouts more deeply green than elsewhere; the oaks broad-spreading, but not deep-rooted; with much strength, but little sap; the earth clayish, variously coloured, here white, there yellowish, there blue, and the ways therein in a clear night glistening like glass; symptions which first suggested unto him the presumption of minerals, and of alum most properly.

Yet some years interceded betwixt the discovery and perfecting thereof; some of the gentry of the vicinage burying their estates here under earth, before the alum could be brought to its true consistency. Yea, all things could not fadge with them, until they had brought (not to say stolen) over three prime workmen in hogsheads from Rochelle in France; whereof one, Lambert Russell by name, and a Walloon by birth, not long since deceased. But, when the work ended, it was adjudged a mine-royal, and came at last to be rented by Sir Paul Pindar, who paid yearly to the king £12,500 to the earl of Mulgrave £1,640; to Sir William Penniman £600; besides large salaries to numerous clerks, and daily wages to rubbishmen, rockmen, pit-men, house-men or fire-men; so that at one time (when the mines were in their majesty) I am credibly informed, he had in pay no fewer than eight hundred by sea and land.

Yet did not the knight complain of his bargain, who having the sole sale of the commodity to himself kept up the reputation thereof, and the price of alum at six-and-twenty pounds the ton. This he did the easier, because no better, and scarce other (save what from Rome and Rochelle) alum in all Europe.

But the late long-lasting parliament voted it a monopoly; and restored the benefit thereof to the former proprietaries, who now pursue the work at five several places: 1. Sandsend, and 2. Ash-holme, belonging to the earl of Mulgrave: 3 Slapywath, Sir William (formerly Penniman's) Darcey's: 4 Dunsley, Mr. Thomas Fairfax's: 5. Whitby, Sir Hugh Cholmley's.

Such now the emulation betwixt these owners to undersell one another, that the commodity is fallen to thirteen pound the ton.

Great the use hereof in physic and surgery, as a grand astringent. Besides, much thereof is daily employed by clothiers, glovers, dyers, etc.: so the same will maintain that another thing in England, as white and far sweeter than alum, may of the two be better spared, with less loss to the commonwealth.

15. The Inland Salt Production

From *The Itinerary of John Leland in or about the Years 1535–1543*. ed. L. T. Smith (London, 1906–8), Vol II, pp. 93–4, Vol. IV, p. 4,

Droitwich

The great advancement of the town is by making of salt; and yet though the commodity thereof be singularly great yet the burgesses be poor for the most part because gentlemen have for the most part the great gain of it and the burgesses have all the labour. There be at this present time 3 salt springs in the town of Droitwich whereof the principal is within a butt shot of the right bank of the river . . . and this spring is double as profitable in yielding of salt liquor as both the other. There be a great number of salt 'coots' or furnaces about this well wherein the salt water is decocted and brought to the perfection of pure white salt. The other two salt springs be on the left bank of the river . . . at the very town's end and at these springs be also divers furnaces to make salt but the profit and plenty of these 2 springs be nothing comparable to the great spring. I asked a salter how many furnaces they had at all the three springs and he numbered them . . . 360 saying that every one of them paid yearly 6s 8d to the king. The truth is that of old they had liberties given them for 300 furnaces for a fee farm of £100 yearly. The fee remains as it was but now the number of furnaces is increased to 400.

There was of late search made for another salt spring at the Wich by means of Mr. Newport . . . and the place where it was appeared and the wood and timber that had been set about it for holding up the earth for falling it in. But this pit was not occupied since, whether it were for lack of plenty of salt spring or for letting the profit of the other three. Men think that if wood and sale of salt would serve they might dig and find more salt springs about the Wich. I heard that of late years a salt spring was found in another quarter of Worcestershire but the Wichmen have such privilege that they alone in those quarters shall make salt. The Wichmen use the commodity of their salt springs in drawing and decocting the water of them only by 6 months in the year, that is from Midsummer to Christmas, as I guess to maintain the price of their salt or for saving of wood, the which I think to be their principal reason, for making of salt is a great and notable destruction of wood and hath been and shall be hereafter except men use much coppicing of young wood. The lack of wood is now perceived in places near the Wich for whereas in places near about they used to buy and take their wood, the wonted places be now sore decayed in wood. They be forced to seek wood as far as Worcester town and all the parts about Bromsgrove, Alchurch and Alcester. I asked a salter how much wood he supposed yearly to be spent at the furnaces and he answered that by estimation there was spent a 6,000 loads by year. And it is young pole wood, for the most part, easy to be divided in pieces. The people that be about the furnaces be very ill coloured. The just rate of every furnace is to make 4 loads of salt yearly and to every load goeth . . . quarters. If the furnace men make more in one furnace than four loads it is (as it is said) at their own avail.

Northwich, Middlewich and Nantwich

Northwich is a pretty market town but foul and by the salters' houses be great stacks of small cloven wood to boil the salt water that they make white salt of. The salt water pit is hard by the brink of Dane river, the which within a good butt shot beneath runneth into Weaver.

There be two salt springs at Middlewich that standeth as I remember upon Dane river and one at Nantwich the which yieldeth more salt than the other three, wherefore there be at Nantwich three hundred salters. A mile from Combermere Abbey in time of mind sank a piece of a hill having trees on it and after in that pit sprang salt water and the abbot there began to make salt but the men of the Wiches compounded with the abbey that there should be no salt made. The pit hath yet salt water but much filth is fallen into it. The pits be so set about with canals that the salt water is easily derived to every man's house . . . They boil the water in furnaces of lead and lade out the salt some in cases of wicker through the which the water voideth and the salt remaineth. There be also a 2 or 3 but very little salt springs at Dertwich in a low bottom where sometimes salt is made.

16. Salt Works near Tynemouth, 1634

From Sir W. Brereton, *Travels in Holland, the United Provinces, England, Scotland and Ireland, 1634–1635*, ed. E. Hawkins, Chetham Soc., I (1844), pp. 86–9.

Resting here 23 June [1634], I took boat about twelve clock, and went to Tynemouth and to the Shields, and returned about seven clock; it is about seven miles. Here I viewed the salt works, wherein is more salt works, and more salt made, than in any part of England that I know, and all the salt here made is made of salt-water; these pans, which are not to be numbered, placed in the river-mouth, and wrought with coals brought by water from Newcastle pits. A most dainty new salt-work lately here erected, which absolutely the most complete work that I ever saw; in the breadth whereof is placed six rank of pans, four pans in a rank; at either outside the furnaces are placed in the same manner as are by brother Boothes, under the grate of which furnaces the ashes fall, and there is a lid or cover for both; and by the heat of these ashes, there being a pan made in the floor betwixt every furnace, which is made of brick, for which also there is a cover, there is boiled, and made into lumps of hard and black salt, which is made of the brine which drops from the new-made salt, which is placed over a cistern of lead, which cistern is under the floor of the store-house, which is in the end of the building: these great lumps of hard black salt are sent to Colchester to make salt upon salt, which are sold for a greater price than the rest, because without these at Colchester they cannot make any salt.

These twenty-four pans have only twelve furnaces and twelve fires, and are erected in this manner, all being square and of like proportion. They are placed by two and two together, one against the other: the six pans in the highest rank, the bottom equal with the top of the lower. The highest pans are thrice filled and boiled till it begin to draw towards salt; then a spigot being pulled out, the brine thus prepared runs into the lower pans, which brings it to a larger proportion of salt than otherwise, gains time and saves fire, because it must be longer boiled in the other pans, and would spend fire, which is saved by reason of the heat which derives from the furnace of the upper pan, which by a passage is conveyed under the lower pan, which passage is about half a yard broad in the bottom, and is, at the top, of the breadth of the pan, which rests upon a brick wall which is of the thickness of one brick at top;

and this concavity under the lower pans is shaped slopewise like unto a kiln, narrow in the bottom and broad at the top; and this heat, which is conveyed under and makes the lower pans to boil, comes, together with the smoke which hath no other passage, under these pans through loop-holes or pigeon-holes, which is conveyed into a chimney (a double rank whereof is placed in the middle of this building), betwixt which is a passage for a man to walk in. In the middle of every these chimneys is there a broad iron-plate, which is shaped to the chimney, which, as it stops and keeps in the heat, so it being pulled out abates the heat.

It is to be observed that the twelve lower pans are only to be drawn twice in twenty-four hours, and by that time they are ready to be drawn; the brine in the higher pans will be sufficiently boiled and prepared to be let into the lower, which are only to be drawn, and that twice in twenty-four hours; they yield every of them every draught two bowls, which is worth 2s a bowl, and sometimes 2s 4d, so every pan yielding every day four bowls at two draughts, which comes to 8s, all twelve pans are worth every day £4 16s; so as all the twelve pans in a week make salt worth £28 a week; which in the year amounts unto £1,400, accounting fifty weeks to the year. Two men and one woman to get out ashes, and one to pump their brine, manage and tend this whole work. The men's wages is 14s a week, besides he that pumps. This salt is made of salt-water, which out of a brine pit made, which is supplied at full sea, is pumped, and by pipes of lead conveyed into every pan: the wall of this house is stone, and the roof of this and all the rest of the houses wherein are brine-pans, are boards. Touching the proportion of fuel here spent, and some other particulars, Dobson's letter is to be perused, and some further directions are to be received from him.

Here at the Shields are the vastest salt works I have seen, and by reason of the conveniency of coal, and cheapness thereof, being at 7s a chaldron, which is three wain load. Here is such a cloud of smoke as amongst these works you cannot see to walk; there are, as I was informed, about two hundred and fifty houses, poor ones and low built, but all covered with boards. Here in every house is erected one fair great iron pan, five yards long, three yards and a half broad; the bottom of them made of thin plates nailed together, and strong square rivets upon the nail heads, about the breadth of the batt of your hand: these pans are three quarters of a yard deep; ten great bars there are placed on the inner side of the pan, three square, two inches thick; every of these great pans, as Dobson informed me, cost about £100 and cannot be taken down to be repaired with less than £10 charge. Every pan yields four draughts of salt in a week, and every draught is worth about £1 10s. Spent in coal: ten chaldron of coal at 7s a chaldron, which amounts to £3 10s in coals; deduct out of £6, there remains £2 10s besides one man's wages. So as in these 250 pans there is weekly spent in coals £775. Every pan yielding £6 weekly, being 250, total of the worth of the salt made in them amounts to £1,500; gained £735; deduct of this £120 workmen's wages for making it, £120; clear gain about £600 a year.[1] A wain load of salt is here worth about £3 10s, and a chaldron of coals, which is worth 7s is three wain load.

[1] This ought to read a week and the total of costs is miscalculated. It should be £875 so then the gain is £625 less wages – £505.

17. Observations for Glass

From Nottingham University Library, Middleton MSS 5/165/92.

Observations for Glass
One case is a horse load, whereby it appeareth that after the rate of two hundred weight to a horseload ten horseloads or ten cases is a ton.
Witch ash, beanstraw ash and green fern ash are all good and are about 8d the strike.
Peas, straw ash and gorse ash are not so good.
Dry fern ash is not good.
Two good workmen will make 16 or 18 case of glass weekly.
For the number of coals and quantity of ash they must be proportioned according to the bigness of the furnace.
Broad glass spendeth both more coals and ash quantity for quantity than drinking glass doth.
The furnace for drinking glass spendeth above 20 strikes of ash weekly and about 10 or 12 loads of coals.
Particular rates of some parts of this business meet for your worship's understanding.

For every rook of coals	5s 6d
For ash of every sort a strike	4s 0d
For carriage from your lordship's to Bridges a ton	4s 0d
For water carriage to Hull a ton	7s 6d
For houseroom at Bridges for a ton and wharfage	6d
For the clerks' wages yearly	£20
For sand a strike	2d

For their complement of ash enough will be had with sufficient gain at the former rate.

The making of 800 ton of glass yearly will spend above 60 ton of coals weekly.

For land carriage I put down 4s 0d a ton because that glass is a goods of great stowage and will not be contained in an ordinary carriage.

There must be one way house erected by two furnaces and another at the Bridges for the receipt of the glass as it is made.

There must be either 8 furnace houses having but two master workmen apiece in each, or else four double furnaces when there be four master workmen apiece if they do make the complement of 800 tons a year. There be some 3 or 4 men apiece in each furnace besides which are employed about the making of fires and tempering of metals et talia.

Look what the charge of a single furnace is that double is as much more.

For aught I understand, they sell a case of glass for 20s 0d.

A conjectural arriving at the profit and charge of glassmaking

A single furnace may well	charge	
make 80 tons of glass yearly	for rent of the furnace	£10
which is worth being sold	For five men's wages	£100
but 16s 8d a case that is	For ash	£50
£8 a ton £640	For coals	£125
	For sand	£6 13s 4d
	For carriage to London	£80
		£371 13s 4d

The freight for glass or any such goods of like stowage will cost for the water carriage between Nottingham Bridges and Hull:

per ton	7s 6d
from Hull to London	10s 0d
houseroom and wharfage	6d
	18s 0d

The convenience for carriage by water is much to further the sale at an easier rate to many market towns viz:

Southwell	Boston
Newark	Towksall
Grantham	Retford
Lincoln	Gainsborough with many others.

No other places is so convenient being two miles from the water.

18. The Fitting-out of a Fishing-Boat Carrying Forty Men

From R. Whitbourne, *A Discourse and Discovery of Newfoundland* (London, 1622), pp. 81ff.

	£	s	d
Outfit of a ship for the fishing for forty men			
11,000 cwt biscuit bread 15s 0d per ton	82	10	0
26 tun of beer and cider 53s 4d the tun	69	6	8
Two hogshead of very good English beef	10	0	0
Two hogshead of Irish beef	5	0	0
Ten fat hogs salted cask and salt	10	10	0
30 bushel peas	6	0	0
2 firkins butter	2	10	0
2 cwt cheese		6	0
One bushel mustard seed	1	5	0
One hogshead vinegar	1	0	0
Wood to dress meat withall	2	0	0
One great copper kettle	2	0	0
Two small kettles	2	0	0
Two frying pans		3	4
Platters, ladles and cans for beer	1	0	0
One pair of bellows for the cook		2	0
Locks for the bread rooms		2	6
Tap, borer and funnels		2	0
1 cwt candles	2	10	0
130 quarters of salt at 2s 0d the bushel (15 gallons to a bushel)	104	0	0
Mats and dunnage to lay under the salt	2	10	0
Salt shovels		10	0
More for repairing of eight fishing boats 500 ft of elm boards of 1″ thickness at 8s 0d the hundred	2	0	0
2,000 nails for said boats and stages at 13s 4d the 1,000	1	6	8
4,000 nails at 6s 8d per 1,000	1	6	8
2,000 nails at 5d per 100		8	0
5 cwt pitch	2	0	0
One barrel of tar		10	0
Two cwt of Clack oakum	1	0	0
Thrums for pitch mabs		1	6
Bowls, buckets and funnels	1	0	0

Two brazen crocks	2	0	0
Canvas to make boat sails and small ropes filling for them at 25s 0d each sail	12	10	0
Ten boats' anchors' ropes	10	0	0
12 dozen fishing lines	6	0	0
24 dozen fishing hooks	2	0	0
Squid hook and squid lines		5	0
Fourpots and liver mands		18	9
Ironwork for ten fishing boats	2	0	0
Ten keepnet irons		10	0
Twine to make keepnets		6	0
Ten good nets at 26s 0d a net	13	0	0
Two seines a greater and a less	12	0	0
Two cwt of lead	1	0	0
Small ropes for seines	1	0	0
Dry vats for nets and seines		6	0
Flaskets and breadboxes		15	0
Twine for store		5	0
So much hair cloth as may cost	10	0	0
3 tun vinegar cask for water	1	6	8
Two barrels oatmeal	1	6	0
One dozen deal boards		10	0
One cwt spikes	2	5	0
Heading and splitting knives	1	5	0
Two good axes, four hand hatchets, four short wood hooks, two drawing irons, 2 adzes		16	0
3 yards good wool cloth		10	0
Eight yards good canvas		10	0
A grindingstone or two		9	0
An iron pitch pot and hooks		6	0
1,500 dry fish to spend thither wards	6	1	0
One hogshead aqua vitae	4	0	0
2,000 good Orlop nails	2	5	0
Four arm saws, four handsaws, four thwart saws, three angles, two crows of iron, two sledges, four iron shovels, two pickaxes, four mattocks, four claw hammers	5	0	0
Other necessaries	3	0	4

If ten men winter they will require of the above, 5 cwt biscuit bread, five hogshead beer or cider, half a hogshead beef, four whole sides of bacon, four bushels of peas, half a firkin of butter, half a cwt of cheese, one peck of mustard seed, one barrel of vinegar, 12 lb. of candles, two pecks of oatmeal, half a hogshead of aqua vitae.

19. Tobias Gentleman on North Sea Fishing

From Tobias Gentleman, 'England's Way to Win Wealth', *Harleian Miscellany*, Vol. IV (1745), pp. 396–408.

Wherefore, seeing the great benefit that this business by the busses, bonadventures, or fisher-ships, by erecting of this profitable and new trade, which will bring plenty unto his Majesty's kingdoms, and be for the general good of the commonwealth, in setting of many thousands of poor people on work, which now know not how to live; and also for the increasing of ships and fishermen, which shall be employed about the taking of fish and herrings out of his Majesty's own streams, as also for the employing of ships and increasing of mariners; for the strengthening of the kingdom against all foreign invasions, and for the enriching of merchants with transportation of fish and herrings into other countries; and also for the bringing in of gold and money, which now is grown but scarce, by reason that the Dutch and Hollanders have so long time been suffered to carry away our money and best gold, for fish and herrings. . . .

Those poor boats and sorry nets, that our fishermen of England now have, are all their chiefest wealths; but, were their ability better, they would soon be employing themselves: for that it is certain, that all the fishermen of England do rejoice now at the very name and news of building of busses, with a most joyful applause, praying to God to further it. For what great profit and pleasure it will bring they do well understand, and I will hereafter declare. . . .

I think it now best, truly to show the true number of our English fishermen, and how they do employ themselves all the year long; first beginning at Colchester, nigh the mouth of the Thames, and so proceed northward.

I can scarce afford these men of that water the name of fishermen, for that their chiefest trade is dragging of oysters; yet have they, in the summer, some eight or ten boats in the North-seas for cods, which, if that they happen to spend all their salt, and to speed well, they may get some twenty pounds in a summer clear. But, here by the way, I will make known a great abuse that is offered to the commonwealth, and especially to all the herring-fishermen of England, only by those men of Colchester water.

For these men, from St. Andrew until Candlemas, and sometimes longer, do set forth stale-boats, amongst the sands, in the Thames-mouth, for to take sprats, with great stale-nets, with a great poke; and, they standing in the Swin, or the King's Channel, on the back of the Gunfleat, they do there take, instead of sprats, infinite thousands of young herrings, smaller than sprats, and not good to be eaten: for one sprat is better worth than twenty of those bleaks or young herrings; but, because they do fill the bushel at Billingsgate, there they do sell them for sprats, the which, if that they were let live, would be at Midsummer a fat summer-full herring; and a peck is sometimes there sold for two pence, which number of herrings at Midsummer would make a barrel of summer herrings worth twenty or thirty shillings. . . .

If that these men will needs use their stale-boats and nets, let them go where the good sprats be; they must then stand at Orfordness and in Donwish-bay, where there be excellent sprats; and, for the good of all the herring fishermen of England, I wish that they might be prohibited to sell that which is not wholesome to be eaten, which is as much as to sell hemlock for parsnips.

The next to Colchester is Harwich-water, a royal harbour, and a proper town, fit for the use of busses, no place in all Holland comparable; for there is both land and strand, and dry beach enough for four-hundred sail: but the chiefest trade of the inhabitants of this place, is with carvels for Newcastle-coals; but they have three or four ships yearly that they do send to Iceland for cod and lings, from March until September, and some years they get, and sometimes lose; but, if that they had but once the trade of busses, this would soon be a fine place; but those carvels and ships, which they now have, are all their chiefest wealth.

Six miles up Harwich-water stands Ipswich, which is a gallant town, and rich; this town is such a place for the busses, as in all England and Holland I know no place so convenient. First, it is the best place in all England for the building of busses, both for the plenty of timber and plank, and excellent workmen for making of ships; there are more there, than there is in six of the best towns in all England. Secondly, it is a principal place for good housewives, for spinning of yarn, for the making of poldavis, for there is the best that is made; which town, with the use of making of twine, will soon be the best place of all England for to provide nets for the busses.

It is also a most convenient place for the wintering of the busses; for that all the shores of that river are altogether oozy and soft ground, fit for them to lie on in winter. . . .

For when our fishermen come home, the first voyage from the North-seas, they go either to London, Ipswich, Yarmouth, Lynn, Hull, or Scarborough, and there they do sell at good rates, the first voyage;

but the second voyage, because that they, which be now the fishermen, have not yet the right use of making barrelled fish wherewith they might serve France as do the Hollanders, they are now constrained to sell in England; for that it is staple fish, and not being barrelled, the French will not buy it.

But, if that our fishermen had but once the use of pinks and line-boats, and barrelled fish; then they might serve France as well as the Hollanders; which by this new trade of busses being once erected, and pinks and line-boats, after the Holland manner; there will be fishermen enough to manage the pinks, for barrelled fish, from November unto the beginning of May, only the most part of those men that shall be maintained by the busses; for that when the busses do leave work in the winter, their men shall have employment by the pinks, for barrelled fish, which men now do little or nothing: for this last winter at Yarmouth, there were three-hundred idle men that could get nothing to do; living very poor for lack of employment, which most gladly would have gone to sea in pinks, if there had been any for them to go in. . . .

Now to show truly, what the whole charge of a buss will be, with all her furniture, as masts, sails, anchors, cables, and with her fisher's implements and appurtenances, at the first provided all new, is a great charge; she, being between thirty or forty lasts, will cost some five-hundred pounds.

By the grace of God, the ship or buss will continue twenty years with small cost and reparations; but the yearly slight and wear of her tackle, and war ropes, and nets, will cost some eighty pounds.

And the whole charge for the keeping of her at sea for the whole summer, or three voyages, for the filling of a hundred lasts of casks, or barrels:

	£
For one-hundred last of barrels	72
For salt four months	88
For beer four months	42
For bread four months	21
For bacon and butter	18
For pease four months	3
For billet four months	3
For men's wages four months	88
	335

A hundred lasts of barrels, filled and sold at ten pounds, the last, come to one-thousand pounds.

	£
Herrings	1,000
The whole charge	335
Gotten	665

Here plainly appeareth, that there is gotten six-hundred and sixty-five pounds in one summer; whereout, if that you do deduct one hundred pounds for the wear of the ship, and the reparations remaining for clear gains, by one buss, in one year. . . .

Now to show the charge of a pink of eighteen or twenty lasts, the pink being built new, and all things new unto her, will not cost two-hundred and sixty pounds, with all her lines, hooks, and all her fisher appurtenances.

	£
And fifteen lasts of barrels will cost	10
Five weighs of salt upon salt	15
For beer and casks	7
For bread	3
For butter	1
For the petty-tally	1
For men's wages for two more months, and all together	20
	57

Fifteen lasts of barrelled fish, at fourteen pounds and eight shillings the last, which is but twenty-four shillings the barrel, amount unto two-hundred and sixteen pounds; whereout, if you do deduct fifty-seven pounds, for the charge of setting her to sea, there is still resting one-hundred and fifty-eight pounds, clear gains, by one pink, with fifteen lasts of fish, for two months. . . .

And when his Majesty shall have occasion and employment for the furnishing of his navy, there will be no want of masters, pilots, commanders, and sufficient directors of a course, and keeping of computation; but now there is a pitiful want of sufficient good men to do the offices and labours before spoken of; all which these men of the busses and pinks will worthily supply.

And to the art of sailing they may happily attain; for hitherto it hath been commonly seen, that those men that have been brought up in their youth, in fishery, have deserved as well as any in the land for artificial sailing; for at this time are practised all the projections of circular and mathematical scales, and arithmetical sailing, by divers of the young men of the sea-coast towns, even as commonly amongst them, as amongst the Thamsers. . . .

And, last of all, if that there by any of the worshipful adventurers, that would have any directions for the building of these busses, or fisher-ships; because I know that the ship-carpenters of England are not yet skilful in this matter: wherefore, if that any shall be pleased to repair to me, I will be willing to give them directions, and plain projections, and geometrical demonstrations, for the right building of them, both for length, breadth, and depth; and also for their mould under water; and also for the contriving of their rooms, and the laying of their gear, according to the Hollanders' fashion.

20. The Boats at Milton, Kent, 1580. D593/S/4/9.

The certificate of Thomas Randelye, William Crounes and Willian Lavyn justice of peace of the county of Kent and John Stanford water bailiff of the port of Milton next Sittingbourne in the said county viz. of all such shipping boats owners, masters, mariners, fishermen and seamen as be belonging and resident to the town and port of Milton aforesaid 19 November 1580 23 Elizabeth certified unto the right honourable Lord Cobham, Lord warden of the five ports.

From Sutherland County Record Office, Sutherland MS. D593/S/4.

To Rainham, parcel of the said port of Milton do belong these vessels

Name	Burden	Owner	Master
One hoy called the George	40 ton	William Elmeston Thomas Marshall Geoffrey Watson	Thomas Marshall
One hoy called the Hart	38 tons	William Elmeston Hugh Rowe William Taylor	Robert Green of Lee in Essex
One hoy called the William	26 tons	William Elmeston	The said William

Name	Burden	Owner	Master
One hoy called the Hare	28 tons	Hugh Rowe John Young	The said John Young
One hoy called the Jonas	20 tons	Robert Holmes	The said Robert
One hoy called the ——	8 tons	Robert Holman	The said Robert
One hoy called the Crab's Claw	10 tons	Hugh Rowe John Beach	The said John
One ketch called the John	14 tons	Hugh Rowe Richard Rowe	The said Richard
One ketch called the Edward	20 tons	Hugh Rowe	The said Hugh
One ketch called the Peter	6 tons	Thomas Broune	The said Thomas
One ketch called the James	10 tons	John Bradley Richard Sheete of Gillingham	The said John
One ketch called the Marie	8 tons	Robert Watson Richard Pennett	The said Robert

Unto these ships and vessels being occupied in the trades of fetching coals from Newcastle, fishing and carrying (in time of year) fruit to London do appertain 24 persons above the age of 18 years dwelling and resident in the said parish of Faversham viz: [all named].

21. Protest of Trinity House Against the Building of the *Sovereign*, 1634

From Public Record Office, State Papers, Domestic, Charles I, SP 16/273 No. 25.

Right Honourable, – Being informed that his Majesty is minded to build a great ship of these dimensions (namely) 124 foot by the keel, in breadth 46 and for draught in water 22 foot, these strange and large dimensions gave us cause to all into discourse, and in our discourse fell on these particulars following, namely:

That a ship of this proportion cannot be of use, nor fit for service in any part of the King's Dominions; and as unfit for remote service: our reasons –

First, there is no port within this kingdom (the Isle of Wight only) that can in safety harbour this ship, then it followeth, if she be not in port then is she in continual danger, exposed to all tempests, to all storms, that time shall bring. In a desperate estate she rides in every storm: in peril she must ride, when all the rest of her companions (his Majesty's ships) enjoys peace, rides quiet and safe in port: for example, we have the Prince in her voyage to Spain for his Majesty in foul weather, when all the fleet harboured in the Port of Plymouth, the Prince she only might not, for she could not, being too big, her draught too much, the wild sea must be her port; in the Sound of Plymouth must she ride, her anchors and cables her safety. If either of them fail, the ship must perish, 4 or 500 men must die, and the King must lose his Jewel: and this will be the state of this ship.

That she cannot harbour is her great draught in water, and less in draught she will not be, but could she be made to draw less water, yet anchors and cables must hold proportion, and being made, they will not be manageable, the strength of man cannot wield nor work them, but could they do it, yet the ship little bettered in point of safety, for we are doubtful whether cables and anchors can hold a ship of this bulk in a great storm, for we have more in our seas to add stress to cables and anchors than the wind and forming sea. We have strong tides which strains both cables and anchors equal to wind and sea, besides the particulars there are many things which must concur; for if either fail, the rest hold not, for example if the cables fail, the anchors are of no use, if the anchors fail, then neither cable nor anchor is serviceable, may if the ground be not good then is all the rest to no purpose, so that if either of these fail all is lost, the ship lost with all her provisions, the men lost, and it may be some great and noble Peer in her.

Thus far so much as may concern the safety of this ship being built.

Now for the force of this ship; it will not any way hold proportion with her bulk or burden, for the aim must be for three tier of ordnance, the lower tier which must carry the greatest ordnance and be of greatest force must lie of necessity so low that in every gale of wind the ports must be shut in, or else the ship will be in great danger, or sink as did the Mary Rose in King Henry the VIII's time at Portsmouth.

Or if you will lay them at 5 or $5\frac{1}{2}$ foot, then must the third tier lie at that height as not to be serviceable, nay this third tier will rather endanger the quality of the ship (as the too high building hath in some of the king's ships lately built made them unfit for any good service). Therefore three tier of ordnance must not be, neither can the art or wit of man build a ship well conditioned and fit for service with three tier of ordnance.

But if it be force that his Majesty desireth, then shall he do well to forbear the building of this ship, and with the same cost or charge to build two ships of 5 or 600 ton a piece, either ship to have 40 pieces of good ordnance, and these two ships will be of more force and for better service and will beat the great ship back and side.

These particulars, Right Honourable, falling within the compass of our discourse we held it our duty to his Majesty to impart the particulars unto you, and with your wisdom to leave them either to impart them unto the king, or otherwise as it shall seem best unto your wisdom. And so we rest.

Your honour's ever at command,
T. Best
Walter Coke
Ro. Salmon

From Ratcliffe
9th of August 1634
To the Right Honourable Sir John Coke, principal Secretary to His Majesty

22. The Valuation of a Ship, 1579

From Public Record Office, Exchequer, King's Remembrancer, Special Commissions of Enquiry, E 178/1112.

[The *William Bonaventure*, a hundred-tonner but very old and with her masts broken, was valued in 1579 as follows]
Hull and masts £23
3 cables and an anchor £11
sails: a main course and bonnet
forecourse and bonnet main topsail
foretopsail and spitsail and mizzen
three parts worn £6 13s 6d
tackle and cordage not serviceable £5
4 old quarter slings of iron with 4 chambers and 1 falconet of iron £6

23. Inventory of Peter Courtopp, 12 November 1567

From *Kentish Sources III: Aspects of Agriculture and Industry*, ed. E. Melling, pp. 110–11.

	£	s	d
Ready money			
Item in his purse		17	0
Item in his house and at London in ready money	13	14	0
Item four remnants of cloth	8	13	4
In the hall			
Item an iron beam, two pairs of scales, two and a half hundred weight and 16 pounds lead weights		30	0
Item two old tables, two pair of trestles and a form		5	0
Item two wool baskets and 4 old tubs		2	0
In the little parlour			
Item a table, a pair of trestles and a form		2	0
Item a wood net and 32 wool nets		22	8
Item 14 pounds of red wool		14	0
Item eight pairs of shears		2	0
Item twelve wool sacks and 11 sarplers	3	0	0
In the warehouse			
Item 7 loads and a half of wood ash at 15s 0d a load	5	12	6
Item one pipe of oil	13	0	0
Item certain oil in another pipe		40	0
Item half a hundred of madder		15	0
Item a cwt of copperas and five pounds of alum		20	0
Item two bales of wool	13	10	0
Item leavings of yarn 18 quarters	5	0	0
Item 33 pounds of old copper		11	0
Item of list in yarn 8½ quarters		17	0
Item 2,000 bricks		20	0
Fleece wool			
Item in fleece wool 326 tod at 23s the tod	374	18	0
Item in wool ready culled	57	6	3
Item one cloth's wool, a fine blue	18	0	0
Item another cloth's wool, fine blue	18	0	0
Item 11 quarters of green wool		40	0
Item 4 cloths wool of medley in colour	18	0	0
Item 8 quarters of red wool		40	0

Item 6 quarters of red wool	30 0
Item fourteen pounds of red wool	14 0
Item leavings of wool in colour	32 0
Item 9 quarters of yellow list in wool	15 0
Item a cloth's yarn of fine blue	20 0 0
Item a cloth's yarn of russet	13 00
Item a cloth's yarn of white grey	8 10 0
Item 9 score quarters of list wool at 18d the quarter	13 10 0
Cloths ready made	
Item one sheep colour	13 0 0
Item five cloths of medley colour at £19 10s 0d the cloth	47 10 0 (*sic*)
Item one cloth of fine blue	24 0 0
Item one cloth sheep's colour	10 0 0
Item one sad new colour	10 0 0
Item two fine new colours	25 0 0
Cloths unthicked at the mill	
Item 2 sheep's colours	16 0 0
Item two new colours	22 0 0
Item one sheep's colour	9 10 0
Desperate debts	
[3 totalling	45 6 8]

[The inventory total, which includes goods not connected with the clothing trade, and not given here come to £1,880 17s 5d]

24. Quality Control of Cloth, 1594

In 1594, in answer to an inquiry, the practice of the Sandwich, and by implication Norwich, Maidstone, Canterbury, Colchester and other bay manufacturers, was in this regard praised to the skies. No less than four seals were attached to such cloths by the makers themselves and impressions made on them by twelve duly appointed viewers.

From Historical Manuscript Commission, *Hatfield House*, Vol. IV, pp. 573–4.

They visit the said bays twice, first as it cometh from the loom, and again after they be fulled. . . . they have three seals which they generally set upon all sorts of bays, the first is the seal of the crown which they have by authority from the Alnager [all cloths had to be sealed by this royal official, but unfortunately the records he kept are not a reliable guide to the numbers of cloths produced] to whom they pay a yearly composition for it. The second seal is of the town, by which it is known where the commodity is made, for the which the township hath for every piece 2d. The third seal is the number of threads in the warp, whereby is discerned the several degrees of goodness. Fourth, for as much as there are two or three sorts of bays in goodness, the one exceeding the other in breadth and price they have for the fourth lead several prints, to wit, for the best bay a seal with a ship, the second a rose, and the third a fleur de lys. This order so duly observed hath given such credit to the commodities both in the Low countries, Spain and Barbary and all other places as the seal being seen is sufficeth.

25. The Tanner's Costs

The tanner's costs included items of this sort. The values involved may be usefully compared with those of the clothier as illustrated in Document 23.

Bark was an essential ingredient in the liquid in which the hides had to steep.

From (A) Nottingham University Library, Middleton MSS, 5/165/37.
   (B) Stafford County Record Office, Anglesey MSS, D (W) 1734/3/4/219.

(A) A note of bark sold forth of Laundewood at Cossalk to Robert Burton of Nottingham tanner these last two years 1573 and 1574 as followeth:
First delivered the said Robert Burton by Henry Nyxson in the last year 1573 seven loads of bark . . . being 3 quarters in the load which is rated unto 5¼ whole loads and 5s the whole load . . . 26s 3d.

Item more delivered . . . in 1574 . . . 8½ loads rated to six whole loads a quarter and a little at 5s the whole load . . . 31s 3d.
(B) Fells delivered to the fellmonger after this rate:
From Easter till Midsummer the dozen 20s 0d
From Midsummer to Michaelmas a dozen 6s 8d
From Michaelmas to Shrovetide a dozen 13s 4d
Calves' skins all the year long to pay for the dozen 6s 8d

A note what money is due to my lord of the tanner and fellmonger of Lichfield 27 August 1580:

the tanner:	John Mathew the tanner oweth for 2 oxehides at 11s 0d the piece	22s 0d
	the same Mathew for 9 cow hides at 6s 8d the piece	£3
fellmonger:	John Wythers the fellmonger for 11 calves' skins at 6s 8d the dozen	6s 1d
	The same Wythers oweth for 2 dozen and 11 wether skins at twenty shillings the dozen	58s 4d
	The same Wythers oweth for 9 dozen and one odd skin, shorling skins and lambs' skins all at one price viz. for every dozen 6s 8d	53s 4d and 5 odd skins

26. Agreement with a Carpenter for Building Part of a House, 1614

From Folger Library, Bagot MSS, L a 1001.

Article agreed upon between Walter Bagot of Blithfield esq. and Laurence Greaves of Bromley Pagets, carpenter, the 8th January 1613/4.

Imprimis it is agreed that the said Lawrence shall new build the backhouse in length betwixt the kitchen end and the dayhouse of equal height with the dayhouse, in breadth 19 foot double floored throughout. The nether room to be divided into two parts and an entry through at the end next the dayhouse. The middle part to be divided into three parts with a gallery along the foreside to serve those three rooms.

Item the said Lawrence is to make three pairs of stairs, one pair at the end of the entry with a gallery to serve the dayhouse chambers and the chambers over the gatehouse, one other pair to serve the three rooms over the brew house, a third pair to serve the garrets. He is also to make three whole windows to serve the middle story and five dormer windows to serve the over rooms, three on the foreside and two on the backside, all the rest clear lights.

And he is also to make so many doors as shall be necessary to use in the said buildings and to cleave lathes for the floors and roofs and to nog all the walls and to spar the roof.

It is further agreed that the said Lawrence shall build a washhouse at the end of the day house towards the moat 9 foot in breadth and twelve in length of equal height with the brew house, double floored.

Lastly it is agreed that the said Lawrence Greaves shall finish all the said work by him to be done before the feast of St John the Baptist next coming and in consideration thereof to receive £26 23s 4d.

27. Repairs to a Watermill at Bromley Pagets, 1552

Mills were important pieces of capital equipment, which needed frequent repairs and sometimes virtual rebuilding. The following cost, it should be noted, does not include the cost of the timber, which, since ten loads were involved, might have doubled the price, or more.

From Stafford County Record Office, Anglesey MSS, D (W) 1734/3/4/ 20.

Repair of the mill of Bromley Pagets, 1552

Imprimis paid to the wright for the making of a new water wheel and a cog wheel, the shaft and all things thereto belonging:	£3 6s 8d
Item paid for two hundred of great nails for the wheel:	3s 4d
Item paid for two hundred of small nails:	20d
Item for two hundred nails:	16d
Item for one hundred nails:	4d
Item for two gogins and two hoops for the mill shaft end:	3s 0d
Item for seven pounds of pitch and resin:	14d
Item for one pound of tallow:	2d
Item for bread and ale and cheese to the wainmen carrying 10 loads of timber for the mill:	16d
Item for the getting of two loads of alder poles for stakes whereon the wheel was framed:	4d
	sum £3 18s 4d

28. Repairs to the Bridge at Burton, 1569

Detailed accounts of repairs to bridges are not as common as they might be, since little remains of the accounts of the local authorities who were mainly responsible. The following account therefore has some interest, particularly as it shows the masons contracting for a lump sum.

From Stafford County Record Office, Anglesey MSS, D (W) 1734/3/4/65.

Repairs at Burton bridge 12 May by my lord Paget's appointment 1569

First paid to the masons for making a new arch with 6 bows	£12	0s	0d
Item for one of the said bows which they were not agreed with for at the first for lack of stone		13s	4d
Item given the mason in earnest of their bargain to drink			12d
Item for lime for the same work	£5	5s	6d
Item to the carpenters for making 'senturns' for the work	£1	8s	4d
Item for clearing pikes and carriage of them to the bridge		2s	0d
Item to two labourers to carry stone up and 'ramell' when the arch fell down			20d
Item for carriage of timber for the scaffolding		4s	0d
Item for nails for the 'senturns' and making scaffolding		2s	0d
Item for a bucket to draw water and a cowle to carry water			18d
Item to labourers to get gravel and to load wains to fill up the work when the masons had done		13s	4d
Item for carriage of gravel to the bridge			20d
Item for carriage of sand		4s	0d
Item for carriage of more gravel in winter last when a piece fell into Trent			12d
Item for taking up the 'senturns' at the bridge and two days work of the masons where need was		3s	4d
Thomas Mason for mending a place in the bridge in winter last and a strike of lime			8d
sum	£21	3s	4d

29. Trinity House to the Privy Council about the Salt Trade, 1635

From Public Record Office, State Papers, Domestic, Charles I, SP 16/308 No. 11.

The greatest part of these ships are here at home freighted only for an outward freight; for loading or freightage home again the owners expose themselves to fortune. Yet, encouraged by their certain loadings of salt (when all other better employment fails them) . . . commonly benefit by the importation of salt [which benefit] if taken from us, or if some heavy burdens be laid upon it, a third part of the best merchant ships in this land will want employment, which God forbid. . . . If our ships be restrained to bring home salt their outward freight will not defray the charge of the voyage.

30. Problems of the Staplers in the 1540s

Letter sent by John Johnson to Mistress Baynam 29 March 1545.

From Public Record Office, State Papers, Domestic, Supplementary, SP 46/5 fol. 70.

Gentle Mistress Baynam I have me commended unto you, praying you I may be the same to all our friends in Calais. Mr Cave, my wife with all your friends in these parts have them in like manner commended unto you. I am ashamed that I have not ere this time written unto you and given you thanks for your herring and other your gentleness. Howbeit my trust is ye take it well, which makes me the bolder desiring you to hold me excused. I have here shipped for you the pockets of wool of sundry sorts which you shall be certified of hereafter. The fifteen pockets do not amount unto so much money as I had of yours and as I did hope to have had wool here for you. But ye may not blame me as I do serve you no worse than myself. The truth is I had wool sufficient bought here in the country but because I could not get carriage for the same in due time against the shipping (and yet I proffered more money for carriage by twenty shillings a load than in other years accustomed) perceiving the prices of wools to be good in the country and that much time would be lost in tarrying to the next shipping I sold in the country both the rest of your wool and my own also, so that you shall have all your money by Whitsuntide or short after with honest profit, I trust to your contentment, for I will serve you no worse than myself. If I had thought that you would not have been displeased I could have sold here in London all the wool that I have now shipped for you, as I have done my own and therefore I intend not to ship one pocket as ye shall perceive. Thus committing you to the preservation of the Lord I rest.

Yours to his power. John Johnson.

31. Thomas Mun on Foreign Exchange

From T. Mun, 'England's Treasure by Foreign Trade', in *Early English Tracts on Commerce* (London, 1953), pp. 167–8.

To lay our money with gain to any place of the world where Exchange lieth. How can this be done (will some men say) for Amsterdam when the loss by Exchange is sometimes 8 or 10% more or less for one month's usance? The answer is, that here I must consider, first, that the principal efficient cause of this loss, is a greater value in wares brought from Amsterdam than we carry thither which make more Deliverers than Takers here by Exchange whereby the money is undervalued to the benefit of the taker: hereupon the Deliverer rather than he will lose by his money, doth consider those countries unto which we carry more wares in value than we receive from them; as namely Spain, Italy and others; to which places he is sure (for the reasons aforesaid) that he shall ever deliver his money with profit. But now you will say, that the money is further from Amsterdam than before . . . yes well enough; and the farther about will prove the nearest way home if it come at last with good profit; the first part whereof being made in Spain from thence I consider where to make my second gain, and finding that the Florentines send out a greater value in cloth . . . to Spain than they receive . . . I . . . deliver my money for Florence; I direct my course from thence to Venice, and there find that my next benefit must be at Frankfurt or Antwerp until at last I come to Amsterdam.

32. Proposal for the Establishment of a Monte, 1580

The proposal is initiated by a letter of explanation in Italian which is followed by more detailed explanations in English.

From Public Record Office, State Papers, Domestic, Elizabeth, SP 12/146 No. 81.

Information
The bank of augmentation is like to be very acceptable to the queen's most excellent majesty because of the profit and reputation of the crown and for the benefit and commodity of the commonwealth whereby besides these respects shall succeed these consequences very worshipful which shall be manifestly considered and known to be such when they shall be proposed.

If this bank be set up with the stock of 5 and 40 thousand marks for to augment the same to the sum of 4 hundred and twenty thousand and two hundred marks at the end and expiration of seventeen years it shall be a worthy beginning and laying in proportioned to the intent where shall be bestowed this money of the Bank for to make the sum which the bank is worth at the same.

2. Which bank and treasure shall be none other than an open bank assured by the Chamber of London which shall receive and pay all the money appertaining to this Bank which in many sums shall receive to the sum of 50,000 marks the expedition therein comprehended under the name of sons and daughters promising unto them which from the age of forty days downwards shall enter in the Bank at the end and expiration of seventeen years to pay ten for every one received and unto them that shall exceed the same age to pay them at the end of seventeen years nine for every one received if the persons in whose names the money shall have been laid in shall be living at the same time and otherwise if the same do die before the time of payment the Bank shall not be bound to pay anything.

The order which shall be given for to gather this stock of five and forty thousand marks to the increase of four hundred seven and twenty thousand and five hundred marks in seventeen years shall be this. Her majesty finding herself indebted of the sum of a hundred and fifty thousand marks whereof she doth pay twelve for the hundred for the interest in a year upon this debt shall ground the stock of the bank wherein we shall bring the same to ten of the hundred of the expedition which in all shall be 50,000 marks which in the said debt shall bring in profit of 6,000 marks a year whereunto her majesty shall win 2,000 a year and even so the profit of this 50,000 marks shall be 8,000 marks a year and of this profit the rest of her majesty's debts shall be abolished whereof the bank shall become creditor. Which debt when it shall be converted in credit of the bank her majesty shall pay no more than ten for the hundred a year for interest to the said bank. Reimbursing herself also of the 2,000 marks thereunto joined in augmentation of the interest and by this order in seventeen years it shall be brought to the sum of four hundred thousand marks. In case of the death of any creditor the augmentation of his stock shall be taken after the rate of eight for the hundred a year and it shall be converted to the use of the crown leaving always the interest of the first year for the Augmentation to the Bank which instead of the dead taking of those that are living augmenting number after the rate of the increase of the bank the money being converted in a bank of lending by exchange at the fairs for the profit of 8 for the hundred a year the same will shortly be exceeding great and it shall be always full and perpetual.

If it please her Majesty to bring this matter to effect I do beseech her Highness that it may please her to grant me that during seventeen years I may have the administration leaving me for my charges travail and invention the fourth part of the profits which shall be gotten in the same time, so that I, setting the same in frame with good order and true service I shall bring this matter to good effect promising all the days of my life to bind me not to occupy my mind in other things than in the service and exaltation of the crown. [The chamber of London, apparently, was to guarantee the bank.]

33. A Market at Bromley Paget, 1553

From Stafford County Record Office, Anglesey MSS, D (W) 1734/3/4/25.

Market of lord Paget held at Bromley Paget, Thursday 24 August 1553
John Paynford bought two cows of the bailiff of Tutbury,
    within the franchise and therefore free, and paid for toll: 2d
Thomas Tonkes of Belston bought two oxen of Mr Mylward
    within the franchise free and paid: 2d

John Barte of Buckinghamshire bought two oxen of John
   Mason free and paid: 2d
William Cricheley bought ten twinters of Mr Robert Savage
   free and paid: 10d
Master Cater bought two oxen of William free and paid: 2d
Master Stone of Walsall bought ten cows of Mr Rolston
   free and paid: 10d
Gabriel Sumer bought two bullocks of Thomas Smyth
   of Adbaston and paid: 4d
Nicholas Tailor of Yoxall bought one ox of John Nevall
   of Walton and paid: 2d
Thomas Compton of Stafford bought six cows of John Pocar
   free and paid: 6d
Ralf Sheven bought four cows of John Tailor of Utoxeter
   free and paid: 5d
Nicholas Royle free bought 40 cows and paid: 3s 1d
William Dakyn and Edmund Dakyn bought 30 oxen and
   paid: 5s 0d
Master Stapleton bought 53 beasts and paid: 5s 0d
Master Wyghtman bought 40 oxen and paid: 3s 4d
Master Fearn bought four oxen and paid: 4d
Master Belbroke bought two cows and paid: 4d
Master Brettyn free bought ten cows and paid: 10d
John Bayly bought 32 cows and paid: 4s 0d

                     25s 8d

Thomas Frith bought 64 cows of Mr Pole free and of
   Mr Milward free and paid: 5s 0d
Thomas Shepard and John Badger bought 30 oxen and paid: 3s 4d
Thomas Royle bought fifty beasts and paid: 3s 4d
Roger Tetlowe bought 30 oxen and paid: 2s 0d
Master Stoner bought 18 beasts and paid: 2s 0d

                 sum 15s 8d
               total 41s 4d

Payments
Paid to two deputy bailiffs for their wages, meat and drink
   2 days: 3s 0d
Paid to thirteen catchpolls for their wages, meat and drink: 13s 0d

               sum 16s 0d
      remainder 25s 8d

34. Newcastle in 1634

From Brereton, *Travels in Holland* . . . , Chatham Soc., I (1844), pp. 89–90.

Here, at Newcastle, is the fairest quay in England I have met withal, from Tyne-bridge all along Town-wall, and almost to the glass-works, where is made window-glass. Divers havens of stone wall erected to cast out their ballast upon, and they pay for every ton cast out 6d. This is a spacious haven, now naked for ships, but sometimes thronged.

The fairest built inn in England that I have seen is Mr. Carre's, in this town: we lodged at the Swan, at Mr. Swan's, the postmaster's, and paid 8d. ordinary, and no great provision. He is a very forward man to have a coy here erected.

This town unto this country serves instead of London, by means whereof the country is supplied with money; whereas otherwise so much money is carried out of the country to the lords and landlords, as there would be neither sufficient money to pay the tenants' rents, nor would the country be supplied with money. This town is also famous for the walls which compass round the town, about which you may walk, and which is strengthened with strong towers placed upon the wall at no great distance.

INDEX